Blind Joe Death's America

Blind Joe Death's America

John Fahey, the Blues, and Writing White Discontent

George Henderson

The University of North Carolina Press CHAPEL HILL

Set in Merope Basic by Westchester Publishing Services
Manufactured in the United States of America

The University of North Carolina Press has been a member of the Green Press
Initiative since 2003.

Library of Congress Cataloging-in-Publication Data
Names: Henderson, George L., 1958– author.
Title: Blind Joe Death's America : John Fahey, the blues, and writing white
    discontent / George Henderson.
Description: Chapel Hill : University of North Carolina Press, 2021. | Includes
    bibliographical references and index.
Identifiers: LCCN 2020038656 | ISBN 9781469660776 (cloth ; alk. paper) |
    ISBN 9781469660783 (paperback ; alk. paper) | ISBN 9781469660790 (ebook)
Subjects: LCSH: Fahey, John, 1939–2001—Criticism and interpretation. |
    Guitarists—United States. | Musicologists—United States. | Music—
    Social aspects—United States. | Music—Political aspects—United States.
Classification: LCC ML419.F35 H46 2021 | DDC 787.871643092 [B]—dc23
LC record available at https://lccn.loc.gov/2020038656

Cover illustration: Portrait of "Blind Joe Death" / John Fahey, 1962, drawn by
John McIntire. Courtesy of the artist and Matt Ducklo, Tops Gallery, Memphis.

Excerpts from John Fahey's work are used here with permission. "Performance
as War" and Charley Patton (Studio Vista, 1970) used by permission of the John
Fahey Trust. "Charley Reconsidered, Thirty-Five Years On," in Screamin' and
Hollerin the Blues: The Worlds of Charley Patton (Revenant, 2001) used by permission
of Dean Blackwood. Liner notes from The New Possibility, Requia, The Yellow
Princess, The Voice of the Turtle, Death Chants, Breakdowns, Military Waltzes, The
Great San Bernardino Birthday Party, Dance of Death, and Days Have Gone By used
by permission of Wolfgang Frank, Concord. How Bluegrass Music Destroyed My
Life (Drag City, 2000) used by permission of Kathryn Wilson, Drag City.

Excerpts from Kevin Lynch, The Image of the City, p. 659, words from pages 1, 2,
4, 7, 12, 13, 47, 48, 119–20, © 1960 Massachusetts Institute of Technology, used
by permission of The MIT Press.

Excerpts from Erik Erikson, Childhood and Society, © 1950, © 1963 by W. W.
Norton and Company, Inc., renewed © 1978, 1991 by Erik H. Erikson, used by
permission of W. W. Norton and Company, Inc. and, in the UK, by Vintage and
The Random House Group Ltd. © 1995.

Contents

Figures

Acknowledgments

In writing this book, I have accrued a world of debt. I am exceptionally grateful to Melissa Stephenson for very generously sharing her time with me. Through her I was able to view the originals of John Fahey's revelatory "psychological" maps of Takoma Park (see chapter 6), as well as some amazing Fahey ephemera. Melissa kindly permitted reproduction of the maps here. Through Melissa I was lucky to spend an afternoon in insightful conversation with John's friend and fellow guitarist, Tim Knight, and later with John's former wife, Melody Fahey. Melody and Mitch Greenhill of The Fahey Trust generously allowed me to quote from essential Fahey works that have guided the direction of my book. Since John Fahey's passing in 2001, a cadre of researchers, with whom I have been very fortunate to interact, has produced work that I have benefited from fundamentally. Claudio Guerrieri's John Fahey "handbooks" are absolute miracles of dogged research. Through Claudio's work I became aware of Fahey's truly extraordinary essay "Performance as War." (Jenni Kotting's sleuthing skills enabled me to crack the code of that work. Thank you, Jenni.) Claudio also made available to me an essay that Fahey wrote at the end of, or just after, high school. *Dance of Death*, Steve Lowenthal's biography of John Fahey, became available while I was working on this book. It is elegant, insightful, unsparing, and essential. I thank Sam Gould for setting up our afternoon with Steve and for sharing his own personal memories of John Fahey in the 1990s. Glenn Jones, a longtime friend of Fahey's, and immensely talented guitarist himself, writes brilliantly about Fahey's music, attested to by the liner notes he has written to some of the reissued records. My personal interactions with Claudio, Glenn, Steve, and Sam have been crucial in helping me shape a background view of Fahey. Over the past few years I have had helpful email exchanges with Fahey associates from the old days in Berkeley, LA, and various Maryland and D.C.-area stomping grounds: thank you, Barry Hansen ("Dr. Demento"), Max Ochs, and ED Denson for engaging with me, even a little, and thinking a book about Fahey's writings could be interesting.

I am exceedingly grateful to the University of North Carolina Press, especially my editor Lucas Church, who has been outstanding, supportive, and responsive in every way, as have all the staff with whom I've worked at the

Press, including Andrew Winters, Cate Hodorowicz, Erin Granville, and Dino Battista. Production editor Kirsten Elmer and copyeditor Liz Schueler have been a pleasure to work with. The anonymous readers commissioned by the Press were models of the art of peer review, honoring me with thoroughgoing and instructive comments. I owe thanks to Wolfgang Frank at Concord Records and Dean Blackwood at Revenant for sorting through the permissions to reproduce portions of John's album notes. John McIntire graciously agreed to have his wonderful drawing of "Blind Joe Death" from 1962 reproduced on and between the covers of this book. Thank you, Matt Duklo, of Tops Gallery in Memphis, for arranging that. Useful information pops up regularly on the John Fahey Facebook group. Enthusiastic thanks to Malcolm Kirton for helping me date one of Fahey's songs from the *Red Cross* album.

Glenn Jones, Robert Fink, Holly Watkins, and Jason Weideman gave feedback on an early draft of this project, helping ultimately to point the way to the quite different conception found here. I was fortunate to join an outstanding group of faculty and graduate students for a PhD course in cultural landscape study at the University of Lund, Sweden: thank you, Tom Mels, Tomas Germundsson, Don Mitchell, and all the students for creating a stimulating environment in which to share portions of this work.

In Minneapolis I have relied on a loving and supportive community each and every day. My amazing partner Rachel Breen has lived this project with me from the beginning, and I can't thank her enough. She has always been ready to hear the next round of thoughts about Fahey, including the fails. She was right there when I decided the first version of this book had to be tossed in the dustbin. What a day! And she was there again when the new ideas began to gel. (A sabbatical granted by the College of Liberal Arts at the University of Minnesota provided precious time to develop the rethink.) Just as important, Rachel's art practice and teaching, which I hold in the deepest admiration possible, have prodded me to stay close to the question of what art, of any kind, can do and why it keeps needing to be made. I owe affectionate shout-outs to other Twin Cities greats. Max Ritts, Sumanth Gopinath, and Mike Gallope: I am deeply appreciative of the time you gave reading drafts of various parts of this project and talking your responses through with me. Alaina Henderson, Arun Saldanha, Aaron Mallory, Glen Powell, Gloria Raheja, and Sam Gould, your passion for worlds musical help sustain my own. For so many conversations about this project that have kept it alive, I thank my dear colleagues and friends, Bruce, Morgan, Vinay, Marv, Penny, David, Michael Goldman, Rachel Schurman, Danyelle, Marc, Miranda, Erin,

Kate, Lorena, Steve, Rachel Bond, Bridget, Michael Roehr, Elisa, Mary-Karen, and Markus. Many faculty and graduate students in the Department of Geography, Environment, and Society have heard about this mysterious Fahey project: I thank you for your steady curiosity. All these thanks said, I hasten to take responsibility for my interpretation of Fahey's work. I know it will not please everyone.

My family sustains me every hour and minute. The long making of this book has kept time with my getting to know and love the Breen family, who have embraced me, and I you, each and every one: Rachel, Aviva, Stanley, Isaiah, Bennett, Kali, Jenny, John, Solana, Franny, Andrea, Billy, Shira, Tova, and Zev. (Who'd I miss?!) My heart explodes in beautiful emojis at the very thought of my parents and my sibs and all their young 'uns: Suzanne Sr. and Jr., Tom, Sam, Kyle, Sean, Dana, Cory, Samantha, and Ori.

Who is this book for? I will tell you. My daughter Alaina, growing daily in wisdom and courage; Rachel, who scouts the horizon and dreams dreams with me; Mom and Dad, who held up the rafters with books, music, art, and most of all, love.

Blind Joe Death's America

Introduction
New Possibilities

In the winter of 2003 I thought I knew something about the music of John Fahey. True, I owned just one album, but I'd had it for some twenty-five years, and besides, *The New Possibility* was not just any Fahey record. It was his best seller, released in 1968, in the middle of an extraordinarily productive period, and a very reliable find in the used record bins where I found mine in my junior year of college. I now think there was a certain logic at work. Because it sold over a hundred thousand copies—being nothing like the rarity of his 1959 debut, *Blind Joe Death*, now on the Library of Congress's National Registry—odds are that plenty of used copies would be floating around. But because there were plenty of used copies floating around, odds are that a lot of people found it too weird. Especially for Christmas. As the full title says, *The New Possibility* is *John Fahey's Guitar Soli Christmas Album*. On it are some standard carols: two- or three-minute takes on "Joy to the World," "We Three Kings of Orient Are," "The First Noel," and so on. Then there is Fahey's tweaked ten-minute riff on the Episcopal hymn "I Sing a Song of the Saints of God." Fahey titles it "Christ's Saints of God Fantasy." It begins with a slowly strummed chord played way up the neck at the eleventh fret, so the voicing is high and bright. At the end of his fifth pass through the chord, he winds up its highest note from a B to a C, then up to C# on the sixth pass and to F# on the seventh. As he flakes off each note, the music draws you near. It is crystalline, wintry, and so, so delicate. Yet the strummed chord has also become brittle with every pass, a little wrong sounding, and slightly noir-ish as Fahey puts his finger behind the high notes and pushes them toward an icy oblivion. But after some time and further variations on the theme, he quickens the pace and settles into some syncopated fingerpicking more obedient to the hymn's familiar melody. Still, it's a *syncopated* treatment of the hymn.

This adventurousness, which is compositional, performative, and a matter of how he arranges songs, has ensured Fahey a long, devoted following. There he is in *Rolling Stone* magazine's list of the hundred best guitarists. There he is in the concert and record reviews of many a music critic (Paul Nelson, John Rockwell, Robert Christgau, Nat Hentoff, Byron Coley), who have all bid to put their finger on just what it is they hear in Fahey's music — almost all instrumental steel-string guitar music by the way, no verses to be sung. Even after its sources in country blues, ragtime, hymns, spirituals, pop, Western classical music, and so on have been discerned, where is this mystique coming from exactly? It was my thought too: What *is* this I am hearing? In 1978, at twenty years old, this question was inseparable from the more fundamental, What, as such, is *this*? This *life* I was trying to put in order. This *future* galloping toward me instead of staying put in the distance. While it had never occurred to me before to buy a Christmas record (a parent thing, no?), the spell cast by that album was certain. Those songs knew how to *un-name* the feelings you had about familiar holiday music, and indeed, about the holiday, while still giving you that music and that holiday. But it's more fundamental than that. This music gives you a glimpse of your basic estrangement without pretending to solve it, or even to want to. You cannot un-hear that feeling. You are hooked.

That's music, right? That's what the music we love, with whatever kind of sentiment, is supposed to do: bind itself to us and become something we live by, with, to. For a steady stream of people, right up to the present, that is what Fahey songs promise, songs that are helped enormously by having no human voice that ages or goes out of fashion. The music, as guitarist Glenn Jones indicates in his liner notes to Fahey reissues, emanates from just an acoustic guitar (though Fahey did "go electric" late in life) that draws on such diverse musical traditions, it is bound to telegraph something old, something new, something strange, familiar, alluring (cf. Richardson). Not to everyone, but to that steady stream of someones, Fahey's music is past, present, and future all at once. So, by 2003 I thought I had learned what to expect: the syncopation, the slow arpeggios that leave notes hanging, the rich open tunings of the country blues, the wandering off into some dissonant, modernist tonality. Yet also the sense that many of these songs were ones I might learn to play. For Fahey was no John Renbourn, no Leo Kottke, not any of the other players slinging notes at a pace well beyond reach. The music had what Kottke called a distinctive "point of view" that contemporary guitar masters could appreciate, but Fahey's craft often seemed accessible. It had space and time inside it, wasn't in a rush. His approach offered a retracing of the very invention of musical sound, in a progression to which I might (might) follow along.

But in the winter of 2003 I got hold of *Days Have Gone By*, an album Fahey had released a year before *The New Possibility*. All was more or less familiar until the two-part "A Raga Called Pat." The song's "Part One" (on vinyl, the last song on side A) is announced with a blaring steam locomotive, a thunderclap, and the sound of rain. When the guitar kicks in, the strings are struck more than strummed or plucked; and around two minutes in, Fahey settles into some vaguely raga-style playing. "Part Two" (the first song on side B) begins much the same—the train blows, the thunder claps, the rain pelts down—but other sounds quickly take over. These are fragments of . . . what? Alien birdsong? Barks, chirps, full-throated frogs? And now dials are turning; there are abrupt volume changes and wild sound distortions. All the while the guitar playing is often muffled, so deeply is it set within an ecosystem of engineered sound. "A Raga Called Pat" took back everything I thought I knew about Fahey. Not only was it far from the guitar-centered folk and blues inflections that I had gotten used to in his music, but the underlying schema was entirely new. It is not as if no one had thought before to put a thunderclap in a song: just listen to the Ronettes' "Walking in the Rain" (1964). And for bird-like cries and sound distortions, revisit the Beatles' "Tomorrow Never Knows" (1966). Simulated trains are rampant in blues music, while the insertion of actually recorded trains in "A Raga Called Pat" strongly evokes Pierre Schaeffer's 1948 "Etude Aux Chemin de Fer," one of the first pieces of musique concrète. But in stifling his guitar, Fahey seems to be making a point of his instrument being hard to hear, especially in the way we want to hear it: forthright and center stage. In a none too subtle transposition, the guitar playing, which typically is the whole of a Fahey composition, is here a whisper from deep inside the sonic world he has confected. Like any whisper, the effect is to draw us closer.

Once there, we might get that the song is staging something, even many things, and that these might require other knowledges to hear. It might be staging the environmental elements that inspire songwriting in the first place, perhaps in sympathy with blues guitarist Robert Pete Williams. Fahey had produced Williams's record *Louisiana Blues* the year before, and therein Robert Pete explains that his music picks up on "the airplanes or moaning of automobiles" coming in on the wind (Wilson, liner notes 5). Or, given the sequence of sounds, a train in the intro and once again as the outro, Fahey might be whisking his listeners off to Tutwiler, Mississippi, where, waiting for a train in 1903, the incomparable blues popularizer W. C. Handy was famously (and maybe apocryphally) woken from sleep by the first blues guitar he ever heard. Fahey's dogged interest in historical context and source materials, not to mention a delight in planting riddles, could incite many such allusions. But it is no stretch to perceive certain cultural concepts in play too. The waft of "folk" issuing from Fahey's guitar and the blare of "modernity" and "progress" sounded by the train in some sense *add up to* the warning thunderclap we heard. I mean, there's a statement there. Musicologists and cultural critics tell us that an attraction to things "folk" may be mere symptoms of "modern" alienation. We should be suspicious of the idea that "modern" and "folk" can be cleanly separated or that feelings of alienation produced by "progress" can be healed by turning back the clock to an imagined simpler time. Fahey, in multiple writings, shows he was no stranger to these critiques. Therefore, inasmuch as these concepts are interrelated, contemporaneous categories begetting and reproducing each other, Fahey's song tells us about our own musical tastes, down to the big bang of their emergence. The song says, or rather sounds out, that the folkish guitar we must strain to hear can be heard only through the din we ourselves are part of, our own obfuscations creating the interest, including Fahey's interest, in the sort of music Fahey plays.[1]

But "we" is a difficult word in this formulation. The sound of a distant guitar coming from "the other side of the tracks"—the inevitable racialized meaning of this train song, hinted at in Fahey's liner notes—was rocket fuel for the folk and blues revival. So, once more, what's that sound, if not also the racializing sound of the revival itself providing juice for Fahey's career (for dozens of careers), even as he claimed to play the part of no part. It's the sound of white appropriation of African American music, of white fascination with Black poverty, of the fight against that poverty. It's the sound of freewheelin' white song hunters traipsing through Black geographies to rediscover the old "bluesmen," the sound of segregation itself. The sound of mostly white audiences and relatively few Black songsters, of white audiences and white musicians inspired by Black songsters. The sounds of late minstrelsy and 1960s' hipstery and the sound of it's more complicated than that.

To argue that "A Raga Called Pat" does conceptual work is to suggest that it makes sense to approach Fahey's music through other means than its immediate sounds and through other means than the immediate experience of them, *The New Possibility* notwithstanding. It means redirecting whatever defamiliarization the music brings, toward the task of defamiliarizing the music itself, approaching it as part of a larger project that brings to bear Fahey's other creative activities and the knowledges they invoke—and that might also open a new vista on the way we understand certain musical and broader social landscapes of the late twentieth century. Well, had I been paying attention, *The New Possibility* had already said in writing that a larger project was in the offing. On the back cover of the record jacket and most of its reprints are Fahey's notes for the album. In the first sentence, he references the existentialist Christian philosopher Paul Tillich, crediting him a paragraph later with providing the name of the album. "The new possibility" is a translation of *die neue Möglicheit*, Tillich's shorthand for the meaning of Christianity. Fahey calls the religious tenet that Christ was begotten, not made, "non-propositionally significant," a phrase offered with no explanation—it refers to knowing something without knowing how it came about—and a sure sign of Fahey's background in philosophy. The last paragraph begins, "The songs are, whenever possible, syncopated, not because I feel that syncopation or 'swinging the Carols' is more in keeping 'with the times' (about which I could care less—blast Hegel's legacy of PROGRESS!), but simply because I prefer to play them the way I do" (liner notes, *New Possibility*). What authorizes this insistence on self-expression? The assumed confirmation that doing what *he* feels like doing would be not just okay but somehow a distinguishing mark, as if doing your own thing was not a sign of the times already, and as if limits placed on which selves matter was also not a sign of the times? What's up with issuing a statement forsaking "the times," as such, smack in the middle (1968) of the very time of Statements? Why the display of schooled intellect? Hegel. Tillich. The nonpropositional. Doesn't this edge toward obedience and abrade the claim of self-fashioning just a bit? For us, how can paying attention to Fahey's writing—of which there is a substantial amount in numerous genres—help establish the larger project just mentioned? What is to be gained by doing so?

What I would like to suggest in writing this book is that Fahey's writing not only creates new possibilities for listening to his music. It also places Fahey and his music inside important social and cultural shifts in late twentieth-century America, in such a way as to wonder what it means exactly to be *inside* them at all. Some of Fahey's writings concern the seemingly narrow relation of his music to the folk (and blues) music of the time, but they always break out of those confines to court broader concerns such as debates around the making of a self, cultural authenticity, race, the American style of capitalist industrialization, and utopian longings for democratic revival. Other writings are, on the surface, strictly musicological or about his childhood, but these topics too become vehicles for a much broader set of reflections. The whole of Fahey's written work is a bit incongruous; not all of it tallies. But there are touchstones. The two around which this book is organized are the influence on Fahey of that shapeshifting formation most strongly linked to the 1960s, an amalgamation of the new left, the counterculture, and civil rights struggle called the Movement, and Fahey's use, his canny use, of different genres of writing by which readers can trace any of these linkages I've just mentioned. Fahey is a challenge to read, and sometimes a challenge to listen to. These challenges may themselves be considered symptoms of our own received ideas that emanate from Fahey's time—the idea that folk music is and should be sincere, the idea that feelings are there to be expressed and validated, the idea that one is either awake to changing times and in the struggle, or hopelessly behind. The idea that the catchiest way to disavow "folk" is not to be awkward about it but always to be cool, classy, smartly ironic, and witty—like Bob Dylan, say. What we find out, I think, is that Fahey is never where we think he should be. Shine a light on him, then, and the space of his emergence might look different as a result.

Placing John Fahey: Texts and Contexts

Today, among fans and knowing music critics, Fahey's music and the genre it spawned most frequently go by the label "American Primitive." But it has also been labeled "folk," "New Age," "underground classical," and my personal favorite, "different" (Fahey's own adjective of choice on *The New Possibility* album). American Primitive is what has stuck, because it implies a lack of formal training, and because of its unruly but revelatory alchemy of known musical styles (e.g., Schillace, Himes). A superior example is "Stomping Tonight on the Pennsylvania/Alabama Border," which appeared on his 1963 release, *Death Chants, Breakdowns, and Military Waltzes*. The song is the product of phrases borrowed from the fourth movement of Vaughan Williams's Sixth Symphony, the Gregorian chant "Dies Irae," and Skip James's "Devil Got My Woman." Born to two white, middle-class parents and raised for most of his childhood in Takoma Park, Maryland, a suburb of Washington, D.C., Fahey developed a curious mélange of musical tastes. Early on he preferred Beethoven and Sibelius to rock and roll, and white-identified old-time country music—which his parents took him to hear live at New River Ranch, a country music park in rural Maryland—rather than the gospel, country blues, and rhythm and blues made by African American musical artists. The aversion to African American music would change dramatically and permanently in his late teens. In the early 1960s, along with a number of other white blues fanatics, Fahey participated in searching out long-lost blues singers whose "rediscovery" filled out the rosters of many of the decade's folk festivals. (Fahey and friends' success in locating Skip James and Bukka White was covered in *Time* magazine.) His interest, he claimed, was strictly aesthetic: he had fallen in love with the music. Building his own music career primarily during the folk and blues revival of the 1960s and 1970s, Fahey brought together, as I have just shown, the musicality of folk and blues stylings, raga, Western classical, musique concrète, and more. He did this in ways no one had imagined in connection with the steel-string acoustic guitar, meaning there was no audience for his compositions and arrangements until he started playing and recording. To build that audience, he launched his own independent record label, the legendary Takoma Records. As interesting and powerful as the music can be, including Fahey's turn to a post-rock ambient noise style in the 1990s (Ratliff) — he died in 2001 — his writings present problems and possibilities in quite a few other ways.

The first point to make is that Fahey's writing, much dispersed across styles and topics, and very uneven with respect to its "literary" quality, does not initially present itself as a project. Yet the sheer breadth of *kinds* is central to what makes it possible to hear the music differently and to posit a wider audience for the writings.[2] By turns, the writings are scholarly, learned, fictional, but also autobiographical, musicological, instructional; philosophical, cartographic, creatively nonfictional; satirical, parodic, poetic. He produced a monograph on a highly influential early African American blues musician, poems for a small literary magazine, essays that have been collected in two published volumes, and album and liner notes for his own records and occasionally others' records. (The last category includes notes Fahey wrote for a new, fourth volume of Harry Smith's iconic *Anthology of American Music*.) He wrote inside book covers and on restaurant menus, and kept a notebook near the end of his life that simply has pages of spirals. A "great American novel" is missing, but other than that he seems to have tried everything at least once. The writings are heady with affect too. Serious, ludicrous, genuine, mocking, morose, offensive, impenetrable. If one asks, as one asks of the music, So, *what is all this?*, it was certainly a "persistent impulse" suggesting that music is just one element of a wider set of creative activities, as Brent Hayes Edwards says of certain jazz musicians (12). But the question answers itself in a different manner too.

It is necessary to home in on the long-term development of a hybridized writing career and hybridized sensibilities as the core of Fahey's writer identity. Here is a brief itinerary. John Fahey was a product of American public elementary and high schools, which, especially after World War II (Fahey was born in 1939), redesigned the teaching of writing, having partly internalized the psychoanalytical ideas of Freud and his progeny, in order to address the anxieties and traumas of a Cold War generation. In other words, Fahey came to writing, and it came to him, in a way that was new to each. Thus, I explore in the first two chapters the stamp on Fahey's writing of self-expressive techniques, the popularization of psychology, and critiques of suburban conformity. Fahey was next a young scholar at American University, in Washington, D.C., majoring in philosophy just as existentialism's popularity among white American youth was growing. Existentialism, I show in chapters 5 and 6, gave Fahey a voice through which to join a widespread liberal critique of the voids of mass culture and, eventually, the commercialization of the counterculture. Fahey's voice was as much performative as intellectual, taking on serious matters with an idiosyncratic, nearly opaque style, thereby deforming the philosophical sources that informed him. At UCLA he graduated from a master's program in mythology and folklore, for which, in 1966, he wrote his major monograph on Charley Patton, a vitally important African American songster from the late 1920s and early 1930s. No other scholar had yet given this Mississippi Delta musician book-length treatment, and Fahey's thesis saw light as a book the next year (see chapter 3). When releasing his recorded music, some half dozen LPs by the time he finished up at UCLA, Fahey wrote copious liner notes and album inserts, parodying the didactic notation style included in folk and blues records, as well as scholarship such as he had himself been conducting (see chapter 4). Through dizzying wordplay, obscure allusions, and fictionalized blues biographies, Fahey's notes were occasions for him to lambast the 1960s' and 1970s' white romance with Black culture and mercilessly ridicule the search for authenticity within folk and blues revival circles. Meanwhile, his Patton monograph made deft use of the latest methods in folklore study and musicology. These led him to a deep appreciation of African American cultural agency in the rural South. But they also reinforced his great reluctance to think of that culture as also a political expression. So intent was he to isolate culture and politics from each other (at least before Martin Luther King's assassination), and like most whites so skeptical was he of the Black Power movement, that what Leroi Jones / Amiri Baraka had already proclaimed in his book on the blues, "Negro music is *always* radical in the context of formal American culture" (235; also Rabaka), would have made little sense to Fahey. Yet, Fahey's writing also expressed an interest in specifying what form he thought race relations ought to take. So, also explored in chapter 6, somewhere along the line, he became entranced with ideas about the subjective human experiences of geographic space in existential philosophy, environmental psychology, and urban planning. In a quite phantasmagoric essay included in *How Bluegrass Music Destroyed My Life*, he used those ideas to address imaginatively (and problematically) racial segregation in his home-town of Takoma Park.

The picture that should emerge from this quick summary is one of unusu-ally strong intellectual appetites hell-bent on the implosion of traditional forms and settled content, and a driving interest in what can be done with the pieces left lying on the ground. It is a far cry from other musicians in-volved in the folk revival, who went on to become scholars writing works of sober reflection (cf. Rosenberg, *Transforming Tradition*). Fahey could be re-garded as an eager heir to American novelists of the 1930s who exposed the political underpinnings of the national obsession with "folk" by narrating it through hybridized genres, such as satire and burlesque (Retman). But Fahey's works make a particular statement about the cultural and social formations of his own time. Fahey's writerly output is distinctly a late twentieth-century, college-educated, white male phenomenon, strongly shaped and opportuned by liberal trends (whatever Fahey's own beliefs) of the late 1950s and 1960s. His young-adult years coincided with the gradual ascent of the new left, some of whose ideas he shared, if the evidence is to be trusted. By new left I mean, as Doug Rossinow puts it in *The Politics of Au-thenticity* (1998), the political and cultural left that "stemmed from white youth participation in civil rights activism" and extended into antiwar activ-ism, feminism, the ecology movement, sexual revolution, liberal theology, and a reassertion of aggressive masculinity (1; also Teodori). I view his writ-ing as also specifically influenced by the counterculture that emerged out of those years. (This is hardly a surprising claim, except maybe to those who hew to a narrow view of Fahey's iconoclasm.) But there is a puzzle here that demands immediate modification of any such claim. When we look closely at, say, the essay Fahey wrote at the end of high school in 1956 and wonder why he did not plunge headlong into the progressive politics of the new left during college or merge body and soul with the counterculture, the question itself is probably wrong. Many people remain attached to the notion that the 1960s redound to a few things—protests, lava lamps, sex, weed—somehow united in purpose. But historians of the new left and the counterculture have for some time been interested in exploring the crumbly edges and margins of these formations (e.g., Rossinow, "New Left" and *Politics*), including, as Rebecca Klatch does, some of the curious overlaps between values and cul-tural styles of youth on the right and on the left. The work of these scholars documents the fluidity and messiness of these movements, the ways that people were partly in them and partly out. Fahey's writing, from its scholarly boasts to its bathetic wandering about, embodies that fluidity and is consonant with these reassessments. It ought even to deepen our sense of the positions and affects made structurally possible by a shifting cultural and political terrain.

Inevitably, Fahey was drawn into that interdigitated space where the new left, the counterculture, and the vestiges of the folk and blues revival eventually met up (Lund and Denisoff; Rossinow, "New Left"; Feenberg; Cohen; Burke). What did he want there? To have a musical career, certainly. (And as we'll see again at length, he also wanted to insert his own voice, his own words, which record buyers would find tucked into record sleeves or as back liner notes on album covers.) But this complex space of cultural and ideological overlaps also wanted Fahey. The 1966 Berkeley folk festival was telling (it is also just one example). Featured were folk and topical-song stalwarts of the old and new left, such as Pete Seeger and Phil Ochs; "rediscovered" blues singer Robert Pete Williams; Jefferson Airplane, counterculture emissaries from across the Bay; and, of course, John Fahey, who was announced on the "artists and folklorists" portion of the program as an "experimental guitarist" working with "traditional guitar patterns," and as "psychedelic" guitarist on the program page containing the large photograph of Jefferson Airplane (Berkeley in the Sixties). If not taken too literally, these are not unreasonable representations of Fahey. As Fahey's biographer Steve Lowenthal has pointed out, psychedelics were not his thing, but in other ways Fahey exemplified the "screwy alliances" of the time, as Rossinow puts it (Rossinow, *Politics*). To the alliance, Fahey brought his existentialist credentials, some interesting references to "ecology," a detour through countercultural yoga and spiritual questing, and, not least, a reassertion of heteromasculinity. A tour de force, if that can be the phrase, for the expression of this jumble of wants would be the introductory essay Fahey wrote for his book of guitar instruction, *The Best of John Fahey, 1959–1977* (cf. Fahey, "Bola Sete"). There, the reader finds a full-page photo of Fahey with his guitar. Atop the guitar is a large desert tortoise (he was a member of a tortoise preservation society in Southern California that was committed to saving habitat amid the state's rampant development [T. Ferris]). Atop the guitar and the tortoise is Fahey sporting a necklace of yoga beads; he had traveled to India, dallied at yoga retreats, and followed the guru Swami Satchidananda. As the reader moves into the essay proper, we learn that "music is a language—a language of *emotions*" (6). As Fahey explains, with detailed instructions as to how it should be done, emotions need to be played authentically and without fear. There should be no "homosexual guitar playing" (13–14), which serves only to demonstrate "guitar angst" (14)—that is, the musician's failure to master and dominate the instrument because of his feminization. A bit of fiction follows, sandwiched within which is a full-page photo of the American existentialist philosopher Walter Kaufmann, beloved by Fahey. Much deeper in the book appear instructions for playing one of Fahey's compositions, "The Revolt of the Dyke Brigade" (140–45).

If it is clear that Fahey seized on the kaleidoscopic potential (not to mention the self-permitted bigotries) inherent in that interdigitated space of the "screwy alliance," it would be a mistake to place him in the center of the new left, if by that we narrowly mean involvement in protests, activist meetings, and preparation of movement literature. What Fahey had were concerns that overlapped those of new-left ideology and counterculture sentiments. The new left was fueled in a profound way by a protean search for authenticity that opened the door to affinities with 1960s' counterculture. "The counterculture," Rossinow writes, "helped the new left project outward its own search for personal authenticity, locating the causes of inner alienation in larger social forces and opening an avenue for all people to achieve authenticity at a societal level." He continues, "The new left and counterculture were two parts of a larger white youth existentialist movement of the cold war era—two parts of a larger historical formation with common roots, even if they were not close tactical allies" (*Politics* 249). What did this search for authenticity in the Movement, as some contemporaries preferred to call the broader phenomenon, fight against (Jacobs and Landau; also Rossinow, "New Left")? It is an often-told story: economic exploitation to some degree, but especially alienation and estrangement from self-determined values and goals as opposed to those pre-given by the dominant institutions of government, school, and corporation.

Here is Richard Flacks, a sociologist who was active very early in Students for a Democratic Society, who describes in 1965 not just goals and values but the inherent tension they manifest:

> If I understand what we are trying to work on when we say we are building a "movement," I think it has to do with two types of goals. One, which we might call "existential humanism," is expressed by the desire to change the way we, as individuals actually live and deal with other people. We speak of the attempt to achieve "community" to reach levels of intimacy and directness with others unencumbered by the conventional barriers of race, status, class, etc. We strive at every occasion to enhance the ability of people to affect their environment,

to be centers of initiative, to be self-expressive, to be free. And the achievement of some of this, on any occasion, we take to be intrinsically worthwhile.

Second, we say that we seek a radical transformation of the social order. In short, that we act politically because our values cannot be realized in any durable sense without a reconstruction of the political and social system. Thus we say that we want a redistribution of wealth and power in the society; that we want to develop new centers of power as a basis for such a redistribution; that we look toward the emergence of new political and social institutions which can authentically provide the conditions for freedom.

It must be stressed that the latter goals are *political* in meaning—they cannot be approached without a profoundly serious commitment to *political* involvement. That is not necessarily true for what I have called "existential humanism"—it seems to me entirely possible for each of us to guide our own way of living according to such standards and consequently strive to approach an ethical existence. And the achievement of some approximation of community for ourselves and those immediately near us seems plausibly independent of political change. (qtd. in Jacobs and Landau 163)

Flacks emphasizes that these goals need each other, that there is as much danger in individuals retreating into personal satisfactions (or dissatisfactions) as there is in a politics that is inhuman. He warns, however, that these differently scaled goals were each poles of attraction on their own and the two would not come together automatically. We might add that when they did intersect, the meeting point itself might be highly idiosyncratic and skewed. In such an angle is where we find John Fahey.

Individuals are often partly in and partly out of a given politics because they are composed of different identities in the first place, which they are faced with attempting to navigate. Social movement scholars working on the question of identities find repeatedly that individuals are *variously* attracted or repelled, or attracted and repelled, by different movement agendas (Stryker et al.; Reger et al.). Fahey was no different. When pressed, he in fact identified countercultural elements he liked. Poet and small press publisher, as well as ardent Fahey fan, Douglas Blazek interviewed Fahey in 1967, when Fahey was finishing up his studies at UCLA. Certain psychedelic rock bands, like Country Joe and the Fish and the Grateful Dead, and some Rolling Stones songs are "pretty nice . . . pretty interesting," says Fahey. Bob

Dylan is "real good sometimes. I like his rock stuff. Some of it more than his early records where he's just doing folk imitations," but some Dylan songs with the "long psychedelic trip-like lyrics . . . are nice too" (Blazek 71). The Beatles are "great," especially the *Sgt. Pepper's* album. Poetry he doesn't like too much. Although, "in D.C. these things were the hippie things to be interested in back then. The coffee houses all had poetry. Ginsberg, Corso and Ferlinghetti came down to D.C. and gave a little poetry recital, and I was curious about it. I liked the first part of *Howl*. . . . I like to hear people read, though, like watching Ginsberg read" (72). We'll see more of Fahey's picking and choosing later. The point is that he made a career of his experimental writing and musicking (Small), and could only have made that career in essential antiestablishment recreational spaces: the cafés, concert halls, folk festivals, and campuses where folk and blues music found their audience, and Fahey consequently found his. Furthermore, as long as the Movement was going to have these two broad goals, it was bound to produce perceived and self-proclaimed outliers, misfits, and naysayers who didn't "properly" belong (whatever that could mean) but didn't exactly belong anywhere else either.

I have already mentioned the relevance of the postwar folk revival in the United States. It figured centrally (albeit not exclusively) as a soundtrack in the counterculture, in the political sensibilities of the new left, and in the civil rights struggle — the Movement at large. But it has a history and logic of its own too. So let's turn for a few moments to a discussion of those and place Fahey in relation to them. Emerging in the immediate post–World War II period and having its greatest commercial success between the late 1950s and the mid-1960s, the folk revival coincides precisely with the formative years of Fahey's musical tastes and his first ventures into music composition and performance. While classical music was played in the house, on Sundays the family often went to New River Ranch, a live-music park in Rising Sun, Maryland, not far from Takoma Park (Lowenthal; also Thompson). Fahey, twelve years old when New River was begun in 1951, got early exposure to country, bluegrass, and other musical styles of the revival. This music, whose deep connective tissue joined it to African American musical traditions, was also, according to the New River Ranch recollections of Mike Seeger (half-brother of Pete Seeger), accompanied by "minstrel/vaudeville dances and routines, barely out of the blackface era" (Seeger 1). Folk's commercial breakthrough, including extensive radio play, top-of-the-chart record sales, major coverage by magazines such as *Time* and *Newsweek*, and television broadcasts (e.g., ABC's prime-time series *Hootenanny*), ensured that the revival would be a staple of Fahey's diet.

It was a diet exceedingly rich in symbolism. "What is important for the folk revival," Robert Cantwell writes,

> is that the minstrel stage, well before the emergence of the romance of the west, was one of the earliest and certainly the broadest imaginative field in which America created its proto-discourse, not only of race and racial stereotype, but of rustic and pastoral life: its folklife. The cabins, cottonbales, wagons, steamboats, . . . all the trappings of the minstrel stage, as well as the piquant genre images of corn and cottonfields, the welcoming old plantation home, the harvest moons . . . all the wistful longings addressed to them, and the very "South" itself, magically invoked by mere names, Kentucky or Carolina or Alabama — are the visual and linguistic coinage of the minstrelsy that has been circulating in America for a century and a half in thousands of forms beyond the stage itself. . . . It is now quite impossible even to think about "folklife" without recourse to the many motifs and images that descend from minstrelsy, which may be said to have formed the core vocabulary of an American vernacular romanticism, one inextricably bound up with the questions of race and racial identity. (*When We Were Good* 24–25)

This is precisely the folk music culture that Fahey lived, loved, and *understood* to be drenched in mythology. Indeed, he picks up the thread directly in his 1984 essay, "Vignettes, Digressions, and Screens." "I really loved these songs. Still do" (14). The nostalgia-drenched "Are You from Dixie?" was one of them, after Fahey heard it on the local country radio station WARL. In the essay, Fahey reproduces the lyrics to an 1890's song, "The Girl I Loved in Sunny Tennessee," including a common racist term of the day that I will abbreviate here: "You could hear the d*****s singing, As they sang farewell to me. Far across the fields of cotton, My old homestead I could see." (Note that Fahey eschews the usual transcription "as *she* sang farewell to me.") "But," he concludes, "what was Dixie, anyway, but a Southern belle you knew . . . a bunch of old songs. It was gone by the time they sang about it. If it ever was. But in Hyattsville [the town neighboring Fahey's Takoma Park, Maryland] and places like that they sure thought it had been . . . and maybe still was . . . something great. Dreams. Air" (14).[3] Of course "Dixie" was more than just a Southern belle. It was, as the lyrics suggest, a much broader representation of the southern plantation economy, as Fahey knew and would write about in numerous other texts. The question is (a subject for parts 2 and 3), Why would his love for that music, its sources, its mythic world, survive his critique of them, and perhaps even rely on it? "The parodist," if Fahey is one here, "is always in effect advancing a theory of what he parodies, however shallow or deep," writes Robert Cantwell (*Bluegrass* 270; cf. Retman). But toward what end?

The long march from minstrelsy to the folk revival is discontinuous and diffuse. In Robert Cantwell's account, *When We Were Good*, retracing the steps involves a multitude of cartographies, many with uncanny connections to Fahey's life and career. It involves following the historical migration of rural people to industrial cities. It involves the rediscovery and distribution of old musical recordings, including the refashioning of tastes that would find these interesting and entertaining. The minstrel legacy traveled along the vaudeville circuit, an outlet for countless African American performing artists, and over the airwaves of commercial broadcasting, which fed white nostalgia for the old South. Crucial also were white song hunters, scouring the southern landscape for remnants of disappearing musical traditions and then, with seemingly endless energy and often a "benevolent," paternalistic racial attitude, championing their discoveries to whomever would listen, usually other white audiences. The route led to the Smithsonian Institution and to "folk" record labels and imprints. An intersecting path leads to the nineteenth-century "genteel" socialists and reformers of the U.S. Northeast and the interest in folk music they developed as part of their critique of a growing mass culture. The route also crosses through early twentieth-century and later male sexual anxieties—founded in a rejection of the perceived feminization of American culture and a barely disguised homoeroticism— that produced newfound interest in "strenuous" living, "traditional" arts and crafts, and summer camps. Folk festivals and the tourism that they fed on and promulgated between the world wars and after also composed the route. The route was illuminated by a very specific sort of ideology through which revivalists claimed they were themselves folk-identified: close to, intermingling with, and of the people whose work they brought to the stage.

The singular fact of the folk revival is that, per Cantwell, while it is steeped in a representational world, its representations appear to be real: real performers, real instruments, real people, real voices. So, unlike the more obviously fictional pastoral representations found in paintings and narrative fictions, folk figures have a particular appeal and a particular presence. They are semiotic and material at once. And this presence made for certain other illusions that only added to its power, the illusion that the folk revival was not a political, power-laden phenomenon. For Cantwell, "folk" is thus a way to imagine that the culture one is complicit with killing off still actually exists. Its existence, he argues, seems to be the cause for which the revolution against industrial capitalism or mass culture or crass materialism is fought, when it is instead very much its product. As he also notes, to be caught up in the folk revival "resembles a recovery of self—but is at the same time a revolution against the forces that constitute the self," an individual self, one is required to be (39–40). That is to say, the notion of the individual who is charged with the necessity of self-fashioning finds in the folk revival the illusion of a choice, unrecognized as illusory. Especially in parts 2 and 3 of this book, we will see Fahey's complicated relationship with these dimensions of "folk," including a complete rejection of the label for himself. But suffice to say that Fahey was caught up in, and reflects quite well in his writing, the contradictions and loopbacks so well outlined by Cantwell (see also Filene; Cohen; Rosenberg). Moreover it is the illusions and contradictions of the folk figure idea that gave birth to Blind Joe Death, John Fahey's blackface alias.

Blind Joe Death

Blind Joe Death is not a pervasive, ubiquitous presence in Fahey's writing, or even in his music. But the social and cultural logics of a presumed racial intimacy, out of which Blind Joe Death emerged, are. Blackness plays a very particular role in folk figure formation. The cultural historian Eric Lott argues that blackface emerged in the context of working-class whites' anxiety over the subsumption of their labor by industrial capitalism and their forced participation in an internally competitive proletariat. In this process, African Americans were constructed as a cultural, social, racialized Other, at once peripheral to this system and yet in it as proletarian competitors. Via blackface, then, white performers and audiences may imagine themselves as having accessed a world lost to them while besting their competition. This was not, or at least not exclusively, about white racial hatred plain and simple; it was a vehicle especially for the white working class to explore its social and cultural location vis-à-vis the broader society. In Lott's words, minstrel artists and audience members who followed them "immersed themselves in 'blackness' to indulge their felt sense of difference" (53).[4]

White participants in the folk revival, whose songs and performers drew from minstrelsy's wellspring, continued this exploratory tradition. Following Lott, Cantwell argues that the white middle class constructed itself as oppressed by postwar industrial capitalism's demand that each person become an upstanding, hardworking, self-reliant individual (*When We Were Good*). Yet such an identity slid easily into the idea of the individual who revolts, for perhaps I can be a liberal self who is not also a wage slave. Lott traces this notion back a long ways: "[With] antebellum blackface performers a set of racial attitudes and cultural styles that in America go by the name of bohemianism first emerged. . . . We ought to recognize . . . the degree to which blackface stars inaugurated an American tradition of class abdication through gendered cross-racial immersion which persists, in historically differentiated ways, to our own day" (52). The model for this economy is the Black musical artist as a figure for, Cantwell argues, the *universal* folk (*When We Were Good*). Still, the operation of the model can't escape the idealization of racial difference it depends on. On the one hand, it matters that Blackness is the source of folk, since in the white imaginary Blacks are figured symbolically as outside, or not quite captured by, capital. On the other hand, whiteness is reasserted as the identity not quite captured by or marked by the domain of color. And yet the *ideology* of the model is that racial difference has been mooted: folk is figured as universal, inclusive. Song styles and gestures can be borrowed, can be blended, and are free for the taking. As the musicologist Robin James argues, the hipness that white male folk artists acquire in the process appears to return to them an arena of choice that a pacifying bureaucratized capitalism has taken away.

Fahey's first experiments with minstrelsy were recordings, some of them guitar *and* vocal recordings, he made as "Blind Thomas," with Joe Bussard for Bussard's Fonotone label, in Fredericksburg, Maryland, outside Washington, D.C. The Blind Joe Death figure (styled after once-popular African American recording artists such as Blind Blake, Blind Willie McTell, and Blind Boy Fuller) came along shortly thereafter. *John Fahey / Blind Joe Death* is the title of Fahey's first self-produced LP, on his own Takoma label, from 1959. The ruse is that the music of Blind Joe Death, a deceased Black country blues musician, appears on side A, and John Fahey's music appears on side B. But both sides are Fahey, Blind Joe Death being merely his "minstrelized persona" (Lowenthal 28). Not until the 1967 printing, and several Fahey albums later, did Fahey remove Blind Joe Death from the album's credits. Fahey played the part of Blind Joe Death in an obvious ruse in person too. I say obvious because there was no blackface makeup involved, only other racial markers, sunglasses and (feigned) blindness. John McIntire, owner of the Bitter Lemon coffeehouse in Memphis, sketched portraits of Blind Joe Death in 1962 (see figure 1) and recalls one of the performances:

FIGURE 1 "Blind Joe Death" / John Fahey at the Bitter Lemon, Memphis, Tennessee, 1962. Drawing by John McIntire. Courtesy of John McIntire and Matt Ducklo, Tops Gallery, Memphis.

These two guys were sitting in the audience, I didn't know who they were. They were writing and talking to each other real loud, they didn't pay any attention to her [the local performer]. They were going, Yech. But it was the only coffeehouse at the time. One of 'em picks up a guitar I had lying around and starts strumming it. I said, "You guys can play?" He said, "You want us to play something for you?" They started playing and nobody could believe it. They played this open-tuned blues guitar, and they went into their act. John Fahey was Blind Joe Death. He wore dark glasses and Bill Barth would lead him up onstage, and they would play together. When he was done, he took his glasses off and he sat back in the audience. (qtd. in Gordon 123–24)

Fahey and Barth reportedly performed the same routine at the 1969 Memphis Blues Festival (Sullivan). Regardless of how many Blind Joe Death performances there were, Fahey was clearly poking fun at, even while participating in, the apparatus that white hipness requires.

My sense, which I hope to convey over the course of this book, is that Fahey would have understood all too well the contradictions that Cantwell, Lott, and James write about, and would have been aware he was also their product. Fahey saw ways to use these contradictions in certain writings, both to sincerely explore his affective attachments and to provoke his audiences who might not know what was going on. I doubt Fahey would challenge Cantwell's view that a continuous line connects the Black minstrel tradition to a figure like himself, although he would want to complicate it by pointing out the importance of other musical traditions to his musical performances and compositions. The same would be true regarding the assertion of self-determining masculinity that comes through in Fahey's Blind Joe Death persona, which he once pronounced had much to do with his anger over middlebrow prohibitions against too much emotional expression. As we will see later, Fahey also ultimately claimed his Blind Joe Death invention had to do with sympathy for Black rage in America's cities.

It is important not to simply read off John Fahey's career from a general "origin" theory of minstrelsy. By the time Fahey's relationship to the folk revival began, the Cold War had changed the terms of what the political uses of the folk idiom could be. As the music historian Marybeth Hamilton notes, interest in the music of old blues figures, including the revival of some of their careers, "formed part of broad-based depoliticization [I prefer to say different politicization] of cultural inquiry in the Cold War USA, part of a movement of intellectuals away from radicalism and towards a new role as 'guardians of the self,' champions of the personal, the individual, against the forces of political conformity" (154; see also Denisoff; Roy). Had he still been alive to encounter Hamilton's argument, Fahey's face would have lit up.

That Fahey's introduction to the music of the revival occurred where it did—that is, in the music scene of greater Washington, D.C.—creates additional significance. Both factors (the Cold War timing and the D.C. location) possibly combined to increase the likelihood that Fahey would balk at getting involved in the more overtly political activities of the Movement, after he moved to California in the early 1960s. Historically, D.C. had already built a strong infrastructure of folk music patronage. During the 1930s and 1940s "folksong collectors in the Library of Congress, the Works Project Administration, and the Farm Securities Administration" spearheaded a "nationalistic cultural project, a government-sponsored 'folk revival' based on locating an authentic, homegrown, non-European national identity legitimized by the culture of people living at America's margins" (Lorenz 41). The Cold War environment steered these doings in a particular direction, however. According to the cultural historian Stephen Lorenz's detailed portrait of the cultural politics of D.C.'s folk music revival: "Highly segregated Cold War Washingtonians had a strong penchant for typically apolitical forms of folksong, such as spirituals, ballads, and the blues, and a long familiarity with the talented rural artists who came from nearby Appalachia to the city looking to work, such as the Stoneman and Carter families. This created a taste for folksong marked by a depoliticized artistry that highlighted the city's own sophisticated, politically refined 'folksense' of its own powerful cultural traditions and place in the region, the country, and the world" (15).

D.C.'s geography played its part. Cosmopolitan and sophisticated, on the one hand, the city was, on the other hand, "culturally still connected to a hierarchical, agrarian past. The city as regional magnet for poor migrant black and white folk musicians, combined with a local resistance to overtly political messages in folk music as a sign of worldly corruption, produced a depoliticized 'folk consciousness' that centered on issues of ethnography and authenticity" (23). Depoliticized doesn't mean full compliance, though; "anxieties about suburbanization, consumerism, racial integration, and the atomic bomb" helped fuel interest in "roots" music and living folk singers (22).

The well-known Lomax and Seeger families were part of this D.C. scene, including having been Cold War targets, but Lorenz emphasizes that the revival involved other key actors too. A local radio station, WARL, hosted the largest country music program of any major metropolitan area. Station DJs Connie Gay and Dick Cerri were at the heart of the city's folk music revival.

Gay's program in particular, "Town and Country Time," which expanded into a TV show in 1955, was adept at addressing rural and urban audiences. Don Owens, who appears in Fahey's *How Bluegrass Music Destroyed My Life*, also joined the staff (Lorenz). (Fahey, we'll see in chapter 6, credits Owens with said destruction.) New River Ranch, mentioned above, was another significant local site where urban and suburban people could experience country music on its own turf, courtesy of its founders, the musicians Ola Belle Reed and her husband, who had migrated from New River, North Carolina. The audience sat outdoors on wooden plank seats, enjoying relatively unrestricted access on any given night to Bill Monroe, Flatt and Scruggs, the Stanley Brothers, Johnny Cash, Ernest Tubbs, Hank Williams, the Carter Family, or Loretta Lynn (Lorenz 122–23). In Lorenz's words, Ola Belle Reed and her husband "specifically tried to recreate a sense of organic community lost in the transition to modern city life" (121). D.C. had a fine share of clubs and cafés at which to hear revival music too. Fahey was no stranger to these, nor to the Seeger family home, where he met and learned from the African American songster Elizabeth Cotten (Lowenthal; also Guerrieri, *John Fahey*, *vol. 1*, rev.).

Finally, Fahey attached himself to a coterie of highly influential blues aficionados, the so-called East Coast Blues Mafia (Dunlap; Hamilton). This group was not a creation of Washington, D.C., alone but included a healthy number of D.C.-area contingents: record collectors Dick Spottswood and Joe Bussard; Fahey manager and cofounder of Takoma Records, ED Denson; independent record label founders Gene Rosenthal of Adelphi Records and Joe Bussard of Fonotone; Fahey friend and later a member of Canned Heat, Henry Vestine; and still others. Lorenz describes this group as off by itself, uninterested in "folkies with nylon string guitars" or topical folk songs. They were after a "real" country blues set in the raw ground of "the most marginalized, disenfranchised folk in America, those who were publicly highlighted by 1960s grassroots voter registration efforts in the deep South. They wanted access to the emotionally sincere, masculine, rebellious, darkly exotic world of the 1920s Mississippi Delta" (Lorenz 195).

Not all of these individuals' interests were so narrowly defined, but it was nonetheless out of this ferment that Fahey developed an interest in seeing if some of the old legends might be found alive, believing, as Mary Beth Hamilton describes it, that the "Delta is alive in ways ours is not, rich in a sense of community and in a music—the blues—that is an intensely personal expression of a living and breathing way of life" (197–98). Such a feeling did not exclusively belong to song hunters like John Fahey. Hamilton may as well have been referring to Tom Hayden, a preeminent voice of the student new left, whose feeling was precisely the same, that southern Blacks simply felt things on a deeper level than whites (Brick and Parker).

With fellow travelers, Fahey toured the Delta and helped rediscover Bukka White and Skip James, but he practiced more locally too. As an older suburb, Takoma Park, Maryland, while segregated, saw Blacks and whites living close together. Its segregation, Lorenz observes, "heightened the sense that" right close by "was an undiscovered black folk world, unseen and ignored in black homes, churches, and clubs." Very easily Fahey and friend Dick Spottswood could "cross racial lines to access the new musical territory" (Lorenz 250). And they certainly did, as we will see in chapter 6: the two befriended the musician Elmer Williams, who lived in one of the segregated neighborhoods along Sligo Road. Spottswood would record duets of Williams and Fahey, and Fahey would write at some length about his "adventures on the edge," as he called them. It is clear that Fahey benefited from accidents (accidental to him, that is) of Washington, D.C., history and geography, with which to get started on a vocation of music and writing. But he was a person of his times reflecting broader formations too.

The Structure of This Book and the Question of Its Stakes

A look at the table of contents shows I have grouped the book's six chapters into three parts with their own introductions. Consider each part as a particular take on Fahey's writing and music. In the chapters of part 1, I set Fahey's Movement-ready teenage worries about the loss of individual autonomy against his much later, adult reflections on the psycho-political corruption of childhood innocence by agents of U.S. capitalism looking to cultivate its next generation of workers. The object is to pinpoint the key affects that crop up in many parts of the Fahey archive and place them in relation to the possibilities inherent in the Movement's culture. In part 2, we find Fahey in the 1960s applying the interpretation of rural Black music he developed back east to his UCLA-based study of Charley Patton and to his album liner notes. That the former is a work of scholarship and the latter tend to be prankish and parodic only means Fahey found a way to use the two genres to express a consistent viewpoint about that music and its muddled reception by largely white coffeehouse and folk festival audiences. In writings of the 1970s and later, explored in part 3, Fahey doubles down on his fixation with individually felt emotion and its expression as virtually a human right, the right to be an "existential humanist" to use Richard Flacks's expression. At first,

Fahey explores the difficulties such radical individualism presents for a society that would propose to found itself on such a philosophy of scaled-up individual expression. Then, we discover him making an about-face, exploring emotion's potential to create a shared, multiracial community space. I propose that Fahey's turnaround is not really a contradiction so much as both positions attempt to reconstitute and extend the ethics of the Movement, to describe on his own terms the balancing act proposed in Richard Flacks's interesting formulation. (Let me suggest too that if, as Karl Hagstrom Miller argues, it is imperative to understand the importance that the Jim Crow era had on the development of folklore studies and modern racial concepts of the folk, then John Fahey's writings and his crucial choice of Charley Patton as a focal point are an example of how those studies and concepts begin to shift when Jim Crow—the old Jim Crow—was being toppled [Miller, *Segregating Sound*].)[5]

The introductions to parts 1, 2, and 3 each conclude with a short "listening session" of selected Fahey songs. Take these as an attempt by one person who is not a musicologist or music theorist to link Fahey's two primary creative vocations. Links between the music and the writing are not always obvious; rarely is the evidence strong for consistent demonstration of a cause-effect relationship between music and written text, or topics shared by them. Yet once one plunges into Fahey's writings, the prompts for what new meanings his music might hold are too irresistible to ignore. My aim is to take some interpretive risks and make what I think are honest attempts to hear and read musical and prose (mostly) texts across each other's differences. I like my University of Minnesota colleague Mike Gallope's suggestion that Fahey's music and writing may be considered in counterpoint to each other. We need not see them as strictly "about" each other, but this does not mean we cannot think about them simultaneously. Readers may feel that it would have been better to place my ruminations on Fahey's music at the end of each of the three parts (i.e., to read after their chapters have been read). In that case, there is nothing to prevent anyone from waiting until just those preferred moments.

A special note about the selected songs: most of the songs I have chosen to write about are readily available to stream on YouTube or Spotify, or elsewhere as indicated. Where a live version of a song I write about may be hard to find, I have tried in my own writing to evoke the difference from the studio recording. Readers familiar with Fahey's music will probably see my selection as not very representative of Fahey's best work, as they understand it. (I'm a little disappointed myself!) For one thing, there are just too many such works to write about in a short book. More accurately, the choice of texts I have written about, chosen because they reflect the scope of styles and intellectual traditions Fahey drew from, and the themes I have found in them, simply pulled me toward particular songs and not others. In fact, a few of these I had not even taken the time to listen to carefully before reading Fahey's prose—"Charley Bradley's Ten-Sixty-Six Blues" being a premier example. That a study of Fahey's writing brought these songs further to my attention is one personal example of the value research like this can have. I hope others might be moved to pick up the baton and run with it as they too see fit: there is a great deal to explore in Fahey's writings and music, more examples of which are not hard to find.

The relationship of Fahey's writing to the "real" Fahey is an issue that is bound to arise. I do not want to claim that the writings grant unmediated access to him. If we do not want to read Fahey from theories about certain strains of postwar American culture, but instead discover how he works on these strains himself, we also do not want to commit the fallacy that Fahey's writings and Fahey the person are the same thing. I view the writings as experiments and explorations in making a self at particular points in time and place, in which we also understand that a self is not an isolated, self-determined being (Hees). Selves are always already social, always already in the making, without being simply mirrors of their environment. A self is like a shifting answer to the world, something someone performs; recalling Cantwell, a reflection or deflection of the many ways one is addressed by others in the world. If readers of this book are bound to see that there is something in Fahey's writings of the confessionalism that swept through numerous cultural media in late twentieth-century America, it would be smart to recognize that, as Christopher Grobe writes, "confessional performers don't just chronicle the events of their lives; they also dramatize the tension between their inchoate selves and the media they use to try to capture them" (23). These different media are partly constitutive of performing selves; they, their conventions, and their adaptability to the bending of conventions make performance possible. Thinking, for instance, about the treatment of race in Fahey's writing, his decisions about what to write, to think, to compose, and his various use of liner notes, a master's thesis, and a fantasized memoir never escaped the brokenness of the racialized social relations into which John Fahey was born. The resources with which to think and write about this are products of that very brokenness. So, when Fahey acidly rejects the models of racial intimacy dreamed up by counterculture and folk revival peers and aims to be a better white ally, he has not somehow gained access to a position outside social conventions. He performatively deploys other such conventions that have their own faults.[6] At least some of the performances redound to genre: received ideas about liner notes, memoir, fiction, and scholarship enter into the production of Fahey's authorial performativity just as genres of music—the blues, for example (Mack)—help any musician construct a performer self. We should not think a look at Fahey's writings is going to cut through the performative net and draw a portrait of the man as he is. (If I will seem to stray from this commitment, I hope it is only in a moment of enthusiasm for a point I want to make.) These things said, nothing about the perspective I am conveying here should be taken to diminish the social power relations from which Fahey benefited. He was afforded more self-performances than most people ever get, and as a white male probably got away with much more than would have been the case otherwise. Nor should anything about the perspective I am conveying here be taken to diminish Fahey's stature as extraordinarily creative either. These two points complement each other, as it is a whole host of white, male privileges that granted him access to the resources he had, and a commitment to his well-being on the part of a succession of women, which kept him afloat for years on end (Lowenthal; Hopper).

Finally, what is at stake in a book about the writing of John Fahey? For one, no account of his career can be complete without considering his writing. Why should that matter? When richer accounts emerge of the people who interest us, the stories told through those people stop being only those stories. Fahey's own music is foundational in the history of American Primitive guitar music, and he has garnered attention in the history of the blues for his monograph on Charley Patton (cited but not much studied or placed in relation to his other texts) and for his "rediscovery" of two important Depression-era African American blues musicians. But, as with Daphne Brooks's reassessments of Zora Neale Hurston's song performances and of the underappreciated intimacy of Geeshie Wiley and L. V. Thomas's creative partnership, Fahey's writings, viewed as a body of work, necessarily widen the telling being told: what looked like the history of the folk and blues revival, or invention of a musical style, feathers out into other histories, potentially changing how we view them (Brooks, "'Sister Can You Line It Out,'" "See My Face"). In Fahey's case, it is significant that his writings tell a story he apparently did not intend to tell. That story, it seems to me, goes like this. Fahey, the musician and composer, was a committed historian and fairly prolific commentator on the music he loved—music that a significant demographic slice of white America loved—but his exceedingly cautious attitude toward the political dimensions of the music means that, even though there are some intimations to the contrary, he too easily settled for its mystery rather than its history, as one reader of this book aptly phrases it (see also Rabaka). This is important because the domain of history as an unending search for what really happened and who said so, for the sorting of fable from fact and who benefits, is a political domain. The gravitation toward mystique, toward ineffable genius and inexplicable emotional depth in the musicians he cared most about, especially Charley Patton, set a mood for much of Fahey's writing generally. But trafficking in mystery shows itself to be a way of imagining the political anyway. Therein the story Fahey tells in spite of himself. Seizing especially on one, the self-creative, strand of Movement culture paradoxically becomes the way that Fahey's writings imagine a deracinated democracy might work, although on his terms and never quite stated as such. Over the course of these chapters I will have to make the case. I do not claim Fahey's writings are unique in their vision, but in tracing the long writerly durée of his concerns, across all the messiness of the writing itself, I want to show how such a position, among others possible, can be built and sustained across a variety of genres bent to that task. Fahey had extraordinarily rich materials with which to hybridize his pen (cf. Retman). There was the reformation of writing pedagogy in post–World War II America and the florescence of the counterculture, shaping and sanctioning his sensibilities. There were many popularized blues figures fighting their singular battles, and revival festivals that seemed to bring each one to life. There was an audience for these figures that Fahey could do battle with. Not least there was an accumulating scholarship on folk and blues, to draw on and give to; a historiography, still being made, with which to contend and within which he is an understudied subject.

Fahey's position, to be clear, is deeply problematic. It has the basic fault Theodor Adorno pointed out long ago in *The Jargon of Authenticity*: when authenticity is claimed to be located in the individual subject, subjective experience is accepted as the ultimate arbiter of authenticity. The individual subject tends to project their own subjectivity onto the world with an unacknowledged silencing of others as the result. Fahey's writings do not cave all the way, though. They exhibit a struggle toward a *critical* self-definition: among nonconformists, Fahey insisted on his own nonconforming (thanks again to my anonymous peer reviewer for that succinct phrasing), even if the telling tended to founder on bathetic denouements. In Fahey's writing there is a certain amount of "not knowing what to feel" or confessing feelings of ambivalence and emotional wandering. The trouble is in not grasping what a luxury this is and what it might look like to people who do not have it, *even as one sees those people.* That is, Fahey's writing sees and does not see them at the same time. Whether, as "art," such writing has to have done better is debatable. But the matter speaks directly to the issue Adorno identifies: that a certain problematic configuration of authenticity would endorse and stabilize even that ambivalence as long as it is "authentically" related. This, after all, is how one can become a white American male person. It is not faint praise to say the matter is revealed with refreshing clarity in Fahey's written work, at least in part because its art does not always aesthetically please. But it's not all on Fahey. His position, along with the affects he records, is a structural result of a misdirected war against capitalist individualism by means of individualism, meaning that at least in part this war chose Fahey, and within it he found some limited room to move.

Over the course of working on this book it became clearer to me that the question of how Fahey was situated with regard to the Movement, or the counterculture, was necessary to pose directly. But it might make his fans and many of the people who knew him personally cringe or laugh or both. But doesn't the question depend on what we think the Movement was? Consider this assessment by Peter Braunstein and Michael William Doyle from the introduction to their excellent book on the counterculture (their term of choice) of the 1960s and 1970s, *Imagine Nation*:

> The term "counterculture" falsely reifies what should never properly
> be constructed as a social movement. It was an inherently unstable
> collection of attitudes, tendencies, postures, gestures, "lifestyles,"
> ideals, visions, hedonistic pleasures, moralisms, negations, and
> affirmations. These roles were played by people who defined them-
> selves first by *what they were not, and then, only after having cleared that*
> *essential ground of identity, began to conceive anew what they were. What*
> *they were was what they might become — more a process than a product, and*
> *thus more a direction or a motion than a movement.* (10; emphasis added)

I think there is a lot of John Fahey in those words. If it is difficult to see him *in* the Movement, I hope Braunstein and Doyle clarify that he is *of* it. And being of it, as defined here, there is still some of its history and significance to be shown. Direction, motion, and process do not always make a clean break of it after all; they can sputter anticlimactically and get stuck in the work of "what they were not." And even embrace it.

PART I | Where Did You Go, John Fahey?

Introduction

It's 1967 and John Fahey has the music critic for Stanford University's student newspaper right where he wants him. In late October, Jerry Fogel had written about Fahey that "there is no relative standpoint from which one can assess his significance or influence." Fahey is incomparable, a "genius in contemporary music." Fahey's new record, *Requia*, was coming out the following month, in time for his campus concert. "Fahey's music is intensely personal," Fogel warns. "Each person interprets it differently, his own emotions contributing directly to the total effect. It is possible for one person to be wholly absorbed in a composition, while another is completely unaffected" (Fogel, "John Fahey: A Guitarist Like" 6). A few weeks later, the day of the concert, Fogel found the comparison he'd been looking for earlier. At the very time of Fahey's concert, Nicholas Katzenbach, President Johnson's undersecretary of state, would be giving a lecture on campus. While Katzenbach will be "bringing a message of concern," Fogel says, "those in the Tresidder Large Lounge will be hearing a different, perhaps more significant message. John Fahey will be performing" (Fogel, "John Fahey: The Guitarist of Relevance" 6). Katzenbach was one of the architects of U.S. civil rights legislation, a man who as deputy U.S. attorney general had stood down Governor George Wallace at the University of Alabama when Wallace physically tried to rebuff court-ordered integration. At Stanford, however, Katzenbach would be defending Johnson's Vietnam policy (Rolph; Kitsman). There were ample reasons, therefore, for every student to attend his lecture and certainly for many to protest it. (A planned protest never materialized.) Compared with the under secretary, though, "there is an inscrutable quality in John Fahey and his music," writes Fogel, "something beyond his appearance and his talent. It is something that almost invariably leaves the listener with the idea that he has experienced something very relevant—more relevant, perhaps, than the temporal message of an Undersecretary of State" (Fogel, "John Fahey: The Guitarist of Relevance" 6).

Fahey, Katzenbach—what a rich comparison. But it was hardly far-fetched in its context. Fogel simply invokes that branch of Movement dialogue concerned with inner fulfillment while keeping the concern with social justice at bay. (In other writing, Fogel would change lanes, decrying "imperialist war, loss of personal freedom, prejudice" ["Baez"].) In fact, as if in perfect alignment with Fogel, Fahey's liner notes for *Requia* make virtually the same ploy, although he finds a substitute for Katzenbach. Fahey directly asks readers to favorably compare his personal experiences and struggles with those addressed by the "social-action theologians." The point is not really that Fogel and Fahey are making rich comparisons. The point is to ask how, for someone like John Fahey, did writing become the place where self-expression is learned as "good"? Once learned as "good" where could that appetite go? With an essay from 1956 as its focus, chapter 1 situates Fahey within the history of the idea and practice of written self-expression, self-awareness, and self-actualization as values that were institutionalized in public schools, especially during and after World War II.[1] In that essay, titled "My Dear Old Alma Mater"—Fahey either was in his senior year of high school or had just graduated—are the seeds of the balancing act between personal and social values he would perform later, in writings like the *Requia* notes. I show in chapter 2 how the fields of psychology and psychoanalysis, which broke wide into the public sphere in the 1950s and were each concerned with American, capitalist childhood, explicitly shaped Fahey as a writer too. His essay "Communism," written well after the 1960s, is a wistful memoir of a raucous childhood spent in a white suburb of Takoma Park, deeply informed by a psychoanalytical framing.

The *Requia* notes enrich our reading of each essay. They contain some of the same interest in self-expression as Fahey's 1956 work but also show he had not become the "agitator" that work seemingly foretold. Just the same, *Requia* furtively glances at the social and political activism of its day, as if Fahey wants to justify his absence and distance himself from his own distance. The *Requia* notes enrich our reading of the "Communism" essay of later years too. For that essay gazes wistfully at past ideals concerning liberation, direct action, and restored innocence, which Fahey might still harbor. Yet there is zero chance he will act, hence the moody return to the "matrix of solitude"—Berman's pitch-perfect phrase—already flagged in *Requia*.

In the notes to that album, Fahey writes about feelings and experiences in a confessional but also performative way for his Movement audience, serving himself up as the *one who has feelings*. He is not interested in moving on from feelings when they are bad. He is interested in tarrying with them, in demonstrating that a struggle should be going on within individuals over their very existence and what its meanings could be. But he also evaluates his situation in light of proclamations made by the "social-action theologians." They are a beloved foil, much as Fogel had suggested Katzenbach was. The questions Fahey raises are implicit: Why shouldn't existential struggle be counted among other struggles of the day? Why should one feel pressured to join a protest or a sit-in, to renew one's alarm with every awful headline, when one must also be doing the work of accomplishing just being a person—which is made difficult by the very society that creates headline-worthy racial, class, and imperial oppression?

Requia was John Fahey's first album for a major record label, Vanguard (Guerrieri, *John Fahey, vol. 1*, rev.). So, one imagines he felt a warrant to tell all to a hoped-for expanded audience who would want to know what brought Fahey to music.[2] It goes like this: "Since 1948, after seeing the movie, *The Thief of Bagdad* [John was nine years old] I composed cerebral symphonies every day. It was a pleasant pastime. But suddenly in 1953 I needed a full orchestra at my command." As a pubescent fourteen-year-old speeding toward adulthood, he needed "to drown out with music, the new disturbing sounds I heard emanating for [sic] my own fear and ignorance of the ways of men and women." But he was also *pissed* he didn't have his driver's license yet, and he needed music to drown out the tempting sounds of car traffic "on the road east." In lieu of a full orchestra, "I made an orchestra out of the guitar," which he taught himself to play. He would have liked a teacher, but "I could tolerate none, nor they me." And he would have liked a teacher "who knew the music of men and women." Alas, still no teacher. "So I taught myself all these things, and now I must play" (Fahey, liner notes, *Requia*).

Why "must play"? To express feelings, for one thing: "I can temper the guitar as I like. I can make my own tunings. I can do whatever I like with it. I am quite free with my guitar." But also needing the money the music brings, he is not free of the guitar itself: "For some remunerative neck-strap has strung me to it." Freedom with the guitar is no more free "than one of the strings" on his guitar, whose only freedom is "to be tuned up and down—or to break." This limited freedom may even be futile, a nonstarter: "A broken string is thrown away even if it was 'dead' before, being no longer of any use to anyone at all. No not that" (Fahey, liner notes, *Requia*).

On and on Fahey goes: profundities fall to earth, possibly to rise again, but only to fall once more. Confession unfolds and stops short of expiation;

accusations are hurled without vindication. There's a story brewing here, never truly to get off the ground, about ineptitude, failure, rejection, or castration and impotence, if we follow the double entendre of a string tuned up and down, possibly to break. Existence is all about up down, up down. Performance is about the undercutting of performance. Fahey doesn't want you to think he is extraordinary; he wants you to think he is really good at being extra ordinary, one with the muck of life. And that's extraordinary. But not.

And then comes the Fogel moment as Fahey pivots:

> The new social-action theologians (and many laymen as well) speak frequently of freedom these days—a new kind, they say. But I know of only one perfect freedom—and that comes to us instantaneously, at one time or another, or not at all, when we are given a chance to gamble. You hear about the game (which might frighten you) and then either you play or you don't. If you do play you find you are free whether you win the game or not. If you don't play, then you become (or remain) a slave. There is no middle way. And it is a rather grisly kind of gambling too, because you don't even know what the stakes are. . . . You have to take a chance—a big chance. But if you don't take that chance, don't choose to gamble, you lose your freedom until the next game—if there is one. There is no fall *up* (Tillich notwithstanding), and the pressing need for social-action is self-evident to anyone who is awake. (Fahey, liner notes, *Requia*)

This moment is packed with allusions, and a few, such as "freedom these days," stand out as especially legible. What "anyone who is awake" in America would have noted in the fall of 1967 is that just that summer, in city after city, African Americans had been in revolt, as they had been before that, such as in Watts in 1965. (Fahey approved his liner notes for *Requia* in the fall of 1967, time, in other words, to have been fully aware of that summer's events [Guerrieri, *John Fahey, vol. 1*, rev.].) Whether Martin Luther King Jr. is the "social-action theologian" Fahey has in mind, King cannot be excluded as an example Fahey would point to if asked for a name. Regarding the "many laymen" propounding freedom, they are too numerous to count. It seems clear Fahey is alluding to the struggle for civil rights and why the struggle is a worthy one. "Social-action," he argues, is a "pressing need" and a "self-evident" one at that. Not one to trumpet the cause of civil rights ("No not that"), Fahey, if quietly, gets the idea, or at least feels the need, to acknowledge it publicly on his first Vanguard record. (A year later Fahey's second record with

Vanguard came out, *The Yellow Princess*, which I'll discuss below. By then King had been assassinated, so Fahey included "March!" on the album in King's memory, regretting, in his notes to the song, that he had never marched in protest himself.)

But, in *Requia*, he is also right away saying that the always-already more profound idea is that, whereas racial injustice is obviously wrong, *less obvious* is how to set and keep a course for taking a "gamble" on individual freedom. So, yes to civil rights, but once obtained, then what? What task remains? Surely, the struggle to understand and act on the fugitive meaning of one's own existence. But—here is the implicit question—why is that struggle hard to see? Why might a person fail to recognize their chance at it?[3] This was Fahey's concern at least since his high-school-era essay and continuing into college, where he found new language to express these ideas as a philosophy major (see part 3). And we'll see him return to it in his "Communism" essay. His idea, shared by many social critics, is that the same postwar American society that individuates people for purposes of turning them into "workers," "students," "fathers," and "mothers," whereby they may have their civil rights, throws enormous obstacles in the path of their actually seizing their uniqueness as human beings—cue the philosophers learned about at college.

I am arguing that Fahey's pivots toward social conscience are, like Fogel's pivot from Katzenbach toward Fahey, much less jarring than they may seem. Ideals about individual liberation and social emancipation were part and parcel of Movement culture and at the center of its messiness. As the Movement scholar and activist Richard Flacks wrote, the problem is that the relationship between the politics of social change and the urge for individual, existential freedom defines two poles of attraction that are difficult to draw together. Tom Hayden, a founder of Students for a Democratic Society and principal architect of the Port Huron Statement, articulately states the necessity of their combination in a 1962 "manifesto" he distributed to the student activists a few months before they were to meet in Port Huron. "Freedom is more than the absence of arbitrary restrictions on personal development," he insists. It "must be a condition of the inner self as well, achieved by reflection confronting dogma, and humility overcoming pride. 'Participation' means both *personal initiative*—that men feel obliged to help resolve social problems— and *social opportunity*—that society feels obliged to maximize the possibility for personal initiative to find creative outlets" (Hayden 28–29).

The problem for Fahey, even as he strongly gestures toward the mutuality that Hayden and Flacks speak of, is that even if his ordinary feelings and his struggle to deal with them may have been personally profound, the civil rights struggles and the gamble for *life* that Fahey alludes to cast those feelings in a rather pale light. Fahey has not, in the *Requia* notes, found a way to convincingly charge his personal details with significance and depth sufficient for the "gamble" that so interests him. Nor has he identified in *Requia* a compelling social basis for his feelings that will help his readers understand how personal feeling and experience can in fact have social significance. Not having a driver's license just will not qualify—although this does say something about middle-class suburban circumstances that I will get to in chapter 6.

And yet is the game Fahey plays in *Requia* necessarily about holding himself up as a good, ennobling example of existential struggle? It may instead (or also) very well be an expression of interest in the sort of social change that prizes individual emotional honesty in whatever form it arrives, with the possibility that such courage on the part of individuals is the very source of social change and not the other way around. This reversal is implied by Fahey's hat tip to Hegel. Fahey is interested in what happens when one commits to a freedom that is genuinely authentic: "perfect freedom," he calls it. The only way forward with such a commitment is to risk leaving behind what one is sure of, in order to enter into a fearful "game" one might lose, but through which one finds genuine freedom. One even looks for opportunities to place oneself at risk; failing to do so ensures one remains a "slave," a reference to Hegel's master-slave dialectic, slave being the term for anyone unable to move beyond their limited self-conception or self-activity (see part 3 for Fahey's engagement with Hegel and existentialism). How to exceed one's limits? Not by the self alone, claims Hegel, but through encounters with others: "I wonder what my game is," Fahey muses, "and if I'll be given a chance to play it with a worthy opponent. I certainly hope so" (liner notes, *Requia*). Sure enough we will see his hopes play out as he fights against "false gregariousness" (see chapter 1) and mass conformity (see chapter 2). The point though is that with his nod to Hegel, whose philosophy urges dialectical movements of ideas, as much as persons and society, we cannot be certain that the idea of "social-action" with which Fahey began this passage is the same "social-action" he means at the end. For it is now "self-evident" that if existential struggle inherently takes two to play, it is itself a form of social action, a nifty end run around the problem worrying Flacks and Hayden.

Fahey has no actual program in mind here. His writing quarrels, explores, tries things out, shoots from the hip, and generally forges ahead in the manner of what the left cultural historian Peter Clecak calls the "ideal self" of the 1960s (and 1970s): a self who seeks, on the basis of their *own* sense of identity and their *own* desire for a "piece of justice" that postwar movements were making possible, to form community with *others* who may feel similar (see Clecak). The exercise is far from innocent. For if one is going to write in 1967 of social action and freedom, toss the American legacy of slavery into the mix, which is surely Fahey's intended double entendre in invoking Hegel, and suggest one has been a kind of slave oneself, one and the same word suiting both cases, one indeed risks a lot. In short, there are too many desires at work in Fahey's associative style. Should the reality of Black struggles be seen in parallel with Fahey's personal struggles? And should the self-deprecating representation of those personal struggles not end up minimizing the struggle for civil rights? Fahey's ask is just too much and the result is flatfooted, just as the Blind Joe Death joke could only go so far. Yet all of this seems utterly symptomatic. The case I want to make is that Fahey is performing in accordance with school lessons, using self-expression to create an "ideal self," which he can leverage so as to remain legible and relevant to the Movement. For Fahey the Movement became the proving ground for what he was already becoming, almost inevitably so once he began to make a career of music with the acoustic guitar. What other cultural environment would there be for him with such a career? He pushed against it constantly. But his writing shows its hold over him. This environment of largely white campuses, cafés, small concert halls, and record buyers and listeners was where major influences on Fahey's own becoming as a postwar self met and intertwined. This environment gave him a language with which to communicate to an audience, even if an imagined one, and through which to distance himself and claim special status as unique (see part 2). Without this environment and its grammar, could Fahey even misfire as he does?

Fahey seems to be insisting—in a pattern that was repeated over and over again—that any platform for social change is going to be judged against its capacity to make room for how individual people actually encounter and value their own lives. This may after all be the way in which he posited a substantive relation between a politics of social change and one of personal freedom and self-actualization. A person really is, in every instance, an emotional being and a thinking being; a person really does arrive on any given scene with a past that has been consequential. If there is a conclusion to draw, then for Fahey it seems to be that his reader should be allowed *to catch him in the act of feeling,* even if that feeling is the ho-hum of ambivalence or the querulous resignation of the cynic. Only in vain may we wonder what the payoff is for him. To read Fahey over time is to sense a deep discontent with his own discontent, and rarely the self-satisfaction at having had his say.

Moreover, Fahey's oppositional stance will place community chronically out of reach. To read his writing as a teenager—in 1956 the writing is rebellious, demanding, angry, and smart—is to wonder why it was not to be preparatory to a radical, activist future. When that future prospect arrived in his late twenties, he no longer knows what his "game" is, even as social injustices have become plainer for him to see. By the time of his much later reminiscences (the "Communism" essay), he is framing his life in terms of some radical alternative he might have lived. Do these "almosts" and "might haves" bespeak failure, or if the Movement is looked at in its microspaces and moments, do they amount to another way of being involved?

Listening Session One

"Sligo River Blues" (*Blind Joe Death*, 1959)
"March! For Martin Luther King" (*The Yellow Princess*, 1968)
"The Singing Bridge of Memphis Tennessee" (*The Yellow Princess*, 1968)

One of Takoma Park's defining geographic features is the Sligo Creek. It carves a long diagonal through the city, not too wide, not too deep. During high school, years of intense guitar learning, John Fahey lived with his mother in an apartment overlooking the Sligo (Guerrieri, *John Fahey, vol. 1,* rev.). The apartment is on New Hampshire Avenue along the eastern edge of Takoma Park near where the creek crosses over to Hyattsville and disappears into the Anacostia River. Fahey memorialized the Sligo on his first LP, *Blind Joe Death*, three years after graduation. "Sligo River Blues" is a *hard* song to get just right. It is less a blues than a rag, with zero margin for error if you're going to get it to bounce perfectly along. It is, in a way, a beginner Fahey song. But it is also a real player-piano of a tune, from start to finish possessed of an animating inner mechanism. Considering Fahey only began playing guitar at fifteen and had no teachers as such, his impressive accomplishment was to have mastered the alternating-thumb style of Piedmont guitar players like Elizabeth Cotten and Blind Blake. The determination, care, and self-discipline that "Sligo River Blues" embodies give the lie—or at least offer a counterpoint—to the rebelliousness and insouciance Fahey projects in his writing. That Fahey could play the song at all is a product of that nerdier side that knows how to pay attention, how to focus, and how to steal himself away from the "false gregariousness" he complains of in his "Alma Mater" essay. The same could be said of Fahey's 1958 rendition of Sam McGee's "Buck Dancer's Choice" on Joe Bussard's Fonotone label (Fahey,

Your Past). But the latter is not Fahey's composition and, while utterly thrilling, lacks the subtlety of rhythm and mood of "Sligo River Blues."

Most of the magic of Fahey's song is in the right hand while the left hopes it can hold steady for the three minutes demanded of it. The whole song is played in first position (at the first fret), where the song's only three chords can be accessed: C, F, and G. Variations on the chords can also be done from that position, including a single strum of C maj7 to end the song. On top of the chord changes, Fahey plays a melody anchored by a series of alternating B, C, B, C notes, accomplished by moving the index finger of the left hand off and on (and off and on) the second string at the first fret. It is partly the tension of the left hand nailed into place with the left pointer finger moving up and down during many of the chord changes that makes the song deceptively easy and accounts for its subtle mood shifts. For a beginning player, almost nothing could be easier than playing C, F, and G chords, although it is a bit harder to get the ups and downs of the pointer finger timed just right. Harder still when the finger will have to speed up its work later in a slightly more up-tempo portion of the melody, even as the tempo of bass notes goes unchanged. All along an elusive syncopating rhythm has to be delivered by the finger-picking right hand to give the song the bounces and skips it needs. Provided these mechanics all come together, "Sligo River Blues" sounds as though it simply plays itself, unfolding out of some inner inevitability. The little *miracle* of the song, though, is the quiet, never overstated joy it signals—dreamy, wistful, happy within limits. (This is not to say the song can't be interpreted differently, as Devendra Banhart does on a Fahey tribute album.) As far as I know, the song is not copied from anything, although Fahey did record some standards for *Blind Joe Death* (e.g., W. C. Handy's "St. Louis Blues"). It is, in 1959, Fahey's perfect three minutes of invented innocence.

Allow me to make a pivot of my own now. On April 9, 1968, every American could have listened to the sermon the Reverend Martin Luther King Jr. gave at his own funeral. King's "The Drum-Major Instinct" had been tape-recorded barely two months before at Ebenezer Baptist Church in Atlanta, and so the entire country could tune in to hear the sermon in the same church, where the first part of his funeral service was held.[4] The drum-major instinct, King preached, is the instinct all humans have for recognition by other human beings. King's sermon dwells on the perversion of this instinct and subsequent warping of human personalities. He warns against the drive to keep up with the Joneses, the propensity for selfishness and exclusivity, and the evils of an oppressive economic system that creates artificial divides between people. Was *this* the moment when Fahey decided to compose a march for King? Perhaps King's sermon sparked some renewed interest in similar worries Fahey had himself nurtured for more than a decade, even if he was never especially outspoken about civil rights per se. Did Fahey sense the year before, when working up his notes for *Requia*, that even though he was no frontline civil rights activist, not on campus and certainly not on the streets, he was actually in the minority of white college-educated students, let alone whites generally, who actually had a favorable view of King at all? Most college-educated whites had no such view, and huge majorities of whites with less education felt the same or worse about King (Appleton; also Virella).

In analogous ways the final two songs on the first side of Fahey's second Vanguard album, *The Yellow Princess*, released months after King's assassination, are remarkable and unremarkable. "March! For Martin Luther King" and "The Singing Bridge of Memphis, Tennessee" stand out because they are favorable statements of a kind, in the face of white majority disapproval. But they are unremarkable in being grand understatements of the subject matter they engage. Fahey's headnotes for the songs suggest they work as a single composition, although the instrumentation is dramatically different. For "March!" Fahey asks, "Why didn't we all? Maybe some of us will now; maybe it's too late." For "The Singing Bridge" he writes, "Pan chases away the assassin, but the city remains unredeemed." "March!" is unusual in that Fahey hired musicians to play with him. The song leads off with very slowly picked and strummed guitars accompanied by drum rolls that gradually become more prominent until a fadeout at the end. The song deliberately counts out its four beats per measure. At the start the drummer strikes the snare once and does a quick roll, strikes double time and quickly rolls again: tap, roll, tap-tap, roll. After a minute, it's roll, tap-tap, roll, tap-tap. At fairly regular intervals a fill on the toms and cymbals breaks the solemnity. Save the drum fills, the song is somber and restrained, asking you to reduce your voice to a whisper or, better, to hold your tongue. It provides the soundtrack for whatever you have going on in your mind as the funeral procession goes by.

A brief moment after the fadeout of "March!" an abruptly new sound appears. Even without the "singing bridge" title, you know from the approaching and quickly fading whine that a procession of passing cars has been caught on tape and is being played back. Since you know the traffic is going over a bridge, the regular *thwomps* you hear are courtesy of tires hitting the expansion joints on the road. Twenty or so seconds in, some stressed metallic part of the bridge sounds off like a tuning fork. *Piiiiiing! Ping-ping!* Those notes hang high in the air, while the traffic whines on and the joints give off their muffled *thwomp-thwomp*. The concerto, Fahey's alternate title for the piece, no sooner comes together than the low moan of an electric bassoon creeps in. It modulates ever so slowly—low, lower, back to low—a menace that has been lying in wait now snaking through the ensemble. It is the assassin, we guess, coming out from hiding. Or it could be the approach of Pan readying to "chase away the assassin," or the sound of the two together: criminal (and impending) justice. It isn't long before we hear the trill of pan pipes, two minutes snatched from Big Boy Cleveland's "Quill Blues" that were spliced into the mix (Guerrieri, *John Fahey*, vol. 2, 5). Those notes are reedy and light, but also aloof and unforgiving.

Although the idea for "The Singing Bridge of Memphis, Tennessee" apparently came before King's assassination, Fahey's headnotes secure it for a new purpose.[5] "Pan chases away the assassin, but the city remains unredeemed," reads Fahey's note, the note itself reading like a headline of a news daily, large and in bold print. We cannot pretend we do not know the story that follows. It is not just of one criminal and his apprehension but a token apprehension that fails to root out the deep corruption, the rot at the root.

CHAPTER ONE

Manufacturing Discontent

Aggregate Execrable Nemesis. Saying this phrase out loud—why not give it a try?—is like getting gum off the sole of your shoe or taffy out of your teeth. That is how its creator, John Fahey, no doubt wanted it. The phrase is a pseudonym he devised sometime during or just after his last year of high school for an essay, "My Dear Old Alma Mater." With that title and that pseudonym, you know the essay has begun before you get to the first sentence. (This is the first of several pseudonyms—Blind Thomas, Blind Joe Death, Elijah P. Lovejoy—Fahey adopts.) But how is the pseudonym supposed to work exactly? *I'm the accumulated unpleasantness that is your downfall?* Your *cumulative unpleasantness is my downfall? Of all downfalls coming due, this is going to be* really *bad?* The name reeks of book learning, of real and feigned attempts to impress, of "I'm going to tell you exactly what I think" but also "You don't understand me!" It reeks of a gathering belief in the power of words. Sure enough, resentment, alienation, betrayal, superiority, desperation—all these themes surface in abundance.

Part thesaurus, part comic-book villain, the pseudonym Aggregate Execrable Nemesis is a perfect concoction for a seventeen-year-old nerd twitching in his skin. "Schools are factories," Nemesis soon instructs, "which . . . produce neurotic gregariousness, fear and hatred of the unknown, mass hysteria, hypocrisy, general mild insanity, and above all, conformity in the minds of their product, their students." In 1956, publication outlets were few for a resentful teenager to get such a surgical evisceration into print. *IOTA*, the journal that published Fahey's work (and another of his essays the previous year), was the brainchild of Fahey's friend Anthony Lee (Guerrieri, email). It shut down after just two issues, and was strictly DIY, having the slightly wobbly look of a typewritten ransom note. Oh, and on the first page, there is a ruler-drawn, two-dimensional runic figure of indeterminate provenance. It is a diamond shape, bisected by a vertical line, balanced on top of a rectangle. Could it be a TV antenna, or mind control device? A spoof of the binomial and trinomial theorems, whose visual proofs were taught in geometry class and that Fahey ridicules a few pages in? A riff on the lines, boxes, and triangles used for teaching sentence diagramming and parts of speech? Under

41

the figure Fahey writes, in droll senior-year lingua franca, "This symbol represents." (Symbols always represent *something*. This one represents . . . uh . . . nothing.) Full stop. We get it. Twelve years of symbols just . . . representing.

What student has not felt it: the universal, unholy, refluxing impatience of the American senior year (or junior or sophomore or freshman year)? In addition to senioritis, though, whole literatures cheer Fahey on. By 1956, who knows how many junior Holden Caulfields J. D. Salinger had launched. (His *Catcher in the Rye* appeared in 1951.) By 1956, very few had not heard of the previous year's *Blackboard Jungle* and its explosive story of teens in revolt. Questions: Should we read Fahey through the permeating effects of best sellers and films? Or through the universal disease of senioritis? Whatever reading we decide—and there are many choices, of course—we would not want to miss the obvious, yet nontrivial, fact that we are reading a writing. What happens if we simply put Fahey in that light? That is what I would like to do here: simply see Fahey as the recalcitrant male high school student (all-white school), product of a formal American education, who has learned to write and been encouraged to write. What, here, has he written about? How did he come to it? Why do most students in high school write? There are banal answers. They write because they are asked to, often required to. But they also write because somewhere along the line, and in the context of their education, the idea has been transmitted that it is good to write. Emotionally good. Developmentally good. Psychologically good. Politically good. This particular bundle of "goods" is of relatively recent vintage. It has a history, and my first purpose is to put Fahey in it. If the whole of this seems banal, well, Fahey's banality is also our own. The moment that made him is still making us. Is there anyone who has not been taught that getting one's thoughts out is a good idea? Are there not racks of blank books and journals in every bookstore, gift shop, and airport? Is it not the case that in that serial killer movie you saw, the scene where we are homing in on the perp, there will be a journal (or wall) filled (filled!) with the perp's tiny scrawl, often legible only to himself, and that this excess is on the spectrum of "good" writing and its purposes?

The endeavor will have to be speculative. I will not be able to connect all the dots of cause and effect that led to Fahey's essay. (Yes, it seems Fahey's friend asked him to contribute to his magazine, but this only prompts again the question of the learned value of writing.) While the essay is fascinating, it is not to be too much an object of fixation in itself. The essay is really a marker pointing elsewhere. The point is to reconstruct a certain discourse about writing that helps make Fahey's essay explicable, so that when Anthony Lee asks if seventeen-year-old Fahey has anything to contribute to his magazine, something has already been happening above and beyond, and around and in, Fahey—a whole environment of writing has emerged that in conjunction with Fahey answers, *Yes, he does*.

Let's linger just a moment, though, over what it might mean that Fahey's essay is a marker pointing elsewhere, and also over why it could actually be intellectually stimulating for us that the Fahey "archive" contains very few early works. Later, as Fahey moves into the worlds of music composition and recording; record collecting, folk festivals, and concerts; and musicology and folklore, many more writings are available. But this is the first, it sets a pace, and it is worth making some attempt to gauge what work it is doing, what work environment it likely emerges from, and what these two things have to do with each other. First, Fahey's essay—its diction, orderliness, and frankness—marks the cumulative reinforcement of the "good" of writing and the cumulative impact of many writing assignments over the years. Fahey writes with skill, wit, and aplomb. He has been practicing. To extrapolate from Fahey's comment about the factory, no one would build a car factory to build one car, because the point is to build many. Just the one essay implies there are many others, grade level upon grade level, essay upon essay. The existence of just this one essay, an ostensible takedown of the school factory, points in all directions toward what the school factory is in the business of making in the first place. Much more importantly, therefore, Fahey's willingness to reveal what he feels demonstrates precisely the value placed on postwar teenage writing in the first place. His essay is imminent to, the very warrant for, the environment of writing. Note the logic: as Fahey reveals his troubles, which he writes is his "burning desire" (11) to do, he reaffirms that youth are troubled and shows there is a need for writing to reveal these troubles. And what any one writing by any one individual confirms, in this particular mind-set, is that depth of feeling is only the provenance of single individuals alone. And since this environment, as we'll see, is in the business of producing individual subjects capable of identifying and communicating feeling, Fahey, even as he will condemn the school environment, produces the warrant for it in that very act. The work Fahey's essay does is recursive work and social work; it is partial cause of the very discourse that asks him to write. The original warrant to teach writing is reproduced, all the more when this piece by Fahey was published outside, and after, school. What better justification for writing than to have produced a student who can and will do it on their own?

A Brief History of Creative Writing

Starting during World War I, the teaching of writing in American schools entered a sort of prolonged crisis, with different approaches and justifications jostling for favor. Before the war the purpose of writing (i.e., a skilled activity to be taught in English classes) emphasized "classical studies and drill." Scholarship and its representation in writing was a pure pursuit to be transmitted to high achievers. World War I seemed to change this. It produced a desire that writing instruction emphasize practical goals ("practical forms of service" [Brand 63]). Writing should address itself to the needs of industrial growth, the consequences of international upheaval, and the realities of social change. By the 1930s reaction again set in. Progressive educators veered away from the emphasis on practical writing toward writing as a mode through which to elicit children's innate creativity and to develop ("unfold") their unique personalities. Creative potential — John Dewey's influence was clear — was the property of every human being, not just the talented few. The essential task of writing, in this romanticized view of childhood, was to help students integrate their various experiences, so that their unique, best self would result. Writing, as creative expression, had fundamental psychological value too: "Composition was liberating. It organized experience. That is, writing rehearsed experience and interpreted and evaluated consequences, thereby resulting in greater personal integration" (Brand 65).

John Frederick, a writer and teacher of English at the University of Iowa, Notre Dame, and Northwestern University, is worth quoting at some length. Here is his case, made in the middle of the Great Depression, against the overvaluation of "business" writing in the schools, in favor of a more balanced approach:

> *Creative writing occurs when the pupil recognizes the dignity and value of his own experience, and when he imposes upon that experience the discipline necessary to an attempt to transfer it to others.*
>
> Creative writing is differentiated from other forms of composition by the absence of an external or utilitarian motive — by the fact that it is done for its own sake alone, and proceeds from experience which is recognized as possessing intrinsic rather than practical or utilitarian value. . . . We may say with a considerable degree of accuracy that we *realize* an experience by naming it; that the attention directed upon the experience in the process of attempting to share it results in our own fuller and more permanent possession of it.

. . . [But when] material and utilitarian motives become paramount—when a prize or a grade becomes the whole reason for the writing—the work ceases to be creative. . . . Great writers speak of the "mysterious compulsion" the "obscure inner necessity" which impels and directs their work. . . . The impulse for realization of experience, either actual or imaginative, through communication of it, is at once the source of all great art and of the most humble creative compositions of what we call very ordinary children. The most dangerous fallacy in the teaching of creative writing lies in the assumption that it is of importance only to the "gifted few."

. . . Let us say at once that the making or training of professional writers is not the business of creative composition in the schools. The real objective is the development of the pupil's capacity for creative experience. By creative experience we mean experience which is valued for its own sake and not for some utilitarian end or practical consideration. . . . It is not necessary that these be actively opposed to the utilitarian values emphasized in most of our educational processes, but that they be presented as an essential supplement to the utilitarian.

. . . Perhaps never before in the history of the world have men so widely lost the power to recognize and possess those values in life which are not material utilitarian; and perhaps never before have men been so generally disappointed and despairing. In America our educational process as a whole must assume a part of the responsibility for the all but universal currency of material standards. Our school system as a whole has not always combated, has sometimes even fostered, that restless and insatiable desire for *things*—for newer, brighter, more costly things—which has made possible the large-scale commercial exploitation, the "creation of markets," and the consequent disastrous inflation of industry. . . . We have more and more emphasized the practical and exalted the profitable. We have neglected the creative, the non-utilitarian. We have been satisfied if we taught boys and girls how to make a living, and did not concern ourselves with teaching them how to live. And now it appears we have taught them neither.

. . . Many of us feel that we cannot justify ourselves or our system merely by fitting people to do their work in the world, by developing specific skills of practical value in social and industrial and commercial and professional activities. We believe that the function of our schools is not the production of robots—standardized units to be used by an industrial society—but the development of personalities, the education, in the full sense, of human beings for human life. And to this end, no matter how crowded our schools and how limited our resources, we need and can use creative composition.

. . . Whenever we can get the pupil to try to transfer to us what has interested and impressed him, no matter how humble the material of his experience or how crude the form of expression, we are opening the way to wider and more discriminating interests. . . . When we deny him this opportunity we make him a robot indeed; we reduce his life to a mechanical formula of working and eating and sleeping, of getting and spending. And in America at the present moment we should be less than ever ready to accept as final for anyone the utilitarian-material standards which are suddenly revealed as so tragically inadequate for all. Quite frankly whatever we do in creative composition may be viewed as one aspect of our effort to establish in the consciousness of American children some values other than those associated with the unholy trinity of industrialism: wages, goods, and profits. (Frederick 9–15)

Two years after Frederick's impassioned plea that "ordinary" students be allowed to validate their own inner experiences (by enunciating and sharing them), as a source of value beyond that of the commodity, the National Council of Teachers of English released a major document, "An Experience Curriculum in English." (The council was in fact the publisher of the journal in which Frederick's essay appeared.) As Alice Glarden Brand writes, this 1935 report, in proclaiming experience "as the organizing center of public school English studies, recapitulated the functional and psychological goals of writing" (66). The commission, like John T. Frederick, did not think the boundary was impassable between writing for the purpose of communication and creative writing for purposes of self-expression and self-knowledge. The "Experience Curriculum" adjusted these goals for students at varying levels, and for upper-level students especially, "the commission suggested activities aimed at refining the following mutually dependent phases of the creative process: observation (the gathering of sense impressions), imagination, and reflection (personal reaction to sense experiences)" (Brand 66).

During World War II, the argument in favor of expressive writing—and reading—was given a new, therapeutic, and "psychologistic" twist. "Strongly influenced by psychoanalytic theory, a number of educators specifically appropriated therapeutic nomenclature to support this function of reading. They also stressed creative activity early in the child's schooling to help prevent neuroses later in life" (Brand 67). Among the benefits of creative activity, noted by a variety of writers, were the release of war-related stresses and insecurities; the sense that other students were going through the same feelings; the tapping of the unconscious; and the draining of aggression and other destructive emotions. The collective sense among its proponents was that creative writing aided self-exploration and "had therapeutic value for all children, whether or not they had talent or evidenced behavioral problems" (67). One teacher, L. H. Buckingham, felt especially strongly about the value of autobiographical writing:

> This is where the English teacher comes in. If the unuttered experience has a far more illogical effect upon the personality than the experience put into words . . . and this is one of the basic assumptions of psychiatry—we who deal in expression can lend a powerful hand in clearing away these unreasoning and unreasonable influences. . . . With any troubling or imperfectly understood situation the effect of expression is the catharsis toward which the Freudian psychiatry works, and a growth in understanding of oneself, of others, and of one's relations to others—an insight which goes far toward automatically doing away with maladjustments of personality. (qtd. in Brand 68)

The psychological take on students' writing needs intensified after the war. "Adjustment" became the new keyword heard throughout the educational system, along with "reconstructive mental hygiene," "life adjustment," and "tension release." The Education Policies Commission of the National Education Association, already on board with the psychological turn in the 1930s, redoubled its support, advising that teachers develop writing assignments tailored to students' specific backgrounds and interests. In the postwar years, "education periodicals abounded with accounts of the ways by which teachers obtained appreciation and understanding of their students and their students of themselves" (69). By the 1950s, when Fahey was in junior high and high school, a concerted and prolonged effort began to try to resolve differences between the expressive and utilitarian camps, which had apparently hardened. The Commission on English Curriculum published a series of volumes between 1952 and 1965 to address the matter. The first volume in 1952 laid out the basic premise: language development and human growth and development went hand in hand. With the release of *Volume III, The*

English Language Arts in the Secondary School (1956), "personal writings still offered the usual practical and personal benefits," Brand writes, "improving the ability to think, developing communication skills, and promoting emotional stability. But beyond these life skills, personal writing provided a source of entertainment, insight, emotional release, and empathic understanding" (70–71).

No surprise, the psychological benefits touted in the postwar period tracked developments in psychology instruction. Introductory psychology textbooks by midcentury were much more geared toward student readership (as opposed to psychology researchers), emphasizing the value of psychology for the attainment of personal insights and personal adjustment. Textbooks gave greater coverage to social psychology, intelligence testing, development psychology, personality, adjustment-related topics (e.g., frustration, conflict, defense mechanisms, maladjustment), psychopathology, and psychotherapy.

These new emphases did not come out of the blue. Studies showed that students were particularly interested in "personally practical" issues like personality, social relations, mental disorders, and intelligence. The most popular textbook authors wrote to these interests. These authors were also self-professedly concerned with the impact of global war and for that reason, too, gave greater coverage to social problems and to those topics that were personally relevant (Weiten and Wight 477–80).[1] Arguably, there was some convergence between writing and psychology pedagogy. If teachers of writing were going to make claims for the psychological benefits of writing, it would make sense that they would draw on the field of psychology as it was being taught. Teaching in both fields emphasized an approach that was relevant to the lives of students as they imagined those lives to be: psychologically complex, searching for meaning and validation, questing for an integral relationship between self and society, and in need of "adjustment" to new social realities and changing personal circumstances.

As if to index the above changes at least in some measure, Fahey's high school yearbook, *The Compass*, in 1956 shows that Northwestern High offered its psychology course (much reviled by Fahey as we'll see in a moment) in the Social Studies department.[2] Its English department, meanwhile, offered instruction that placed at least some emphasis on contemporary writers (i.e., desiring that students perceive the relevance of their studies, even when teaching historical subjects). On one of the pages devoted to the English department (English appeared first among all the pages devoted to the school's academic departments), a group of students is shown hanging a mobile devoted to the theme of the U.S. Civil War. Shown on the mobile are titles of novels from the 1950s that contained Civil War themes—*Step to the Music* (1953), by Phyllis A. Whitney; *Love Is Eternal* (1954), by Irving Stone; and *The Kentuckyians* (1953), by Janice Holt Giles. Hanging also are the titles *Gone With the Wind* (1939), by Margaret Mitchell, and the poem "Kearney at Seven Pines," a ballad by the nineteenth-century poet Edmund Clarence Stedmen, about the famous Battle of Seven Pines (big casualties on both sides, each side claimed victory). Then, as if in lockstep with the notion that some balance should obtain in writing and reading pedagogy, the facing page of the yearbook shows a row of students working on "reading accelerator" machines. The machines were meant to increase reading speed and comprehension.

My Dear Old Alma Mater

Fahey's essay is in four parts: (a) the pseudonym, (b) a brief section called "Biography," containing an editor's note about the author's request for anonymity (including his "literary history") and a short section of verse, including the runic symbol mentioned earlier, (c) a section called "Statement," and (d) the body of the essay. By the end of the work it is clear that "My Dear Old Alma Mater" is a mash-up of different forms of writing and rhetorical strategies—verse, argument/evidence, parody, and autobiographical narrative—in which Nemesis recounts the variety of injuries and insults done him by teachers, other students, and the institution of school as such. Let's start with the verse, which forms the larger part of the biography (11):

> After three grade schools,
> one junior high school,
> and two high schools,
> I know something about schools.
> Dust be my destiny.
> Dust be their destiny.
> Dust be your destiny.
> (Declension of the possessive pronouns.)

Fahey has been through many grades as well as many schools: he knows whereof he speaks. The lesson? Dust. It's all dust in the end. "Dust be my destiny." Fahey doesn't say that this is the title of a popular film noir of 1939, his birth year. The film tells of a man hounded by the police and the courts for a crime he did not commit, and of his vindication by telling the truth of what really happened. Story of my life, imputes Fahey. (Further in, Fahey writes of having been accused of setting off a firecracker at school. Readers might remember this for the next chapter.) Ergo, dust be my destiny, but then "their destiny" and "your destiny." Everyone will stand falsely accused at some point? Probably not. Besides, Fahey himself does not seem to intend to *falsely* accuse his schools of anything. Perhaps "destiny" now refers to everyone's ultimate and inevitable declension, death as the great leveler. The double entendre of the parenthetical phrase echoes the thought: "*declension* of the possessive pronoun." Each and all are destined for *decline*, for giving up self as the dearest *possession*. Another meaning shows itself too. "Declension" is the technical grammatical term that indicates number, in this case number related to possessive pronouns (e.g., my, yours, theirs). Fahey has learned the rules of the schoolmaster and parodies those rules by repeating them more loudly than anyone else in the room. Now cue the runic symbol that "represents," which I mentioned a moment ago. (It is placed just below Fahey's declension exercise.) Perhaps the intent is to construct a generic symbol, redolent of all things "school": a little grammar, a little geometry, a little symbol representing symbolization as such, and therefore signifying nothing. The beginning of the essay, then, is a sort of hybrid of creative, expressive, utilitarian, and practical writing. A virtual summary of writing pedagogy. Fahey's intentions seem echoed deep in the essay when he taunts, "I learned when, where, and how to dangle participles into demonstrative triads when the binomial and trinomial surds were interjected with various declensions of somnambulistic hyperbolas" (15).

"I have a burning desire to write down and publish some of my experiences and feelings concerning our wonderful institutions of learning," Fahey writes in the "Statement" section (11). A single sentence screed announces his findings: "Schools are factories which, by lack of concern for student body, lack of toleration and understanding, expectation of conformity, disregard of democratic principles, teaching of useless information, lack of diversification, lack of placement according to the student's ability and achievement, lack of intelligence in planning, disregard of student comfort, double-talk and lies, and refusal to face facts and progress, produce neurotic gregariousness, fear and hatred of the unknown, mass hysteria, hypocrisy, general and mild insanity, and above all, conformity in the minds of their product, the students" (11). The rest of the essay consists almost entirely of incidents through which Fahey proves his case, each one concluding with a parenthetical identification of the kind of injury or insult suffered. The time when Fahey was called out by a coach for not enjoying or really understanding football is proof of "(expectation of conformity from superiors)" (12). Being laughed at by students for the same failing proves "(lack of concern for student body. Lack of toleration and understanding)" (12). Fahey failed physics one semester, so he took psychology the next one, since he had already read several books about psychology and enjoyed them. But in class too much time was spent learning concepts he already knew about ("gregarious," "phobia") and had been using "for years." This experience was evidence of "(learning useless information. Lack of diversification, and lack of placement according to the student's ability and achievement)" (14–15). Students aren't allowed to smoke or to drink coffee or tea or Coca Cola, which proves the school's "refusal to face facts and progress." And so on down the long list of findings.

A couple of passages are especially indicative of Fahey's interest in social psychology, and, conversely, this field's interest in him as a possible subject who will see himself through the field of social psychology. The body of the essay begins, "And I went with my friends and we all stayed together because everybody else stayed with their friends and people feel stupid by themselves. They are inadequate individually. A few stayed by themselves, but that was because nobody knew them. (Neurotic gregariousness, and fear and hatred of the unknown.)" (11). The essay concludes somewhat ambivalently. Students wear the same clothes, eat the same food, talk the same way—"in fact, they are not themselves, they are everybody. They are all one person going down a long hall, along which are found classrooms, drinking fountains, and clocks—a hall leading Nowhere." Here is the school as factory, producing its homogenous product. "They are not themselves, they are everybody" is a memorable turn of phrase. It does not jive well with Fahey's opening thought, though. The lone individual is inadequate; groups must form. Fahey has no solution, only a compromise to offer: the massed one person, the selves that are everyone are being led Nowhere, but "at least I am going there by a different path. (Conformity.)" (16). It is not certain whether Fahey means in the end to implicate himself in the "conformity" urged by teachers and students or if the different path (to Nowhere) makes all the difference, as (most readers think) Robert Frost famously posed.

A fundamental theme of the essay is that the form of sociality produced in high school is inimical to the form of individuality promised. The essay is deeply "psychologistic," in fact tinged with the basic critiques found in the new field of humanistic psychology that was beginning to be popularized and reflecting the fact that by the late 1950s everyone was "speaking the language of psychology" (Grogan 29). Truly "healthy individuals must stand apart" because it is the culture that is maladjusted (17, 20). Fahey's essay is redolent of the ideology that writing is "good," and shows evidence of the different kinds of writing that would have been taught. But writing is used against the school rather than in praise of what a postwar secondary education promises it can deliver. I think it is fair to assert that for all this, Fahey is the very product of this education, that his attempt to show he is no such factory product only stands to show that he has indeed bought into the idea that writing is worth his time. Fahey is smart and wants to show it. His exposition is clear, and he adduces specific evidence to make his points. At the same time, he stitches into the essay certain obscure references, perhaps to make sure he will remain a singular mystery. Fahey flaunts his anonymity, showing that he is someone with exactly the rich inner life that educational theorists and postwar psychology would say subtends him. With the writing and thinking tools he has been taught, and with the sense of self he has learned to have, he can only reflect these qualities back. We are still prone to think, in reading a piece like this, that Fahey is revealing what's "inside," but he is very much reflecting what is "outside," namely that part of the dominant value structure that prizes the ostensibly individual expression of ostensibly individual feeling. He is, in that sense, as much writing as he is written on. Yet in taking his task so seriously—the task of enumerating and evaluating each promise his society makes to him, and in fact reading his experiences as implicit tests of those promises—he cannot help but array the contradictions that define his environment. For he has found a set of promises that can never be fulfilled, were never meant to be fulfilled, and thus unsettled the very discourse of which he is a part.

The problem here, as anyone might tell Fahey, is that he is supposed to have the common sense to just "go along" with things and not question so much. But the problem also is that we don't know that he cared anyway. He did not necessarily want to help himself so much as he wanted "out." It is the entire dialog between adult and adolescent, student and school—that is, the mutually produced "product"—that seems really to be the subject of the essay. But no matter how much he expresses that desire in this particular form, he will show he is a worker in that very factory. A best-selling psychologist of the postwar period, Erik Erikson would tell us we need to be asking here about the phases undergone in the life of individuals, when values and ideas first seem to matter so much. We need to be asking about the temporalities of individual and social life that come to intersect and shape each other, and about how these come to mesh with broader and deeper historical currents that give values and ideas wider play.

CHAPTER TWO

The Suburbs, or Communism

> It is 1951.
> A long time ago.
> I am in the seventh grade.
> But the torture has started. . . .
> And who was doing the torture?
> You know who.
> If you don't know who it was then there is something wrong
> with you.
> You should go and get psychoanalyzed.
> I'm not joking. You won't be able to understand what I'm writing
> about here.
>
> —FAHEY, *How Bluegrass Music Destroyed My Life*

Fahey again. Seventh grade this time, but not broadcasting "live," as was the case with the essay he wrote during or just after senior year. The passage above is from a remembrance, an essay titled "Communism," crafted many years later. It has the benefit of hindsight and of an analytical structure, a storyline, that reads a certain strain of psychoanalytic theory that came to prominence in the United States in the postwar era. In this theory, adolescence is formative for the development of individual identity and its psycho-political qualities. This is the idea that at a certain stage of life an individual's psychological development encounters and responds to the possibilities for identity formation offered in the public sphere; the idea that becoming a certain sort of individual is also about becoming a person who, through an evaluative process only partly in their control, will (or won't) internalize publicly sanctioned attitudes, values, behaviors, and aims, and so become a "good" national subject.[1]

"Communism" virtually cries out for psycho-political reading (Medovoi). It is a canny piece, moreover, a *knowing* document that reads the very idea of psycho-politics into its story. The essay comes not quite halfway into the better known of Fahey's two books of collected writings, *How Bluegrass Music Destroyed My Life*. It is a culminating piece tying together a number of the collection's themes explored up to that point: white suburban lifestyles, neighborhood "gangs" and their leaders, adults and kids in steady battle, and lingering questions about the aftermath of World War II, especially the rise of mass culture, mass consumption, and the insidious combination of middle-class ennui and middle-class enforcement of its own norms. The essay, which is also at least partly fictionalized, handles these themes as psycho-political problems encountered by the adolescent protagonists. Problem making is a two-way street, however. What happens in adolescence that defines the stakes for Fahey and his comrades cannot be untangled from the developmental moment the nation finds itself in, since the nation, allegorized as Takoma Park, not only seeks adherents to American-style democracy and its investments in property, homeownership, and an ethos of self-discipline. It has also made, as Medovoi argues in *Rebels*, a pact with the "right kind" of edgy cultural figures whose acts warn against slavish conformity to American norms, while never threatening revolution as such. Fahey is interested in disrupting this pact. We will see, though, that his disruptions remain safely locked away in his youth and as memoir. I say safe because through these vehicles Fahey can vent his desires for Movement-like liberation, while at the same time keeping them under his personal control. Moreover, in memoir form Fahey can maintain a kind of innocence regarding racial realities in Takoma Park. By the time of Fahey's writing "Communism," he knew a great deal about racial segregation there, but the subject never comes up in this particular essay, which privileges *his* oppression, as it would elsewhere in the same book.

John Fahey and Eriksonian Democracy

The psychoanalytic urtexts on adolescent identity are Erik Erikson's popular books *Childhood and Society*, first published in 1950, and *Identity: Youth and Crisis*, of 1968. Erikson, who was a student of Sigmund and Anna Freud, was one of the most influential psychoanalysts of the twentieth century. He made the idea of "identity crisis" a household word and took on the lifelong task of trying to understand how childhood and adolescence (rather than infancy) are fateful in the mutual relationship between the ego and social development. Erikson brought psychoanalysis closer to the domain of social theory, and even geopolitics, writing about the variable progress of youth development, according to the affordances of the national political economies with which youth development intersects. *Childhood and Society*, for example, concludes with a striking comparative study of youth psychology in the United States, Nazi Germany, and the Union of Soviet Socialist Republics

(USSR). (For Erikson, it is the Cold War and the "necessity" for the United States to secure its supremacy that produced the practical conditions for the primacy of childhood and adolescence in psychoanalytic theory.)

A central feature of Erikson's thought is its rescaling of human psychological development. If, traditionally, the ego concept names the process through which *a person* unifies "his experience and his action in an adaptive manner," as he put it in *Childhood and Society*, Erikson wanted to understand the "ego's roots in social organization" (16, 17). Erikson views the ego as simultaneously a personal and social process and the psychoanalytic method as "essentially a historical method" (17). It deals with individuals, but these individuals are necessarily part of larger social and historical formations:

> To say that psychoanalysis studies the conflict between the mature and infantile, the up-to-date and the archaic layers in the mind, means that psychoanalysis studies psychological evolution through the analysis of the individual. At the same time it throws light on the fact that the history of humanity is a gigantic metabolism of individual life cycles. I would like to say, then, that this is a book on historical processes. Yet the psychoanalyst is an odd, maybe a new kind of historian: in committing himself to influencing what he observes, he becomes part of the historical process which he studies. (17)

Individual time and historical time are linked and intersect most profoundly during the formation of Identity. The term "Identity" is used by Erikson more narrowly than now, ascribing it specifically to adolescence, but perhaps also more broadly too since he links it to historical change out in the world. As inferred above, Erikson theorizes that "Identity development has its time, or rather two kinds of time: a developmental stage in the life of the individual, and a period in history. There is . . . a complementarity of life history and history" (*Identity* 309). We saw something of this complementarity already in Fahey's sensibilities in the previous chapter. There is even a third time, also inferred above, which is the time of psychoanalysis itself and its potential to change events, for as psychoanalysis and its ideas attain a degree of popular acceptance, it acts as a force of historical change too.

Struggles to form Identity are caught up in the bodily changes that occur during puberty, and it is these changes that also make for the complementarity of life history and history writ large. "Experience is anchored in the ground plan of the body," and it is of course the body that changes so noticeably and memorably during adolescence (*Childhood* 108). These changes indicate to the person undergoing them, as well as to the surrounding peers and adults, the future outside the family that imminently awaits. Erikson therefore wants to ask how this period of change will comport with external historical realities. He puts it like this: "Between the id and the superego, then, the ego dwells. . . . Balancing and warding off the extreme ways of the other two, the ego keeps tuned to the *reality of the historical day*, testing perceptions, selecting memories, governing action . . . integrating the individual's capacities of orientation and planning" (*Childhood* 193; emphasis added). If the id is "everything that would make us mere creatures" (192), the ego is a process that is effectively "an 'inner institution' evolved to safeguard that order within individuals on which all outer order depends. It is not 'the individual,' nor his individuality, although it is indispensable to it" (194).

Different societies afford ego development in different ways. Erikson stresses that capitalism (postwar American democracy) is an individuating process, where self-reliance, self-determination, and self-actualization are ideologically crucial. It therefore has to afford the ego its best chances of successfully becoming capitalism's matching "inner institution." Erikson's sensibilities regarding the scale of individuals' psychic life mesh quite well with Fahey's own sensibilities, even though they are in important ways precisely the ones against which Fahey pushes back.

In Fahey's "Communism," the torturers are the adults. Fahey writes that to the adults, he is "a nothing," "not recognized as being sentient." Even to himself he was not sentient. Erikson, as if to confirm what Fahey says, writes, "To be tolerant of the child's play the adult must invent theories which show either that childhood play is really work—or does not count. The most popular theory and the easiest on the observer is that the child is nobody yet, and that the nonsense of his play reflects it" (*Childhood* 215). The first adults Fahey mentions are his parents, with whom he is going to the home of his teacher, Mrs. Anis, and her husband Mr. Anis ("har har," snickers Fahey). Fahey complains of being ignored and, worse, of nobody noticing the transformation taking place in front of them: "And I? I was busy daydreaming of other places; things; colors; smells; tastes; tones; music; other people; other planets . . . other objective, invisible domains. Something had happened and as a result, *I* was no longer a pure spirit wandering around in the ether. No, *I* had, by virtue of testosterone, become grounded in the earth by newly grown, but invisible, roots and sap. I was intoxicated by strange, new alien secretions from recently matured glands" (84).

In sum, "I was a secret monster," and, while not yet a threat to the adults, what all monsters do is to wait. And so he does, knowing he is "an earthling" but a different species from the adults. What "species" they are, he has no idea except that they are a threat to him. The familiar suburban environment is now suddenly strange and menacing: "The other inhabitants of this dismal, pastel, Ethan Allen furniture-filled dwelling place sat around and spoke of polite, civil matters. They smiled at each other nefariously, hiding their teeth as well as their genitals, waiting until they could politely consume each other and 'me' in some mysterious and unseen monster-manner. By some occult, covert process, probably psychic absorption or something of the sort" (84).

Adults ask each other, How are you? They talk about the weather, football, inflation—"a parade of non-sequiturs." Friendship among adults is a ruse, and the PTA is an "organization of gourmets primarily concerned with the best methods of preparing and seasoning their favorite dish—children." What surprises Fahey is that the adults never stop to wonder if any of the children would, in the future, suspect the adults had been plotting their demise. They never suspect some of these children would likely revolt. "Virtually omnipotent, many of the creatures, 'teachers,' 'advisors,' 'principals,' 'guidance counselors'—can you believe in the existence of such salutary, grandiose titles they gave themselves?—were not too bright, despite their pretensions of being . . . 'educators'" (85).

The essay notes the combustible mix of testosterone and forced socialization by the "world-system school"—"A system within a system. Systems measureless to man" (88). Fahey lambasts adults who presume that teenagers eventually will sublimate their drives into socially acceptable forms and adapt to adult reality. And he excoriates his fellow students for sorting themselves into "in-groups" and "out-groups."

> I was taught at university that this thing is called socialization. . . . What happened was this. All my friends at school started disassociating themselves from me. Nobody liked me anymore. They were all starting to wear strange, slick clothes and combing their hair and taking two baths a day. . . . They were splitting up into couples and cliques and things. They were organizing the new
> WASP IN-GROUP.
> And I was on the outside with a few other unwanted, oddball rejects, mostly Jews and transfer students who nobody cared about. (89–90)

Socialization was not something kids did on their own. It was an even more malevolent manifestation of the propensity of adults to snuff out childhood. Adults taught kids to compete with each other so that in the future we could cancel everybody else out and be at the top of the pecking order.

And they were teaching us that this was perfectly ethical. Hell, it was good Christian behavior. It was good practice. And one day we would be able to consume large quantities of our fellow beings on this planet. Male and female.

Bite grab snatch kill outdo overdo murder your friends. All of them. And while you're at it, dispose of any older competitors who might be around. Kill them all as quickly as you can. Get rid of all of them. Don't let any of them live. Even the pathetic ones. You never know. They might get stronger and rise up. Kill them. Do them in. Murder them. *Schnell*. Fast. Quick. Move. Destroy. Murder. Rape. Hate. Kill. Love.

Yes, love.

See, they taught us to love each other and at the same time they taught us to kill one another. (90)

A Christian-capitalist upbringing is a complete oxymoron to Fahey.[2] Once puberty set in, and his feeling of monster-like difference grew, he describes being incapable of holding these opposing value systems together. "When I got hormones . . . I gave up trying to do both things [i.e., love and hate] and make them fit together because the testosterone also affected my brain, I guess. Because all of a sudden it was like I woke up. And when I woke up I saw that these two things could not, could never fit together" (91).

When it comes to the question of why the (capitalist) adults want to kill the childhood of (worker) children, Fahey lets the child answer: "I knew there was only one thing that could explain all this torture and insanity. It was the knowledge that adults enjoyed hurting children more, much more, than they enjoyed hurting and hating each other. . . . The true goal toward which everybody worked so hard accumulating wealth was child torture. The more money you had the more pain you could dole out to the kids. And clearly society was organized to promote the wishes of these adults and to insure the preservation of their power and authority" (92).

Accumulation of wealth, power, and authority for the sake of accumulation of wealth, power, and authority: this is all put upon the child. And it is told by Fahey as if from the perspective of the resentful child: *You're doing this to me because you like to do it*. A childish answer by definition. But the strategy makes sense, since Fahey is driving toward an anticapitalist stance armed with the idea that the ego is *readied for capital* at this very moment of its development. And how else would the adult respond to the charge but with a tautological nonanswer that only affirms the basic critique that capitalism is dehumanizing: *It is for your own good. For you will indeed have to fend for yourself in a harsh, competitive world.* As if to warn that his read is also a limited one, Fahey hints at the larger structure encompassing both adults and children. "Clearly," he writes, "society was organized to promote the wishes of these adults" (92). But how exactly this seeming external force of society, which stands apart from yet is connected to these adults and children, comes into being is not clear here. A shortening of the above passage hopefully makes the point—note Fahey switches from active to passive voice in "I knew . . . society was organized."

Perhaps it is this lack of understanding how society becomes organized in this way, yet nonetheless this perception of the feeling of its organization, the structure of feeling in Raymond Williams's coinage, that leaves Fahey struggling with the contradiction between love and hate, the sense that it is impossible to do both at once. Because the result of this incompatibility, Fahey reports, was a kind of psycho-political self-loathing, an internalization of the negative feelings directed at him. (Here it is very wise to remember Fahey's explicit instructions, even if we do not follow them to the letter, to read his essay as psychoanalytic narrative.)

> Being in the out-group was pretty bad. Because all of us in the out-group hated each other. The gruesome thing was that we accepted the values and the aesthetics and standards and morals and goals of the in-group even though we hated their guts.
>
> Because we also loved them and looked up to them.
>
> But they wouldn't have us.
>
> Now, you see, this was just another way the adults got us. They wanted to drive us crazy so they could lock us up in concentration camps. (93)

We have to slow down here just a bit to catch Fahey's drift. What is "drive us crazy" about? It is about self-loathing and social emulation, the loss of self and creation of a motivation to desire what the in-group possesses. Marx, in another time and place, would call this loss of self the primitive or original accumulation that divorced people from their traditional rights and privileges, the subsequent creation of a working class, and the psychological fix of the commodity fetish, whereby social relations are accomplished by (and confused with) the desire for personal acquisitiveness. But here, Fahey will call it the production of a kind of work ethic, rendering it in the most notorious wartime terms possible:

They wanted to drive us crazy so they could lock us up in concentration camps. Then, as in the Holocaust, they could do anything.
Svengali-type experiments, mass graves, ovens, electric fences and
ARBEIT MACHET FREI
just like in Auschwitz.

Yes, the ultimate trip for any intelligent adult sadist who really
wants to make it to the top and have more power, and therefore more
child torture, is the concentration camp. Student government, taxes,
churches, politics, schools, governments, PTAs, Boy Scouts—all
institutions existed so that someday they could start to build the
furnaces. It would begin when they put the razor-wire electric fences
up around the schools, giant smokestacks going up. Teachers would
be issued guns and whips and stuff. (93)

This passage completes Fahey's vision of postwar capitalism as a total institution that orchestrates its cultural infrastructure toward the production
of the worker-citizen. He invokes the ultimate evil known to the postwar
generation in order to dramatize the "genocidal" attack on the freedoms of
childhood. With strong countercultural reverberations, the passage attacks
"establishment" institutions. Worker-citizens must be made by snuffing out
the contrary, playful urges of childhood and putting human energies to work
in a factory that, as many a commentator (Marx not the least of them) would
say, will crush them body and soul. Indeed, one of the arguments to be found
among new left documents of the late 1960s is that U.S. youth make up an
exploited class (Rowntree and Rowntree).

In linking capitalism to fascism, Fahey is breaking down the barriers
between what are supposed to be, for Erikson, entirely separate kinds of
societies, and documenting the emergence of a sort of totalitarian "world
system," as Fahey calls it. It is a partial pushback against the Eriksonian idea
of the youth's ego development *contrasted* across the three separate realms
of European fascism, American democracy, and Soviet-style socialism. I say
partial because the same language of different world powers provides Fahey
with a way to describe his rebelliousness. In the last section of the essay, it
is now a year later—eighth grade. He has "learned how to look handsome,
tough, and a little sadistic." "Things were looking up." Suburban gangs of
various sorts were forming and meeting in schools and parking lots of shop-
ping centers. Fahey was listening to the "angry" works of Shostakovich and
Prokofiev, "Russian, Communist composers" (94). Revolutionary energies

were beginning to coalesce. Fahey and a male friend each had girlfriends; the sexual activity he complained about not having has finally begun:

> There in the safe dark we did things. And it was wonderful. And we became Communists. All four of us. . . . It was paradise. Victory. We were a Communist cell of four. And all the adults in the world couldn't keep us apart.
> And we fought the adults We started a reign of terror.
> The newspapers called what we did "senseless, random acts of violence."
> And random they sometimes were.
> But not senseless.
> We collected dynamite torpedoes off the B and O Railroad tracks and we sent away for cherry bombs. And aerial bombs. And we went out at night with slingshots and shot these bombs at passing cars on New Hampshire Avenue and the top of the Allen Theater. Nobody ever caught us. (96–97)

On and on it goes. Pranks and more pranks, better than the sex, or maybe "the danger enhanced the sex." Fahey—"leader and educator and theoretician of our cell" (99)—and friends "took a stand against the adults," taunting them by having sex where they might be seen (97). They turned to setting off cherry bombs at teachers' and principals' houses. They tried unsuccessfully to get cherry bombs to explode inside passing cars by tossing them into the open windows. Accidentally, they "set a place on fire"; they surprised themselves with "what you can do with rotten apples." Soon the cops were looking for them, however, and they had to cool it, on the advice of a "friend in the police department" (98). "We were on top of the world," Fahey brags, "and on top of its reptilian mesh of systems. And we never got caught or got in trouble. And everybody in town was trying to figure out who it was that was terrorizing the place. And why" (97–98). The victory was short, just three years. The Communist cell of four dispersed into the general population of teenage gangs.

The Puberty of Political Economy

In a sense, this is the youth's version of communism in the cheap, B-movie sense: the communist as mere bomb thrower, disrupter, lurker, opportunist, psycho, terrorist. Or maybe communist as merely the "bad guy" in a children's game of good guys and bad buys. But these possibilities play out against a larger background. For the good question really is, Just how is one to rebel against the strictures of postwar suburban life? The good rebel, Leerom Medovoi argues, resists the authoritarian tendencies of Fordist, postwar capitalism, especially the threat of conformity emerging among the consumers/workers/citizens. In an ideological bargain, such conformity must be resisted since it smacks too much of the conformity demanded in "Communism" and fails to demonstrate the uniqueness of capitalist democracy. The good rebel will demonstrate nonconformity with capitalism but never so much as to edge into anticapitalist politics. The good rebel is functional to capitalism, providing a safety valve in the cultural sphere for contradictions that emerge at the level of economy and politics. But this argument, as compelling as it is, and as much as it partially fits the rebel Fahey (handsome, tough, a little sadistic — Elvis Presley, James Dean, etc.), does not answer well to Fahey's concerns, which emerge more out of the intersection of psychology and capital, where the pleasures of creativity and play are under threat. These concerns are specifically about how capitalism makes workers out of nonworkers. Under capitalism, as Fahey understands it, the id of the child must be dominated by the superego, and both must be transvalued by the youthful ego that would do the work of integrating these forces. Yet this is also a system of domination by adults motivated purely by their own ids. Society, Fahey tells us, is structured so as to feed on these psycho-political energies. But Fahey is lacking, or holding back, or still mulling over the theoretical frame that would explain what exactly that structure is and how it works (for example, a theory of surplus value extraction and accumulation for accumulation's sake). Metaphor (factory, concentration camp) will have to work in the meantime.

Writing itself will have to work in the meantime too. Writing as rebellion. Expression as rebellion. Because of the way writing has been asked to happen — I am recalling the previous chapter — by the very authorities who would compel obedience, revolt can reveal itself "properly." Note below how Fahey exaggerates the writerly quality of what he has to say. He keeps sentences apart that might otherwise disappear into paragraphs. The prosaic becomes incantatory, thought slows down, and he pulls a certain lyricism and rhythm out of his ideas and seeks a possibly relevant audience (see the "I want to tell you" just below). The value of Fahey's "Communism" essay is not that there is a program here for anticapitalist struggle. Its value is more in the way it depicts capitalist society as lacking coherence and trustworthiness. Capitalism must do something to people; it must distort them and begin doing so early. Capitalism must make promises, not keep them, and then refuse to talk about it. To be clear, the "Communism" essay is not the mere self-validating of self-expression as a substitute for real politics, as Grace Elizabeth Hale argues in *A Nation of Outsiders*, for Fahey's representations are indeed about how the self is always already *really political*.

> So finally the adults won. We always knew they'd win in the end.
> But for three whole years we kept them at bay. We were just kids and
>   we beat them through and through, time after time.
> And we had a lot of fun doing it.
> And we were fiercely loyal to each other.
> The adults hate fraternal loyalty among kids.
> They hate it more than anything else.
> Because it is a threat to their hegemony.
> And because they do not have any loyalty themselves.
> And nobody knew anything about it.
> And nobody did anything about it.
> And I want to tell you that this being a gang member and directing and
>   protecting the others was very important in my character
>   development. (99)

Fahey is not simply drawing on psychoanalytic theory, modeling key points of his narrative after it. He is pushing hard against its powerful normalizing aspects, just as he seeks to describe his experiences on its terms.

These normalizing aspects may be nowhere clearer than in Erik Erikson's classic *Childhood and Society*. Writing in 1950, Erikson hypothesizes that each stage of man's psychological development, beginning in the newborn and progressing through adolescence, can be related, at least ideally, to a particular "basic element of social organization" (250), which works to reaffirm the achievements of that particular developmental stage. He viewed the process as a recursive one, whereby psychological development and social structure and/or social institutions are mutually developed (capitalist democracies), or as the case may be, mutually warped (Nazi Germany, communist Russia).

The stages and their corresponding social organization go like this. The trust in parental love that is developed in infancy and retained beyond it, Erikson thinks, "has throughout history sought its institutional safeguard (and, on occasion, found its greatest enemy) in organized religion" (250). At a later stage, if the child successfully balances the need for autonomy with the possibility of shame and doubt, "the lasting need . . . to have his will reaffirmed and delineated within an adult order of things which at the same time reaffirms and delineates the will of others has an institutional safeguard in the *principle of law and order*" (254). A bit later, the capacity to take initiative grows and with it the sense of responsibility for, and possible guilt over, the acts one has initiated. "Social institutions, therefore, offer children of this age an *economic ethos*, in the form of ideal adults recognizable by their uniforms and their functions, and fascinating enough to replace the heroes of picture book and fairy tale" (258). Later still, in elementary school, the ability to take initiative matures into a desire for industriousness and a sense that this can only be satisfied beyond the confines of the family. The sense of inferiority is always possible, however, along with the feeling of entering a world of impersonal forces. This stage, arriving before the "storm of puberty," is socially "a most decisive stage" (260). Industriousness, because it involves work with others, gives "a first sense of the division of labor and of differential opportunity, that is, a sense of the *technological ethos* of a culture" (260). This phase is decisive in the sense that if the child "accepts work as his only obligation and 'what works' as his only criterion of worthwhileness, he may become the conformist and thoughtless slave of his technology and of those who are in a position to exploit it" (260–61). The child's sense of identity comes next, in puberty (a "physiological revolution," Erikson calls it [261]). Right here is where Erikson shows us (and Fahey) the money. "Childhood proper comes to an end. Youth begins. But in puberty and adolescence all sameness and continuities relied on earlier are more or less questioned again, because of a rapidity of body growth which equals that of early childhood and because of the new addition of genital maturity" (261). Youth find it necessary to fight the old psychological battles over, "even though to do so they must artificially appoint perfectly well-meaning people to play the roles of adversaries; and they are ever ready to install lasting idols and ideals as guardians of a final identity" (261). Identity struggle and confusion are virtually ubiquitous. In defense, young people can be "clannish" and "cruel," excluding "those who are 'different,' . . . often in such petty aspects of dress and gesture as have been temporarily selected as the signs of an in-grouper or out-grouper" (262). Just the same, young people thereby help when forming groups and "stereotyping themselves, their ideals, and their enemies" (262). "The adolescent mind . . . is an ideological mind," Erikson thinks. *As if Fahey were directly in his sights*, he concludes that

> it is the ideological outlook of a society that speaks most clearly to the adolescent who is eager to be affirmed by his peers, and is ready to be confirmed by rituals, creeds, and programs which at the same time

define what is evil, uncanny, and inimical. In searching for the social values which guide identity, one therefore confronts the problems of *ideology* and *aristocracy*, both in their widest possible sense which connotes that . . . the best people will come to rule and rule develops the best in people. In order not to become cynically or apathetically lost, young people must somehow be able to convince themselves that those who succeed in their anticipated adult world thereby shoulder the obligation of being the best. (263)

The danger is that the adolescent subjection to ideology may result in cynicism and apathy, should the prevailing ideology fail to convince youth that the best and brightest will prevail and that the dominant form of rule is bringing out the best in people. Erikson's concerns reach around the globe; they are addressed to the entirety of the industrialized world and the world that is becoming industrialized. He warns that in such a world the stakes have never been higher, precisely because human ideals must be engaged in managing a complex division of labor, impersonality, and bureaucracy. "The management of supermachines," he writes, "be they guided by nationalistic [i.e., fascistic] or international communist or capitalist ideologies," poses immense difficulties for the societies at large, but also for the healthy development of youthful ego and the ethics of the adult (263). (Notably, his book concludes with case studies of Adolf Hitler and Maxim Gorky.)

Erikson's itinerary includes two further stages, but I will stop here. His point is that there is no one road to ultimate ego integrity, the formalization of trusting relationships, and so on. Nor is there just one way for societies to go wrong. What all societies are doing, however, is developing institutional "solutions" to the problems that variations in time and place present to the "provocations and prohibitions" of infantile and later stages of human psychology. It is uncanny how much of Erikson's itinerary maps onto Fahey's presentation of his youth experiences. Or at least it would be uncanny had Fahey not told us that his narrative was to be a psychoanalytic one.

Erikson's "impression" (278), which John Fahey "confirms," is that the industrial revolution in a sense selected the identity phase of the ego's functions as particularly important. "And so it comes about," Erikson writes, "that we begin to conceptualize matters of identity at the very time in history when they become a problem" (282). (Erikson would write in his 1968 book, *Youth: Identity and Crisis*, that in adolescence each individual is "closer to the historical day" than they have been previously in their lives. Previous developmental stages remain relatively stable over historical time, but "the identity problem changes with the historical period: this, in fact, is its job" [27].) The maturing of the industrial revolution, because it was so disruptive of agrarian societies and their prescribed roles for individuals, and then the globalization of the industrial revolution together with its quite different development in the United States, Nazi Germany, and communist Russia, which inherently suggested different possibilities for how industrial society might be organized and valued, opened up the question of what to do, what to become, how to be, what to believe in—all matters that come to a head during the identity phase of adolescent development. "The study of identity," Erikson writes, "becomes as strategic in our time as the study of sexuality was in Freud's time" (*Childhood* 282). At stake in each of these contexts is the "need, in the youth of all these countries, for a new, a fraternal conscience and a more inclusive, and necessarily industrial, identity" (283). In the American context, valued most by Erikson, this need takes on a particular meaning.

> Consider our adolescent boy. In his early childhood he was faced with a training which tended to make him machinelike and clocklike. Thus standardized, he found chances, in his later childhood, to develop autonomy, initiative, and industry, with the implied promise that decency in human relations, skill in technical details, and knowledge of facts would permit him freedom of choice in his pursuits, that the identity of free choice would balance his self-coercion. As an adolescent and man, however, he finds himself confronted with superior machines, complicated, incomprehensible, and impersonally dictatorial in their power to standardize his pursuits and tastes. These machines do their powerful best to convert him into a consumer idiot, a fun egotist, and an efficiency slave—and this by offering him what he seems to demand. Often he remains untouched and keeps his course. . . . Otherwise, what else can he become but a childish joiner, or a cynical little boss . . . or a neurotic character.
>
> . . . For the sake of its emotional health, then, a democracy cannot afford to let matters develop to a point where intelligent youth, proud in its independence and burning with initiative, must leave matters of legislation, law, and international affairs, not to speak of war and peace, to "insiders" and "bosses." American youth can gain the full measure of identity and of its vitality only by being fully aware of autocratic trends in this and in any other land as they repeatedly emerge from changing history. And this not only because political conscience cannot regress without catastrophic consequences, but

also because political ideals are part and parcel of an evolution in conscience structure which, if ignored, must lead to illness. (323)

The argument is elegantly distilled in the assertion that "the crisis of youth is also the crisis of a generation and of the ideological soundness of its society" (309). The stakes are not only American stakes. In a Cold War context, the stakes are global. Erikson argues that it is necessary for America to defeat its own autocratic and consumerist trends so that it can become a global model in the fight against communism. (Erikson did not have fascism on his mind so much.) "We must be able to demonstrate . . . that our new and shiny goods (so enticingly wrapped in promises of freedom) do not come to them as so many more sedatives to make them subservient to their worn-out upper classes, as so many more opiates to lull them into the new serfdom of hypnotized consumership" (402). Who exactly is the "we" who will perform this demonstration? To Fahey, there is no one in sight.

The Limits of Memoir

Erikson would in no way disagree with Fahey that his experiences as a youth were extraordinarily important to his "character development" (Fahey's words, recall). Fahey's problem, instead, would likely be deemed his insistence on prolonging or, better, overvaluing the moment. Yes, life is a bore if it has no options, but if well lived it must also consist of fidelity to one's commitments, Erikson says. Without this balance, "identity confusion" results (Erikson, *Identity* 245). The problem for Erikson, I think, would be that Fahey does not identify the communist cell as a problem to be rid of. Sure, experiences and explorations at the social margins are fine, because a sense of social possibilities, tolerances, and limits results. What Erikson claims to see is that in the not too distant past the identity crises "suffered" by adolescents were "more or less" unconscious. "A certain type today," he writes in *Youth: Identity and Crisis*, "tells us in no uncertain terms, and with the dramatic outer display of what we once considered to be inner secrets, that yes, indeed, they have an identity conflict" (26). They even wear it on their sleeves, "Edwardian or leather." Displaying the classic symptoms of "negative identity," "they seem to want to be everything which 'society' tells them not to be" (26). Erikson, who played a major role in popularizing the phrase "identity crisis," demurs that "some young people actually seem to read what we write. . . . Sometimes they merely acknowledge that we seem to know what they are talking about. . . . It is an aspect of the old game of what Freud called 'turning passive into active.'" It is as if youth, who know they are supposed to have an identity crisis, are declaring, "Who says we *suffer* from an identity 'crisis'? We are choosing it, having it actively, we are playing at making it happen" (28). "From Freud's early days onward," says Erikson, and quite eloquently, "enlightened people have adapted to his insights by mouthing the names of their neuroses—and keeping the neuroses too" (28).

The difference is that Fahey, who we must note is figured by Erikson as quintessentially countercultural with no objection from Fahey, in no way desires to supersede his character development. He offers evidence why. Fahey clings to his ability to have ferreted out the contradictions that produce capitalist-industrial values and the social and cultural forms that have grown around them, and insists on living right there amid contradictions, where the "pranks" are most effective. It is as if these contradictions are themselves the only alternative, in the face of such daunting powers. Life in the trouble zone is hard to sustain, however. Note, in what I called Fahey's "literary" passage above, that he switches from describing what the communist cell does to describing what has become of its members. He emphasizes their fraternity and their loyalty, and the emboldening of these values in the face of those agents who want to both split the members up into the competing individuals those agents themselves have become and recombine them into a "false gregariousness," as Aggregate Execrable Nemesis might say. Despite the nostalgic tone of Fahey's desires, it would be a mistake to view them as merely the perpetuation of juvenile longings. Or rather, properly understood, maybe they are juvenile in a radical psychopolitical sense: if there is something to what Erikson proposes about the historical and ideological significance of the "identity" phase, it seems apt to regard Fahey's desire as a wish to prolong as long as possible the very knowledge, even when sunk within the matrix of solitude (Berman again), that one is being subjected to an ideology, made to coincide with "the times" and the sites (home, family, school, work) that index the times most profoundly.

And yet, what else composes the times? Let's pivot again. It would never have been possible for Fahey to comprehend all the social processes to which he was subject. But is it surprising to "hear" in this essay the force of a certain silence joined to the very way that he narrates his innocence and victimization? Amid all the constructed forms of social difference Fahey attends to—between children and parents, home and school, teachers and students, adults and youth, boys and girls—there is no mention that they are all on one side of the "color line." In reading these memories through the rebellious adolescent phase of his desires, and as the preservation of those desires, Fahey reflects (without comment) the fact of his upbringing in a racially segregated school and a racially segregated neighborhood (Hale, *Making Whiteness*). The process and history of capitalist industrialization propagates a racial divide that goes missing *in this essay*.

"Communism" is a certain kind of authorial performance of white innocence, itself segregated from reportage of the racial composition of Takoma Park later in the book (see chapter 6). Viewed from its avoidance of race relations, "Communism," which offers a wide-ranging, highly systematic exploration of psycho-politics, exerts a great deal of control over where its critique is willing to go and where it is not, as if there is a time when race matters and a time when it doesn't and John Fahey knows the difference. Fahey feels oppressed, he reports, but does not communicate how that oppression works in conjunction with other oppressive relations, which, because ignored, allow his emotions to feel as if they are purely his own, and the emotions that circulate inside the "communist cell" to seem purely their own, too (Lipsitz). In this kind of reportage, in which genre is used to select memory, the whiteness of the spaces, school and neighborhood, never have to seem to matter. They can be made to seem unto themselves, unaware of their own "dispossession," as George Yancy calls it (*Look*). That is, these are spaces that appear to their residents as self-made, rather than being produced through a broader set of race-making historical and geographical relationships and forces, imposed upon the youthful Fahey by his elders (without, as I say, any comment from the adult Fahey, who has just written a memoir precisely about the relationships and forces that make a self). A journey away from supposed white self-sufficiency is in order if the fallacy of self-sufficient whiteness is to be exposed—as Fahey will show he knows in another chapter from *How Bluegrass Music Destroyed My Life*. (Even then, Yancy writes, one will not have arrived at some terminal knowledge, some satisfactory angle of repose, some final, absolving awareness of what whiteness entails.)

So, why does "Communism" not connect the dots when it comes to the segregated racial worlds of Takoma Park? Well, one answer is that it doesn't have to; it has other purposes. But perhaps it is because not doing so absolves Fahey from revisiting old ambivalences about how to "do" civil rights struggles, per the days of *Requia*. But in my view, this approach is consistent with a desire to choose (or for Fahey to think he is choosing) how to treat that subject under conditions when he can specify which racial intimacies he feels and which ones he does not. This makes the avoidance of race in "Communism" of a piece with how, elsewhere, he constructs the racial intimacies that do come to interest him. We find these constructions first in his writings on music and the discourse of "folk."

PART II | Delta Haze

Introduction

If John Fahey was to have a career as a musical artist, there was no escaping that the environment of folk music was where he had to be. And in some measure, his many protestations aside, he would need to be and was "folk" himself. (After all, how close can a moth get to the flame without becoming part of it?) This thesis runs against virtually all his statements to the contrary, but it is borne out by his writing in folklore studies, specifically the way he projects a relationship onto Charley Patton, in the Patton monograph and elsewhere, and by the parodic content of his liner notes. His approach was not a matter of utter capitulation to "folk" notions, but rather one of opening up a critical space within them.

Folk discourse followed Fahey as closely as his shadow. He insisted repeatedly that he was not a folk musician, abhorred most folk music, and was dismissive at best of the folk scene as he understood it. Yet on these grounds in the mid and late 1960s he secured a kind of cult status. He was headlining small concert venues, his records were selling, and his music was being reviewed in the music press and in newspapers. Despite the different styles he incorporated into his compositions, there was really no other widely known category to which he could be assigned, if sometimes falteringly, than "folk."[1] After all, here was a guy alone on stage, on a chair, with a mic, rolled-up jeans, and a baggy shirt, looking every bit the part of the folksinger, or at least some kind of folksinger, even if he did not sing, and picking a steel-string acoustic guitar. The problem is that folk music was really the only viable category to pitch Fahey's music to a broader audience. This, even though a number of music critics acknowledged that "folk" was not an apt description. Phil Spiro, reviewing Fahey's second album for Takoma Records in a 1964 issue of the folk magazine the *Broadside of Boston*, concludes, "Fahey is easily the most inventive, original guitarist working in the folk idiom today. One is almost tempted to call him a jazz guitarist when he moves from the folk and/or blues area, but the area he moves into is *not* jazz at all. Perhaps it is best called Faheysville. . . . In all, this is an exciting, if strangely mixed, bag of styles and ideas, presented by a guitarist with extraordinary technics, soul, and imagination" (qtd. in Guerrieri, *John Fahey, vol. 1* 242). Of Fahey's third Takoma release, Spiro finds that it is the "most musically mature." Spiro counts Fahey among the few "experimentalists" (along with Robbie Basho and Sandy Bull) producing a "truly new" musical form, concluding that he "is one of the most imaginative guitarists now on the folk scene, and this record is a fine demonstration of his remarkable musicianship. He is one of the best now, and in time may well become one of the great ones" (qtd. in Guerrieri, *John Fahey, vol. 1* 269). By the sixth Takoma volume—released in 1967, by which time Fahey had branched out into musique concrete, montage, electronic sound effects, programmatic compositions, and atonal experiments—Spiro states, "A problem: What can be said of Fahey that has not been said already in one form or another? . . . The best way to enjoy Fahey is to play the record and forget about the details; perhaps this is the best way to review the record as well. . . . Buy the record; it is healthful and refreshing, and will put a good shine on your liver" (qtd. in Guerrieri, *John Fahey, vol. 1* 319–20). This last review, with its concluding flourish, reels Fahey in with its own folksy idiom. While clearly straining, stretching, and bending received categories, Fahey is "on the folk scene," "working in the folk idiom," good for your liver. Fahey's swerves away from folk may even be the best kind of "folk" indicator. Fahey's friend ED Denson, who was his manager for part of the 1960s, puts it so: "The great folk artists, or perhaps the idea will be easier if I say, the great primitive artists, are not those who rigorously follow their father's ways; they are those who accidentally and eclectically gather certain materials and techniques from their environment and then stubbornly persist in combining them until they have created something. This is the kind of artist John seems to be."

Fahey was also the kind of artist who kept showing up to play amid the very crowd he imagined himself to be against. Let's read here how Fahey attempts to draw blood in a 1982 essay, "The Historical Subjectivity of the Guitar." It is unrelenting critique, which can really only be understood when also engaging with his earlier work in the liner notes and in the Patton book, of what he regarded as the anachronism of the folk and blues revival.[2]

These young acculturated Americans—Ingroupies—have not suffered the necessary humiliation. They are attempting to appropriate the semblance, not the reality, of a bygone era, a dead tradition. Even with sufficient experience in degradation . . . a person cannot, without an extraordinary amount of effort, imagination and research produce the lost emotions and "weltanschaung" of the nineteenth century. This was already the sound of a bygone era when Blind Lemon Jefferson recorded, and *his* last sessions were in 1929. That was a very long time ago, young man with the Martin guitar playing bad imitations of Blind Lemon licks. . . . What we hear in these recordings is their memory and experience of this bygone era and all its ways. These sounds and feelings are remnantal. They were remnantal when they were originally recorded.

There can be no contemporaneity for us with the nineteenth century (Cf. Soren Kierkegaard, Philosophical Fragments, Princeton University Press). (31; Kierkegaard citation in the original)

The offense seems to lie in an imitator's being content with appropriating semblance, in *not caring* about the difference between semblance and reality, or just in not being curious enough about one's influences to gain an understanding of them in their own context. "Guitar playing is looked upon by many as a form of art, or art plus self-expression," Fahey instructs (cf. Bennett and Dawe; Dawe; Evans, "The Guitar"). "The people that make such outrageous claims then proceed to play you plagiarization after plagiarization on the guitar attributing these songs all to themselves or, what is even more disgusting, insinuating the 'artist' from whom they stole this song was (is) a good 'friend' of theirs. Thus they attempt by means of subterfuge to appropriate the being and substance of this or that retired (or expired) 'blues singer'" (30).

Long before this 1982 essay, Fahey was jeering at the folk revival. For the liner notes to his first Takoma album, *Blind Joe Death*, he invented a discography for his invented Blind Joe Death persona. A parody of the value accorded to "rarities," the faked discography consisted of *two* songs, one recorded in 1929 and the other in 1934—therein Fahey's object lesson on the folk revival's fascination with a "remnantal" culture remote from contemporary suffering and contemporary politics. In Fahey's mind, folk musicians of the sixties and their audiences fundamentally misunderstood the music they were supposedly reviving. Revivalists, in tapping into folk and blues, had not discovered the so-called voice of the people. For the voice of the people was certainly not in the music of Black musicians, whose recording heyday was before World War II and whose careers, as David Evans also emphasizes, had lapsed into obscurity ("Charley Patton," *Screamin'*). African Americans had now moved on to other music styles. As Fahey put it in his book *How Bluegrass Music Destroyed My Life*, the acoustic country blues was "in capricious demand by Whitey. Only by Whitey" (220).

But that is not all. In the "Historical Subjectivity" essay, Fahey describes the social deception and subterfuge roiling within the folk scene itself:

> All of this pretense at contemporaneity by means of going to a party with a Martin guitar, all of the imitating John Hurt or old 78's by Sam McGee in a social situation, in a guitar shop, in Baskin-Robbins, jamming in the key of "E" endlessly at Washington Square, all of this is carefully planned obfuscation and subterfuge carried out by the murderous Ingroup, and when I say murderous I am not joking. (The Ingroupie, each and every one of them, is a murderer. Every time one of them purchases a phonograph record he commits an atrocity.) This apparent confusion of ethnic traditions, this attempt by someone to imitate a nineteenth century feeling-sound-emotion through the mechanics of guitar playing, by showing up at a party in dirty Levis with a Martin guitar and playing note for note John Hurt or Sam McGee, this phony democracy of "I'm OK, You're OK" is a carefully contrived plot to confuse the Outgroup, and especially among the Outgroup those few solitary individuals (if there are any left) who are true loners.
>
> But the plot did not fully succeed. Although there are few of us left, I remain. (31)

Hardly the democracy of loners and individualists it appears to be, the folk scene is ruled by a self-anointed, deceitful, and ignorant in-group (with a following of record-buying "in-groupies") who gain status posing as loners and outsiders.[3] Yet it is in the relatively termed out-group where the real loners and outsiders can be found. In becoming mainstream, the in-group is also blind to what it kills off: historical accuracy, genuine contemporaneity, and originality. But all is not lost! Fahey, tongue in cheek (sort of), anoints himself one of the last true outsiders. He has eluded capture, in sly fashion moreover, for his escape strategy has been to pass as a folk musician even while insisting he is not one. My point, though, is that Fahey cannot control how he is viewed, a predicament that thickens the more "himself" and elusive he tries to be. Of course, if Fahey is a loner and outsider, he is also one who wants to be brought "inside" and paid attention to, hinting at a desire to best the folkies at the entertainment game. These contradictory emotions generated sufficient heat to produce Fahey's darkly humored suggestion at the end of the "Historical Subjectivity" essay that performer and audience, having cornered each other into roles that could only lead to self-deception and "bad faith," commit suicide together.[4]

Fahey's soapbox proclamations notwithstanding, he did not rule out authenticity as a goal and a quality of music and musical performance. He just vehemently disagreed with where (he assumed) his peers were looking for it and rejected their motives. In Fahey's Patton book, the tale is told more through asides than direct, extended confrontation. For most of its pages the book is a rigorous, scholarly account of Patton's discography, lyrics, and song styles. But among Fahey's intents, which surface in the offhand comments he makes, is to fend off interpretations of the blues as a kind of political protest song. He considered such interpretations an illegitimate projection of present-day concerns onto a bygone tradition. The country blues ought instead to be appreciated for its aesthetic and emotional qualities. It is unclear, though, what the leading edge of this analysis was. Was it that his distaste for white folk and blues imitators and white fans' proclivity for romanticizing the suffering of Black musical artists led him to deny any political meaning in the blues, because this would endorse the white romance? Or was it that he simply did not see Black songsters of the pre-Depression era as political actors at all, leaving available only an aesthetic and emotional appreciation, or no appreciation at all? And how much did Fahey read his own reticence about political involvement into Patton? I'm not sure these questions can even be separated from each other. It is the tangle of them that perhaps envelops Fahey's defense of white, Depression-era, Southern paternalism that we will see also appears in a one-off comment in the book. But maybe this comment did not signal Fahey's belief system so much as it was a defensive, rhetorical move sparked by Fahey's distaste for white imitators and fans? Maybe he was telegraphing both possibilities.

Such are the looping complexities that arise in Fahey's attempts to, on the one hand, position Charley Patton and his music in such a way as to avoid the white romance about Black musical artists in an oppressive Southern political economy and, on the other hand, to formulate a positive, affective relationship to Patton, who, long deceased, had left behind only his guitar playing and his lyrics for study. Who was Charley Patton? A preternaturally talented songster from the Mississippi Delta, virtually every account agrees. Born in 1891 and a member of the first generation of what the music historian David Evans calls "folk blues singers," Patton influenced a wide range of blues musicians: Son House, Howlin' Wolf, Bukka White, Big Joe Williams,

"Pop" Staples, and others ("Charley Patton," *Screamin'*). Patton attracted white and Black audiences, and was himself of mixed racial heritage. He was active primarily during the pre-Depression era but made recordings into the winter of 1934. Patton was also an idea that Fahey had. To be clear, Patton's singularity, and indeed the singularity of the Delta Blues, is a construction that predates Fahey (Hamilton). But Fahey updates the particulars as well as the purposes. I argue in chapter 3 that Fahey was heavily influenced by a particular theory of folklore, which stated that its logic—that is, the cultural and linguistic processes through which folklore is created—is essentially "associative." Patton's process involved associating together, as he wished, all sorts of lyrics that with his gruff singing and polyrhythmic playing style communicated extraordinary emotional depth. This was a Patton that Fahey, also capable of drawing on a large repertoire of song and a deep well of emotion, could relate to. This is how Fahey becomes "folk" himself.

Not only this, Patton stood out from his peers as a singular figure, just as Fahey aspired to stand out. Each man, in Fahey's mind, was largely outside politics. When Fahey insists that "I remain" in his essay on the historical subjectivity of the guitar, we should understand he imagines Patton's ghost is by his side and that Patton's singularity is a concoction of the folkloristics Fahey uses to single him out. And yet, as I began this book by stating, this conceit of being outside the political points to a story Fahey may not have meant to tell. It is precisely the same, shared common ground between Fahey and Patton, as Fahey understands it, that is the means for an authentic polis to emerge, again, as Fahey understands it. I will explore this theme much more in part 3, but we get a strong taste of it in some of Fahey's liner notes. Chapter 4 focuses on a selection of liner notes that Fahey wrote for his own records. The notes follow some of the patterns already established by other note writers. But in keeping with his *Requia* notes, Fahey took advantage of the more experimental and expressive styles that were becoming popular too. In the selections I discuss, Fahey's parodies of "folk" music and its study are lengthy, wry, and sarcastic. He also works some magic on the infrastructure of prose itself, as when paragraphs, sentences, phrases, and words devolve into a confetti of non sequiturs. Words will be made up and carved up. At their extremes, passages become almost unreadable. Nothing is explained; words and phrases are hurled onto the page. A meaning might announce itself, only to break up when the next assault occurs. Nonsense is partly the point: let's grind all matters "folk" into dust. But nonsense is also a *method*: Fahey produces it by means of the associative process that makes folklore in the first place, the same process that Fahey finds underlies Patton's work. Certain liner notes, in other words, describe a line of connection to Patton. Only when old meanings are demolished can a new kind of conviviality and social integument become possible.

As different as they are, the Patton book and the liner notes could not be more aligned. It is as if Fahey needs to have worked in the two contrasting modes of scholarship and parody in order to build a hybridized critical space, in folk discourse by means of folk discourse, folking with the folk, as it were (cf. Retman). In Fahey's writing, the critique of folk, and simultaneous conjuring of a singular emotional depth that abides in an expressive, mysterious self, is not isolated from the other themes we've already seen in his work. Is it coincidental that this self is more or less compatible with the kind Fahey had learned to be since high school? This is a figure consonant, too, with ideas about the self, embraced in the 1960s' counterculture, *even as* Fahey used Patton as evidence that countercultural and new-left ideas about Black blues music were wrong. Finally, there are pitfalls in deploying the folk idiom in its own undermining. Fahey's prima facie interest in the unfathomable, self-confirming depths of the self and its subjective experiences contradicts his other claim that he (alone?) really *gets* Patton, in both senses of that word. There is a possessive claim here that anchors Fahey's authorship and renders limited the forms of community and intimacy that might follow from it.

Listening Session Two

"Charley Bradley's Ten-Sixty-Six Blues" (*Red Cross*, 2003)

The last musicological study Fahey produced, long after his monograph, was an update of his thinking about Charley Patton. "Patton's recordings have meant so much to me for so long," Fahey effuses, "it is almost as if he were a constant companion to me" ("Charley Reconsidered" 53). Let's suppose this idea and Fahey's musicology explaining it—together written up as an essay included in the sumptuous Charley Patton box set, *Screamin' and Hollerin' the Blues*—is of a piece with the fact that Patton is one of the touchstones for Fahey's own last solo album, *Red Cross*, recorded a few months before he died. (Both *Red Cross* and the Patton box set were released by Revenant Records, an independent label Fahey cofounded with record collector Dean Blackwood, using a $50,000 inheritance from his father [McCord]). I would like to close this introduction to part 2 by putting Fahey's late-life thoughts about Patton in conversation with his last album, and one song in particular:

"Charley Bradley's Ten-Sixty-Six Blues." The conversation is by no means obvious, however. For one thing, Patton's influence on *Red Cross* manifests more as the sound of Fahey's ideas about Patton, or, more remotely, as the sound of the chase after those ideas, than a cover of the Patton sound itself. Some degree of separation like that is necessarily the case, however. Although there are two Patton titles on *Red Cross*, "Ananaias" and "Charley Bradley's Ten-Sixty-Six Blues," the songs themselves were never released. Therefore, John Fahey never heard them, although he did know of them, by title, at least as far back as his master's thesis research. (Patton and his wife Bertha Lee recorded the songs in New York in the winter of 1934 for the Vocalion imprint of ARC [American Record Corporation], but Fahey reports in *Charley Patton* that ARC never released them. Moreover, the masters no longer exist [Evans, "Charley Patton," *Screamin'*].) Who were Ananaias and Charley Bradley? The first is the name of a few different biblical figures; the second was a railroad engineer. Nothing is known about the Bradley song, except for what Fahey himself learned from Son House, who recorded and performed with Patton. Fahey interviewed the elderly Son House while he was at UCLA. In Son House's words, "Charley Bradley, he was a white fellow, an engineer, and the engine number was 1066. [He drove] a train that come out of Memphis going down to Vicksburg late in the evening, and it would be round about 6:30 or 7:00. Everybody liked the way he blowed his whistle, and then they started talking about Charley Bradley and the 1066: We'd better get there and get there quick / So we catch Charley Bradley on the 1066" (qtd. in Fahey, *Charley Patton* 110).

There are further complications. Fahey's versions of the two Patton songs on *Red Cross* were actually recorded by him (under different titles) during a studio session in 1977 but not released until they appeared on *Red Cross*. But when Fahey sent the recordings that make up *Red Cross* to Dean Blackwood, he claimed the material was completely new.[5] Fahey must have marveled at the trick he was playing, rediscovering a lost Charley Patton tune that was really a "rediscovery" of his own. The connection to Patton is a slippery matter, then, made even slipperier by our not knowing how much Fahey might have had Patton in mind when he composed the material. The original title of the composition from which Fahey's "Ananaias" and "Charley Bradley's Ten-Sixty-Six Blues" were edited was "Melody Brenan," Fahey's partner whom he would marry the following year. This doesn't mean Patton's influence wasn't lurking on the fretboard. (Shall we just go with Fahey's insistence that Patton was *always* his companion?) Arguably, Fahey decided that for purposes of *Red Cross*, Patton's influence had been there, or was now through the magic of retrospection. *Somehow*, Fahey deemed these two compositions to be in fitting association with Patton. Just how so will never be certain. My notes below mean to generate some thought about the matter, on the basis that song meanings and song titles do not stand firm at a song's origin but are transformed as they travel into new domains (Rosenberg; Frith). Other matters to note are that Fahey credits neither Charley Patton nor Bertha Lee on *Red Cross*, and neither song is an imitation of Patton's music in the conventional sense. (For an imitation of Patton, listen to Fahey's rendition of "Mississippi Bo Weavil Blues," which he recorded in the late 1950s for Fonotone, under the name Blind Thomas [Fahey, *Your Past*].) When you engage *Red Cross*, either you recognize the provenance of these two titles as Patton's or you do not. And if you do, you have to be ready for a rubbery sense of Patton's sound anyway. The album goes digging for a deeper truth about him, one that opens vistas yet unheard. Meanwhile, Fahey thinks in that last writing of his about Patton that he has come closer than anyone to unearthing the deep truth. Before getting to that discussion, though, let's listen to the opening material of "Charley Bradley."

It is a dissonant chord struck two or three times, slowly enough to hear the individual notes peeling off, then hit more quickly with a few upstrokes tossed in. Fahey slows again until after fourteen or fifteen strums, the dissonance quickly resolves—fifteen seconds and its over—helped along by a few bass notes that carry the melody into more harmonious territory. The opening bears a striking resemblance to Fahey's "Christmas Fantasy, Part 2," from the second album of Christmas music he made in 1975. There also, Fahey announces the song with a struck chord, one very similar to that of "Charley Bradley," but maybe a step down. The point of the comparison is to hypothesize that Fahey means to announce "Charley Bradley's Ten-Sixty-Six Blues" as also a *fantasy*, in the sense we noticed in this book's introduction. It does not seem to me far-fetched to suggest that, given the information Son House provided Fahey, Bradley is a Patton-type figure, an entertainer of great popularity whose appearance people did not want to miss. So, sound the bell, strike the chord, get people to pay attention.

Fahey's writing for the Patton box set is a lengthy recalibration of the basic claims made in his master's thesis, and a rethinking of what he refers to as the "Blues Story." In chapter 4, I show that the conventions for narrating biographies of blues musicians were something Fahey parodied mercilessly in liner notes from decades past. So, here, Fahey has finally pulled these interests together, offering a portrait of Patton that resolves some basic question of what he thinks a life lived as a blues story means. As I read it, the essay represents a mature Fahey steadying himself for a solid reckoning. He puts aside jokes and parodies that in the past he carried to extremes, and writes with confidence and reverence, without being maudlin about it. Considering his ill health and precarious finances at this time (the essentials are recounted in Steve Lowenthal's biography), the essay makes for powerful reading. Not the least of it is Fahey's respect for the research by fellow Patton scholar David Evans.

"Charley Reconsidered" emphasizes that Fahey had always regarded Patton as "a very intelligent, complex, interesting and first class artist . . . a man who inspired many people's love and trust and respect . . . and a man therefore who was serious, a person of good character, someone whom many people found inspiring, including me" (47). Fahey believes Patton had been a "leader of men" (47). It is one of "the (many) transgressions of my youth" that Fahey did not bring these aspects of his understanding to the fore in his master's work (47). The thesis had claimed, among other things, that Patton's worldview was extremely limited and that he lacked even the intellectual resources to develop significant social criticism. This did not mean Fahey thought racialized poverty in the South and throughout the United States did not warrant exposure. We know this from Fahey's comments about the civil rights era on his *Requia* album, and we will see it again in a discussion of his liner notes for *Days Have Gone By*, in chapter 6. The point is that Patton's struggle lay primarily elsewhere.

Can we hear Fahey's renewed appreciation for Patton in "Charley Bradley's Ten-Sixty-Six Blues"? Maybe so. As its discordant opening material dissolves away, Fahey transitions to a melody that is as delightful, catchy, and toe-tapping as anything he ever came up with. With ease and sophistication he produces effortless syncopations of picking and strumming that just blossom from his hands. This section of the song brims with such affirmation and joy that, yes, maybe Fahey means to honor and communicate Patton's profound accomplishments and talent. As the possible sound of "Charley Reconsidered," maybe it also announces Fahey's joy in having found the right things to say about his long-term "companion." Before these possibilities have a chance to set, however, this part of the song is over. It's been maybe forty-five seconds since the song began and Fahey is about to say something new.

In "Charley Reconsidered," the most important point Fahey is compelled to make is that Patton was "a pioneer in the externalization through music of strange, weird, even ghastly emotional states" (47). Patton can certainly be set within the larger economy and race relations of the plantation South, but these did not define him. He was a most profoundly deep self, working around economic and racial constraints to create a life as a successful entertainer, earning the respect of whites and Blacks alike. If Patton battled racial discrimination, and Fahey does not appear to doubt this as he did while working on his master's thesis, the struggles more worth commenting on in 2001, because no one had touched on them to his satisfaction, were with those "ghastly" states of mind.

Strange, weird, and ghastly states of mind are the center of the "blues story." The blues story was an early preoccupation of Fahey's partly because it was such a common motif for liner notes on blues records. It was especially a preoccupation though because the younger Fahey had no patience for the very notion. In a 1966 review of a Mississippi John Hurt album for *The Little Sandy Review*, Fahey fires off a question to Nat Hentoff, who wrote liner notes for the record (and whose notes for Fahey's *Of Rivers and Religion* would later provide some of the best descriptions of Fahey's music to be found anywhere), "What the hell is a 'blues story-teller' anyway, Nat? And who was one?" (qtd. in Guerrieri, *John Fahey, vol. 2* 426). Well, now Fahey thinks he knows.

Fahey returns to the question raised in his master's thesis of why Patton's lyrics are built using an associative method—that is, stringing phrases together in a seeming random fashion (see chapter 3). "Now I think I know the story of the stream and how we can see in these difficult songs some sense and coherence" ("Charley Reconsidered" 48). For one, at least some lyrics are actually autobiographical. More significant, though "unprovable, unless we can have a common understanding of music," is that even without the lyrics the guitar playing and singing "are also to some extent autobiographical, usually evoking a mood or feeling in the listener" (48). Fahey avers that other scholars, notably Robert Palmer, have used the term "deep blues" to describe the feelings expressed and evoked by musicians like Patton. What is "deep," though? Fahey asks. "A 'deep' person does not engage much in small talk. He is not nervous, and is certainly not trivial. He knows things that we do not. He knows himself" (49). As if directly commenting on Patton's associative style, Fahey continues, "He is in touch with his unconscious feelings and inclinations and he is neither cut off from (disassociation) nor afraid of them. . . . He recognizes that we are all subject to the same drives and your unconscious is not so different from his" (49). "Patton was . . . a master in his blues songs at externalizing inner, and for the most part socially unacceptable, emotions [such as rage]. . . . He presents the unacceptable to us in an acceptable manner—in music" (49). These are all fascinating comments, but they are to some extent projections too. Fahey notes that he entered Freudian psychoanalysis after he wrote his Patton book. "It was an eight year journey but it was by far the most exciting trip I ever took. And I'm still taking it. Nothing is more interesting than a trip into the unconscious" (49).

To be in touch with feelings, though, is not necessarily to expel them; the "deep" person does not procure self-knowledge once and for all. "Patton in his lyrics continuously and openly states that he is being controlled more and more by forces outside himself, such as women, trains, the fates, prison. . . . He is always singing about escape routes from these controlling forces." But the secret feeling underlying everything is the worry that these external forces actually come from within him. "What Patton portrays brilliantly, both in words and music, more than any other musician is the *uncanny* feeling that comes only gradually to consciousness that the real forces controlling him are in fact not forces *outside* himself, but dimly beheld, obscure 'jinxes' or ominous feelings which hang over him and cloud his thoughts like a pall" (50). Patton is dogged by "the terrible anticipation that something unnamed yet familiar is going to happen . . . which hasn't happened yet, but which in fact *feels* inevitable" (50). It could be death, castration, separation from the superego, the future, divine retribution—"God knows what else" (51). Above all is the fear of "something unknown within oneself—something that is controlling you again and again, naggingly familiar each time, in the same manner but such that any attempt to escape it results in simply being the shortest path to that very same terrible thing" (51). And then, one day, it simply disappeared. The ominousness, the uncanny, "simply evaporated from his psyche and his art" (51). Fahey writes, most curiously, that Patton "forfeited the obsessions" that drove him to produce his greatest blues works (51). Not so much a victory, then, or even a surrender, just a pass.

But what was it inside Patton that produced the feeling of the ominous and the uncanny—Freud's term, recall, for something one thought was settled and put to rest but turns out not to be so. Fahey suggests that Patton, as a Christian who believed he was saved, might not have believed in his salvation so much after all, nor even, perhaps, in Jesus Christ as savior. For this particular stream of Christian belief, sins past, present, and future are already forgiven so long as one proclaims belief in salvation. The greatest sin from this perspective, Fahey states, is "unbelief" (52). In Fahey's version of the "blues story," all blues are consistent with Christian belief, but they express that belief from the other side, the side where one can continue to sin. What makes Patton's blues special is that belief does not guarantee a permanent victory over unbelief. The implication of Patton's "forfeiture," then, is that he returned to the belief, the faith, that all is well, after all. And with that, the music is also less interesting. By 1934, "Patton can clearly no longer sing angry, ominous blues songs convincingly" (51).

All of this now raises some tasty questions for Fahey's use of Patton's title. Whatever tune and lyrics Patton had given the Charley Bradley blues, its having been recorded in 1934 would place it in Fahey's category of post-ominous music, which Fahey thinks less of. The delightful, toe-tapping portion of Fahey's rendition could be in the celebratory mood I refer to above. But now it could be a critical reflection on the trajectory of Patton's music too. Both are possible (as are other possibilities, of course). Whatever the meaning of this portion of the song, everything changes after it is finished. The music is a whole lot less pretty and a whole lot more interesting. The shifts are dramatic. The nicely affecting fingerpicking continues for a few moments, although Fahey suddenly switches to a different key. He has also now moved up the neck, fretting the strings at the ninth fret. In combination, these changes introduce a great deal of tension into the song. The strong sense is that the truth of the song, what Fahey's composition really wants to say, is about to come. For a few moments he keeps a lid on things by slowing the rhythm, making the song . . . hymn-like? Indicating . . . "God knows what": an acknowledgment of Patton's return to faith or are we moving beyond that "God knows what" to the return of the uncanny? The uncanny's return to whom—Fahey? Patton? Fahey ceases fingerpicking and starts strumming, just the bottom few strings, fast, faster. Exploding the notes with his thumb pick, plastic on metal. Rapid strokes, until all artistry and skill evaporate and the "song" is nothing but tantrum, rant, frustration, confusion. Emotions without lyrics, without singing, without anything that counts as even guitar playing. All that and a punk celebration of "unbelief" too. And then, calm returns. Music is back, the strumming slows, bringing with it the peeling of a dissonant chord: the outro reminding us that this has been a fantasia, a really stunning think-piece on Patton, brought in at under three and a half minutes. Can "Night Train to Valhalla," often considered Fahey's truly fearful work, really compare? "Night Train," which Fahey included on *Days Have Gone By*, has an undeniably propulsive rhythm and chord progressions suggesting great malintent, but it never courts the chaos and devolution that "Charley Bradley's Ten-Sixty-Six Blues" does.

But there is a trap here. Yes, Fahey and Patton are joined in a sense by the one reality of the structure of the unconscious, a form of human community, if we subscribe to that theory and that vision of social change. If anyone wants to believe that, let them at least also believe that Patton, as a Black man in the Delta, experienced things Fahey never would, lived in spaces Fahey never would, and to be successful, experienced struggles Fahey never had to wage. There is no Charley Patton without that difference, and, like it or not, Fahey depended on it as the background against which Patton stands out. David Evans memorably states his difference with Fahey when he insists that Patton excelled in a Black musical form that allowed him to escape the life that most ordinary Black men of the Delta had to live. Patton rejected and fought against, as much as he could, the Delta's racialized economy: his music and incessant touring around the Delta *was* that rejection and *was* that fight (Evans, "Charley Patton," *Screamin'*). For Fahey, was this too obvious to make much of? Did he assume this gave him a pass on developing substantive ideas about it? His choice of focus was on the existential howl and deep psychology of Patton's blues and on Patton as lone individual, a choice representing to Fahey the shortest route of connection. Race for Fahey, we can surmise, is too easy to focus on, or too much of a detour, if the point is to search out what all mankind has in common.

CHAPTER THREE

The Politics of the Songster

It seems simple enough, going to the Mississippi River Delta, land of the "Delta Blues." Just don't make the mistake of actually going to the delta of the Mississippi River. Because the "Delta" is not where you think it is, if you believe it is where the Mississippi unloads into the Gulf of Mexico. No, you have to look instead a couple of hundred miles north of there, around Vicksburg. Mark that spot, and then another up around Memphis. Cut northwest into Arkansas, but only to the western banks of the Mississippi River, barely over the state line. Stop about there and trace the meandering banks back down to Vicksburg. Now you have outlined the elongated and misshapen triangle of the Mississippi River Delta. But the name is a misnomer anyway, since the major rivers of the Delta are the Yazoo and the Tallahatchie, not the Mississippi. It is therefore sometimes also called the Yazoo Delta; and geologically speaking, it is the Yazoo River Basin. Anyway, therein a world.

So that is how John Fahey begins his book on Charley Patton, by setting readers straight on these geographic puzzlers. The Delta is important because of the extraordinary number of "blues singers" and "guitar-playing songsters" who lived, worked, and entertained in and around there (7). Puzzlers are important too, because swirling about these singers and songsters—and no less, scholars' and fans' interest in them—are cultural traditions, social histories and networks, and questions of political economy to reconstruct. "Charley Patton has been dead more than 30 years," Fahey marvels, "yet his name is readily recalled by many Mississippi blacks and some whites. His musical influence . . . lives on to this day in the recordings and performances of such recently popular blues-singers as Howlin' Wolf (whom Patton taught to play the guitar), Lightnin' Hopkins . . . John Lee Hooker . . . and others" (8).

Tucked into this lineage, and no less the lineage it stems from, is a whole other world that during his time in the UCLA master's program in folklore and mythology, Fahey was learning to ask about: What is folk music and does it remain "folk" if it appears on a commercial recording? Are folk songs primarily a "literature" whose meanings are encased in their lyrics, or is their performative context part of what they mean, too, in which case meanings are summoned and shared in the act? What is a blues ballad, and what are spirituals? What is ragtime? Do the blues contain a political message or are they merely entertainment? What is Black music and what is white? Is there white music that is Black and Black music that is white? What are European song traditions and what are African? Fahey has *personal* questions too: *What should my own relationship be to "folk" music, to music of the Delta, to Charley Patton? How should I relate to all that while not letting the mythology that has been surfacing around "the blues" creep in?*

It is also the case that there are a number of different ways one can approach questions like these. With or without sincerity? In what sort of mood—enthusiastic, argumentative, calm, angry, righteous, doubtful? From what sort of stance—superiority, neutral observer, interested participant, parody, ironic distance? Answered through what set of values—scholarly, activist, preservationist, revivalist, comedic? A UCLA master's thesis demands sincerity, neutrality, thoroughness, confidence, equanimity. It wants to set the reader straight on the many controversies that have arisen around a near-mythological figure such as Charley Patton, let alone the genres of song he drew on.

John Fahey was by any measure extremely accomplished before enrolling at UCLA in 1964. Already a field worker, composer, and recording artist, he was well primed for the sorts of transformations that had been taking place in folklore and musicological scholarship. Fahey had been collecting and learning from old, pre-Depression-era records for several years in Takoma Park and throughout the South, and with a few friends had located Delta musicians Bukka White and Skip James and participated in reviving their music careers. Come graduation from UCLA, Fahey had produced the only monograph on Charley Patton to date. Far from just being a statement of known fact and informed judgment, the work represents a certain *kind* of thinking. Its structure, content, and "moods" are the subjects of this chapter, therefore. But at no time during his program at UCLA was Fahey also not writing pages and pages of album liner notes for his own records and his own purposes, notes addressed to a wider audience than his professors. At the start of his master's program, Fahey had already recorded and released two LPs. When he submitted his thesis on Charley Patton in 1966, three more records had come out. By the time the thesis reappeared as a book in 1970, there were five more. Throughout his master's program Fahey was playing folk festivals and clubs, central meeting points for Movement aficionados. His liner notes—wry, parodic, poetic, but also juvenile, supercilious, bullying—call into question everything from his own (and others') sincerity to his own (and others') values.

Very shortly after graduating, moreover, Fahey had also tipped his album notes toward extremes of parody, parody of geography and lineage reminiscent of the Patton monograph:

> Thus it was that all suddenly realized how Magruder Park brought forth to mind, or would bring, or will bring to time, or if found would bring to mind, or will bring to time, having brought forth the unfound, or mind to bring, or finely sing or ring to mind or brought ought . . . but Henry Vestine and Al Wilson were there, which two brought large quantities of One, and John McIntyre brought Steve Kling and wife and baby and the true spirit of Memphis, and Southern Hospitality, and Ralph Doplemeyer and Phil Spiro brought Beautiful Linda Getchell . . . and Mike Hall and Sally O'Connor brought a Whaleing Hand, a Dekadent Wildgoose, three non-existant [sic] blues-ballads, five non-existant [sic] "items" of folklore. (Fahey, liner notes, The Voice)

And on and on this particular set of notes, for The Voice of the Turtle, will go until some dozens of names will have found their place in a lineage that traces back to the Fahey birthplace of Takoma Park, Maryland. As I will argue in the next chapter, notes like these are not nearly as distinct from Fahey's scholarly work as they might seem, all parody aside. (Note that the parody here is not just in reference to writing about the Delta blues. It references the "begats" of the Old Testament, the many gifts brought in "The Twelve Days of Christmas," persons well known in the rock and folk music worlds [like Al Wilson, Henry Vestine, and Phil Spiro], and the spoofed names of Fahey's UCLA professors D. K. Wilgus and Wayland Hand, and much, much else.) Parody aside, then, there is a similarity, and maybe a codependence, of outlook and purpose in Fahey's scholarship and his highly stylized notes that I want to attend to in this chapter and the next.

Folklore and Folksong Study in the 1960s

When Fahey began his graduate studies at UCLA, there was no one way of approaching the study of folklore. There were established and up-and-coming academic stars but no agreed paradigm. A 1961 panel on folksong at the annual meeting of the American Folklore Society is indicative. The panel was a "who's who and who's going to be who" in the world of folksong scholarship. (The papers were collected afterward and published as a book in 1964.) Panelists were invited on the basis of the different views and approaches they represented (Limón; also Ben-Amos; Bronner). The "literary and aesthetic approach" places emphasis on those folksong versions that are the finest examples of their art. The "comparativist" looks at the texts of individual songs and their variation over time and space, hoping to find lines of development and relationships among the variations. The "anthropological" scholar of folksong wants to understand the song's function within the broader cultural system that it mirrors. But one panelist stood out: D. K. Wilgus, a rising star who welcomed Fahey to UCLA a few years later, after being impressed with some of Fahey's comments at the Berkeley Folk Festival in the summer of 1964 (Guerrieri, *John Fahey*, vol. 1). Wilgus's paper "did not fit easily into any particular school but came to be called the 'rationalistic approach'" (Limón 76). Wilgus preferred to call his approach rational, as in sensible: "The approach to folksong must be rational, not rationalistic or absolutist in any form. I have yet to find an approach to folksong from which I have not learned something; I have yet to find one whose dominance is not dangerous" (qtd. in Limón 77).

While recognizing Wilgus's commonsense approach, it is also the case that he defended his preference for *textual* study of folksong. When he became president of the American Folklore Society in 1971, he titled his presidential address "The Text Is the Thing." He was reacting to the ascendance of performance studies in the mid and late 1960s, "asking that we concentrate on the artifacts within their performance and traditional contexts rather than losing sight of them" (Engle et al. 366). It is helpful to know that Wilgus's favored approach to the study of ballads was to home in on their narrative elements—that is, the themes and events found within ballad lyrics—so that new relationships and lines of influence across different ballad traditions might be discoverable. This led him, for example, to discern what he called the "blues ballad." The blues ballad is a ballad "sung in blues style—without stable text and often without a stable narrative (both improvised each time)—but nevertheless balladesque since the events in the ballad 'celebrating' them are stable and known to both singer and audience" (Engle et al. 366). Amid the seeming arcana of folkloristic study, this was an effort to establish a relationship between ostensibly separate kinds of songs (blues songs and ballads), a goal consonant with Wilgus's overall sympathy with the idea that cultural practices travel from one domain to another. Undeniably, songs were sung in particular ways, by particular performers, and in specific contexts, but if textual content was overlooked, so too would be the insights Wilgus also thought essential.

If we follow the drift of that panel convened at the American Folklore Society meeting, and Wilgus's backward glance in his 1971 presidential address, it is obvious that folklore studies was rife with different ideas of how to study its object, and of course exactly what this object was and how to compare it across widely different geographical and historical domains (Bendix). Who counted as the "folk"? How would one answer this question on European soil, home to centuries of peasant tradition, versus in the United States, with a long history of immigration, slavery, colonialism, and American Indian displacement? What did the folk produce that was of interest— written literary traditions? oral traditions? Was it "things" instead? Or performances? Did folk traditions actually arise in the folk, or did the folk participate in some way in the same culture as the "royalty" above? Was folklore study increasingly only the study of survivals? Or is folklore still being made? The questions themselves indicate just how unsettled this field was, but they also communicate a lot about its liveliness and the intellectual heritages it drew on. Different answers to these questions often reflected that folklorists tended to be spread across departments of literature and anthropology (Bronner), and not necessarily housed in independent, interdisciplinary programs of folklore. Different answers may reflect generational differences, too (Ben-Amos).[1]

It is no surprise that, beyond what Fahey gleaned from his friends, from record collecting, and from conversations with African American musicians he came to know (e.g., Elizabeth Cotten, Bukka White, Skip James, Son House, Ishmon Bracey), his scholarly understanding of African American music, and American folksong history in general, was shaped most by D. K. Wilgus. Brought to UCLA in 1963 to start a folklore and mythology studies program, Wilgus had established his reputation in 1959 with the publication of *Anglo-American Folksong Scholarship*. Already the ballad specialist focusing on "narrative elements," he nonetheless extends a hand to other scholars and their approaches: "The limitations of this history," Wilgus writes in his book, "are perhaps balanced by the inclusion of the entire range of folksong scholarship." The book focuses on ballads, but "ballad scholarship no longer reigns alone; it has absorbed or has been absorbed by folksong study" (xiii). If it was possible just a couple of decades before to treat the ballad almost exclusively as literature, "an historian of twentieth-century scholarship can no longer do so. He must consider the song and the singer, the performance and the function" (xiii). This "functional" approach is exactly the one with which Fahey came to have a conflictual relationship in his study of Charley Patton and his role within African American communities in the South, for it touches on the question of, as Wilgus put it, "folksong as an expression of the singer and of the community" (xix). As will be clear later, Fahey pushed against a social protest interpretation of Patton's blues, opting for Patton as highly individualistic in his expressions, and as limited in his ability to express much else.

Yet there is every indication that Fahey subscribed to the broad lines of Wilgus's argument, which underscored the process of hybridization in the development of folksong traditions. In Wilgus's appendix on "the argument over the Afro-American origin of American Negro song," he wants to "dispel the sentimentality, prejudice, and confusion between origin and essence that have obscured opportunities for an important study" (*Anglo-American Folksong* xix). His carefully (under)stated conclusion to the appendix strongly hints at why the dispelling was needed:

> To America from Africa the Negro brought a song tradition differing from and yet in some respects resembling the European folk tradition (with which, in fact, it had some historic connections). From the songs of the whites, the Negro borrowed what was congenial to him, and the whites were debtors as well as creditors. The resulting hybrid is a folk music which sounds African in the Negro tradition and European in the white tradition.
>
> The Negro has preserved, borrowed, and re-created, as has the white. The two races share a tradition which they tend to treat distinctively. In the absence of trustworthy reports from the eighteenth and nineteenth centuries, we can only hope that an increasing knowledge of African music and study of recent field reports from American areas will enable us not merely to sort out elements, but to understand the hybridization of not only the spiritual but all American folk and popular music. (Wilgus, *Anglo-American Folksong* 363–64).

This push against efforts to naively "segregate sound," as Karl Miller memorably puts it (cf. Brackett), marks Wilgus as keen to adapt folklore study to the moment in which it then found itself—namely, that decades of song collecting and recording of songs in the field *and* in studios of record companies had definitively tipped the scales toward musical "hybridization" as the irrefutable truth. (If Wilgus was confident in his conclusion about hybridization, he is less clear, as was Fahey, about whether a shared tradition might mean different things to the people who share it.)

Wilgus was acutely aware of the benefits to (and prejudices toward) academic folksong study bestowed by song-collecting efforts of devoted enthusiasts and also of record producers and record labels. Figures like Alan Lomax, Moses Asch, and Kenneth Goldstein loomed large for Wilgus. Goldstein, moreover, was a pioneer (like Wilgus) in the development of the liner notes and brochures inserted into album sleeves. "He has become a major force in the development of scholarly responsibility in the production of folksong albums," Wilgus wrote in his book. "A Goldstein production almost invariably provides, whether in 'liner' notes or the more extensive booklets provided by Folkways, not only bibliographical references and brief discussion of the songs themselves, but often necessary information concerning the source of the text and tune" (236). "For the scholar and teacher recorded music is a tool" (365; cf. Wade). Wilgus, record reviewer for the *Journal of American Folklore* between 1959 and 1973, eventually amassed his own trove of eleven thousand commercial recordings (Engle et al. 364). Scholars ought to be interested in recordings that are "not always purely traditional," things like "hillbilly and race recording, for example. Indeed, if writers who insist that the current folksong renaissance is spawning a new oral tradition are in any sense correct, the scholar must be extremely interested in current 'citybillies' and concert performers who also represent one of the effects of folksong on the broader cultural pattern" (Wilgus, *Anglo-American Folksong* 365–66).

Not every folksong scholar thought it worthwhile to pay attention to the folk revival under way, or held a positive view of citybillies. Wilgus was interested in musical practices that were current, and later participated in West Coast folk festivals. He kept open the idea that processes of ballad creation and adaptation were ongoing. He was a performer himself and occasionally recorded songs, such as one contribution he made to the compilation album on the theme of "The Unfortunate Rake," produced and notated by Kenneth Goldstein.

In light of Wilgus's expansive sense of "scholarly responsibilities," Fahey was in good company when he went to UCLA to study. Indeed, Fahey thought Wilgus was in good company too. Here's Fahey crowing in his thesis on Patton: "If the only source material for black music that we had was the printed collections . . . we should have but a small fraction of the source material that is available to us. If, in addition, we had the testimony of people who remember Patton and singers like him, but ignored the possibilities inherent in analysing commercial recordings, we should be overlooking an extremely fruitful job of sampling, done inadvertently by commercial recording companies" (8). Without the efforts of record collectors like Fahey *himself*, knowledge of African American music history on the part of the professoriate would be paltry, restricted only to the canonical songbooks, the printed collections referenced above.

There is one more idea Fahey learned in his master's program that is essential for his work on Charley Patton. This is the notion of "associative" thinking as central to the making of folklore. The relevant figure here is Archer Taylor, a prominent folklorist well known to Wilgus, and the PhD adviser to another of Fahey's professors at UCLA, Wayland Hand. Folklore, in the eyes of Archer Taylor, had a big problem in 1952, the year of one of his signature pieces. Taylor, president of the Modern Language Association, lamented that folklore had failed to carve out a place for itself in the humanities that was proportional to its cultural importance. Folklore was still too attached to the "antiquarian and dilettante tradition of collecting curiosities. Proverbs, tales, ballads, customs, or superstitions are thought to be quaint and are recorded and studied for that reason" (Taylor 59). Folklore too much "finds itself in the situation that the natural and physical sciences occupied in the Renaissance and earlier, when men described strange animals, plants, and minerals" (Taylor 59). Folklore needs a "principle"—a concept of *what kind of thinking it is*—not an endless accumulation of examples of a something nobody can put their finger on. It needs a new definition to stand on firm academic footing. None of the current alternatives will do. "Folklore is the lore of the folk, but this temptingly simple definition at once involves us in difficulties," Taylor writes. We see better now that much of the supposed "lore of the folk" descended from higher rungs up the social ladder. "The curiosities of folk medicine were once good medical practice. Folk costume keeps the fashion that once belonged to high society." Tales and songs circulating as "folk" were once the materials performed at court. If we define folklore as precisely that which has descended from on high, this just states a new problem: "This effort is akin to the definition of folklore as the study of survivals in culture, and especially of a prehistoric culture known to us only by comparison with the cultures of so-called aboriginal or primitive peoples." If we emphasize the notion of lore over that of folk, then we run into another problem, that this lore of the folk, supposedly more a matter of oral tradition than the written word, "concerns primarily the accidental circumstances of the way in which these materials have been collected" (60).

What then? The answer to the question of what principle defines folklore is what Taylor calls "associative" thinking. "Folklore deals with materials which associative rather than logical thinking has shaped and handed on" (60).

Take a folk ballad or tale, riddle, superstition, or proverb. What has led to its preservation and its variations over time and from place to place are processes largely unconscious, unplanned, and unintended. It's not that there is never any intent or conscious purpose, of course. It is a matter of degree. To the degree the process is demonstrably, largely planned and intended, largely artful, we are not speaking of folklore but of, for example, literature. Poets look for the exactly appropriate word; the ballad uses clichés and conventional incidents. A novelist "individualizes his characters" and aims for accurate description; the folktale trades in "conventional characters — the brave youth, the beautiful maiden, and the wicked witch" (66). Taylor likens folklore to language and the changes it goes through, when new words, spellings, or pronunciations emerge. These are "almost entirely the result of associative or unconscious activity" (63). Folklore study had a political point to make too, Taylor argued, especially given the abuses of the folk conception by Nazism:

> In the last few years we have seen a very unfortunate and, I think, ominous change in the position of folklore. Men have collected folk materials with a view to perpetuating or awakening hatred and division. Like anything else, folklore can serve bad ends and its deep roots in human nature make its misuse an especially dangerous attack on the dignity of man. Such endeavors have fostered a vicious nationalism or something worse. These perversions have reached beyond the misuse of folk materials to the invention and dissemination of what is intended to be accepted as folklore. . . . These recent deliberate efforts to modify men's thoughts by means of folklore deserve special condemnation. (65)

If we were to want to know, therefore, what it means to study folklore in 1952 and to define it in a certain way, we might find no better passage than this, not because it tells us that folklore is good to study in and of itself as the voice of nonmanipulated peoples, or that it must find a place within the humanities. It tells us folklore is socially positioned at all and is subject to appropriation and misuse (cf. Dorson). We will want to remember this after the long excursus on Fahey, folksong, and folklore below.

Making Way for Charley Patton

Before John Fahey, no one had written a book about Charley Patton. A reproduction of Fahey's master's thesis, *Charley Patton* is stamped by his UCLA education and his goal of fending off what he thought were the misunderstandings of blues singers held by Movement adherents and folk revivalists.[2] His strategy is one of calm, scholarly restraint. "Patton is remembered as a 'songster,'" Fahey observes, specifically because of his large repertoire of many kinds of songs, "blues-ballads, ragtime pieces, and songs derived from either white popular or rural white traditions" (7). In a passage straight from Wilgus's blackboard, Fahey explains:

> Blues-ballads are loose, shifting, and subjective narrative songs which celebrate and comment upon events rather than describe them in a straightforward, journalistic manner. . . . They are usually collected from blacks rather than from whites, and many of them evolve through a long process of "communal recreation" (using the term loosely) among black people. When collected from whites, black influence can usually be demonstrated. . . . In this study, "ragtime" will refer to songs which are textually composed of nonsense stanzas or stanzas referring humorously to sexual matters. Musically, they are characterized by a quick tempo, frequent chord changes in the guitar accompaniment, and melodies which are either chromatically constructed, or are gapped versions of the Ionian mode. (7–8)

I will say more later about the significance of the definition of ragtime Fahey uses. What follows in Fahey's book is a spirited discussion of just what sort of folk document commercially recorded Black music is and what its role must be in folksong study. Yes, the recording studio is an artificial situation that demands songs be kept to a prescribed length and that musicians unfailingly keep time together. (For folk music diehards [i.e., not Fahey], these were two strikes against the idea that recorded music could be folk music.) Moreover, only songs considered to have commercial potential were recorded, never the whole of African American music as actually practiced in everyday life. Various sorts of other directions and prohibitions may have been given before and during the session. The final product is a compromised social document, not folk expression.

But this is not something Fahey cares terribly much about, preserving some essential folk quality. Let's put worn out caveats aside, he would urge, and finally notice what students of African American song, from way back in the 1920s, had failed to see but that Fahey himself now knew. If the scholars and collectors of Black song in the 1920s

> had gone to their local race record stores in 1929 and had listened to some of the recently issued race records, they would have discovered a

new phenomenon: recordings of individual singers accompanying themselves with only guitars or banjo-guitars. They would have heard many traditional (as well as many non-traditional) blues-verses that are not contained in their printed collections. Nor in any others. They would have discovered recordings of traditional spirituals, blues-ballads, and folksongs of which they were totally unaware. And they would have been able to collect further traditional stanzas of songs which they knew already existed. Many of these songs and verses had never been issued on any previous record and thus could not have been learned by the recording artists from previous factory products. (10)

Boom! Never mind that blues ballads are a Wilgus coinage of post-1929 vintage, Fahey's point speaks for itself. For all its artifice, the recording studio had captured songs, with little-known precedent, performed in an unheard style. Moreover, as solo performances, the songs were allowed greater stylistic latitude: performers could break time, improvise on the spot, and compose lyrics on demand. Anyway, careful research "can in many cases determine where . . . controlling factors were exercised" (12). On top of all this, certain record companies made a habit of recording "virtually anyone who could make any kind of musical sound." Paramount, Vocalion, Victor: these companies "allowed their artists a great deal of freedom in the hope that the artists themselves would know what would sell" (12).

Karl Hagstrom Miller's careful reconstruction of the way record companies preselected and racialized the musical feel they were looking for would have some trouble with Fahey's generous assessment of artistic freedom, but the point is that Fahey and Wilgus are of the same mind concerning the singular value of record collecting (K. Miller). The records were a treasure trove of historical material, signaling that the search for blues and other African American music had only begun. With very rare exception (e.g., Alan Lomax), no one thought it necessary to look for anything recorded after the mid-twenties. So it was, until the late 1950s, when for aesthetic reasons record collectors like Fahey, and a few academics like Wilgus, hit the road, benefiting enormously from the fact that no one previously thought that "race records" counted as a source of "folk" music. Add to this the fact that records present the obvious opportunity to have not only song texts but the sound of the song itself. It is, therefore, "a sad commentary on American scholars of folk music that between 1927 and 1962 the commercial recording industry did an infinitely better job of collecting, preserving, and making available to the public native American folksong—especially black folksongs" (15). Just how Fahey came to have the aesthetic interest he refers to, I will discuss in chapter 6, although recall some of this background from the introduction. The remarkable coincidence is that he would enter the field of folklore study at such a propitious time and study with an ecumenically minded scholar similarly attuned to the value of the "factory product" and the fieldwork necessary to find it. It is also fortunate that Fahey chose Charley Patton as his touchstone. Unlike a number of Patton's contemporaries who played only the blues, Patton had a repertoire that was extremely wide, greatly helping Fahey to see that a firm color line between Black and white music was impossible to draw.

From Sense to Nonsense and Back Again

With the status of Patton's recorded music now secure, and Fahey's own status as an authority asserted too, much of the rest of his book is devoted to three different classification systems for Patton's music and what they tell us about the kind of music it is and the social purposes it served, if any. One classification sorts the songs according to structure: the scales, modes, keys, and metrical configuration the songs fit into. Another assigns his songs to different "tune families," where songs are grouped according to shared melodies. The third is a textual analysis of the lyrics, by which Fahey discerns whether a song is categorized as blues, blues ballad, ragtime, or miscellaneous. Each song, in other words, is classified three times. To a nonspecialist it is an obsessive, belabored piece of work. The categories are a mix of what was acceptable in musicology and folksong/folklore study at UCLA and Fahey's adaption of these standards for his purposes. They were not the classifications used by Patton or the record companies, however, as Fahey's goals were different. A substantial part of the thesis is devoted to Fahey's explanation of the system he used to musically transcribe Patton's recorded songs. Because of the traditions Patton drew from — Anglo-European, African, and quite likely Arabic — the received categories of Western music analysis, scale, key, mode, pitch, and so on had to be used flexibly and adapted to Fahey's purposes. It was not a question of forcing Patton's songs through some unyielding sieve but rather one of getting at the empirics of the songs by adapting categories as necessary. The project was all the more difficult because Fahey often had to contend with records that were worn out, and sometimes had to struggle with songs recorded at varying speed due to poor recording technology. Nor was Fahey an expert at musical transcription; he credits his friend Al Wilson (vocalist and guitarist for the blues-inspired rock band Canned Heat) with providing guidance and corrections.

In his analysis of musical structure, Fahey makes a crucial distinction between mode and scale, two often conflated concepts. In this he followed the method devised at UCLA: "Mode exists as a theoretical concept in the mind of the musician or composer before he creates music using that mode" (32). Mode sets the possibilities for what notes and pitches will likely be heard; scale is the choice actually made. (Following this method, Fahey claims to have discovered that Patton employed a musical structure no one would have been able to guess had they followed the analysis of African American folksong that then prevailed, Henry Edward Krehbiel's *Afro-American Folksong*, dating back to 1914.) Using this framework, Fahey proposes that Patton's music was "determined by" (43) two traditions: the tradition of field hollers and religious songs (largely African American) and "a tradition (or traditions), probably white, of singing with instrumental accompaniment utilizing frequent chord changes among at least the major I, IV and V chords" (44). Patton's songs rarely represent only one of these traditions. While the first predominates, his recordings represent "a continuum" (44). Fahey goes on to speculate that the songs from the field holler tradition are "older in black tradition" (47) than songs at the other (white) end of the continuum, because of their infrequent appearance on records after 1931. But at the end of the discussion he returns to "continuum" as the primary message of Patton's musical structure.

The book's discussion of tune families is much shorter—a tune family consists of a group of melodies whose pitch sequences and pitch stresses are similar—but it seems to point in a similar direction as the analysis of song structure. Fahey is looking for some sort of evidence of songs that have originated in either a Black or a white tradition. In my read, and I hasten to add I am not necessarily interested in whether Fahey is technically correct, Fahey is thinking through in both cases what Wilgus above called the difference between origin and essence. The origin of Patton's songs is frequently African American; the essence of the body of work is that in its reshaping and development it runs along a continuum of cultural influences and traditions. The implied conclusion, also reached by Fahey's analysis of song structure, is that Patton's music is not a political music protesting against social conditions. Its roots are deeper than present-day concerns: whereas these concerns emphasize the rift between Blacks and whites, Patton's music describes a continuum of racial traditions.

In Fahey's textual analysis of Patton's songs' gone are the speculation and informed guesswork we have seen so far. Fahey now descends on the page with both feet, bold in his assertions, more certain than ever of his findings. As if to take Archer Taylor's "associative thinking" thesis one step further, Fahey finds that Patton's lyrics are "random." If one goes looking for the lyrics to be a coherent representation of thought, Fahey advises that one will discover the "incoherent" instead. If one searches for a sensible narrative whose elements and arc comport with each other, like part and whole, one will search in vain. (Refusing to see Patton make sense as a socially aware, politically savvy performer, Fahey will get called out on this when fellow music scholar David Evans writes his album notes for publication in the 2001 Grammy-winning Charley Patton box set, *Screamin' and Hollerin' the Blues*. Recall that Fahey, too, contributed album notes to the box set. But they are odd in admitting he may have overstated his original case while also reemphasizing his view that Patton's "associative" lyrics and flamboyant guitar playing *primarily* sought to make an emotional impact.) Fahey here bucks the white middle-class trend to revere the grassroots wisdom of old Black blues singers. In such a romance, as Fahey critiques it, every ounce of hardship endured by the Black bluesman must produce an ounce of wisdom to revere. But Fahey defines a different economy through which to understand Patton. If Patton is simply reduced to his social circumstances, there is nothing original about him. To only read him off our own interpretation of what those circumstances are robs Patton of anything unique he might have to say. Yet to define what Patton says as irrational and nonsensical, as Fahey does, is to willfully underread him, to deprive him of a potential political voice at precisely the moment, of civil rights and folk revival, when consensus is building among Fahey's peers that Black voices matter politically.

Specifically, then, how does Fahey read Patton's songs? Patton recorded five kinds of songs that Fahey recognizes, based on their lyrics (note now a Wilgus-like attention to text): blues, blues ballads, ragtime, traditional spirituals or church songs, and miscellaneous songs that don't fit any of the categories. (Fahey also lists a number of songs, such as "Charley Bradley's Ten Sixty-Six Blues," he has not heard or located, admitting the possibility that other categories might exist.) Fahey reserves all his substantive comments for the blues and blues ballads, saying virtually nothing about any of the songs in the other categories. The ragtime songs deserve little comment since they are, by Fahey's definition, "characterized textually by nonsense verses (which can accordingly not be construed as either coherent or incoherent) referring to sexual matters" (68).

Most of Patton's blues songs use the AAB stanza form, common to blues music. Patton also makes liberal use of what Fahey calls "commonplaces," formulaic verses used by many Black singers and also recorded in printed collections of African American songs—for example, "I'm worried now but I won't be worried long" or "Vicksburg's on a high hill, Louisiana's just below" or "I think I heard [a certain train or boat whistle] blow" (58). In none of Patton's songs do these refrains play an important role in the rest of the song's lyrics, Fahey argues. Sometimes, they exist only to sound out a sound where a more sensible word is missing. "Patton uses the words, 'Lord,' 'Lordy,' and 'babe,' 'baby' in most cases for metrical reasons to fill in a portion of the melody" (59). In the song "Mississippi Bo Weavil Blues," "Lord" or "Lordy" is sung twenty-eight times, and not once does it play a "rational part of the text." "Baby" is sung fourteen times in "It Won't Be Long." Again, the word is inessential. "In fact, the use of it in this song creates confusion by giving the impression that the singer is speaking to someone. But the stanzas indicate that he is not" (59). Words serve the performance, not a particular, coherent message; they arouse emotions but rarely in a rational way: "It is as though Patton, at each recording session, had a series of random stanzas concerning different subjects running through his mind—a stream of consciousness composed of numerous disjunctive blues-verses—and that what the recordings did was register certain segments of this thought process" (62). A song's first stanza might introduce a particular idea or observation that we would expect to be further developed. Not only does this not happen, but the last stanza (e.g., "Rattlesnake Blues") introduces some new thought, having no relation to any of the previous ones, and leaves the listener hanging as to how the event might resolve.

Listeners will fare no better when they look to see if the emotions produced by the tune of a song match the emotions generated by the lyrics. Fahey bears down on the technicalities of the matter: "From a musical point of view, songs such as 'It Won't Be Long,' played for the most part with one chord accompaniment and with the use of a bottle-neck technique, a tune contour consisting of a quick ascent to the minor third and a gradual descent to the fifth, minor third, and tonic below it (a total range of a tenth), *produce a generally depressing psychological effect*" (63). The words of the song convey a different, more wandering set of feelings. The first stanza is "happy," the next four are "sad." The sixth stanza is "neutral," and the last is "happy." Fahey constructs a table with these data and concludes the song is "ambivalent" and "non-sensical" (63).

Stanzas in many other songs are considered by Fahey to be "enigmatic," meaning that "external events" are mentioned but never explained in the song; their significance remains a matter of conjecture. "An attempt to attribute some significance to any stanza or to search for some sort of hidden or implicit coherence among the stanzas implies that there is a pre-supposition in the mind of the analyst. . . . The presupposition that all songs must have coherent stanzas thus represents an attempt to apply an external standard, probably derived from familiarity with popular (composed) songs of Western Europe and America, to a genre to which this standard is perhaps completely inapplicable" (64–65).

The supreme and overriding quality of Patton's blues is that their textual contents are plucked "*at random*" from the "large storehouse of them in his mind" (65). The description probably pushes Archer Taylor's notion of associative thinking in the production of folklore about as far as it can go. Taylor's own analysis of folktales is not struck by incoherence within tales. Rather, his analysis stipulates simply that tales are replicated, altered, or adapted in an unconscious way or, better, in accordance with tradition, which has no particular goal outside itself. Fahey's insistence on reading Patton the way he does also tests Taylor's implicit assumption that folklore should be studied and appreciated in an unbiased way, devoid of any external social intent.

Patton's blues ballads lead Fahey to a similar conclusion. They are narratively incoherent. Blues ballads are defined by the fact that they represent known events. Patton's blues ballads share this characteristic, although he also recorded blues ballads that contain references to events that his audience did not have knowledge of, such as Patton's imprisonment by local police in small Delta towns. When Patton's blues ballads suffer from incoherence, Fahey wonders if Patton is just not capable of putting together an orderly, coherent journalistic account. To make his point, Fahey offers a brief on Patton's version of the classic blues ballad "Frankie and Albert." We should remind ourselves, of course, that the blues ballad is Wilgus's invention and that there is no necessary reason for Patton to follow its formula. Anyway, when we look at what Fahey has to say about the last stanza of Patton's version, we can see that Fahey is quite obstinate in his interpretation. Here is the stanza:

> Well, Frankie's mother come running,
> Come a' whooping, screaming, and crying.
> "Oh, Lord, oh Lord,
> My only son is dying."

In most versions of the song, Fahey notes, the young woman Frankie and the young man Albert are understood to be lovers. Fahey complains that when

Patton sings that *Frankie's mother* laments the death of her *son* (Albert), it must mean that Frankie is Albert's sister and not his lover. But if Frankie has no brothers and her mother has come to think of Albert as family, it might make perfectly good sense that she refers to him as her "only son." In fact, Fahey writes that Patton's own first wife was a "common-law" wife and that he "married" (Fahey uses scare quotes) two other women (20). So, Fahey had some sensitivity toward alternatively defined family relationships. He is also bothered that this stanza comes after the stanza referring to Albert's burial. In the song, therefore, Patton has put Albert in the grave before he is actually dead. Fahey is confused by the verb tense in "Frankie's mother come running." He doesn't imagine that it could be a description of an event that happened from the standpoint of its happening. It simply is not unusual to employ the present tense in a recollection when describing past occurrences.

We begin to get some purchase on where Fahey is likely coming from when we read the biographical chapter of the book. Here, the geographical limits of Patton's life loom very large in Fahey's imagination. Patton, Fahey tells us, spent nearly his whole life in and near the Delta, even when performing. He left only a few times, to cut records. The records therefore reflect his "limited picture of the world" (26)—by dint of his limited travels, the place-names noted on the records (almost all of which are Delta place-names), and no one outside Mississippi or anyone "of more than local prominence" ever being mentioned (27). "Patton was dependent upon, and a product of, the prevailing socioeconomic conditions of the southern cotton production economy, a semi-feudal society" (28). Fahey's informants in the field (fellow musicians, Patton's extended family, and others) tell Fahey that Patton hated manual labor and avoided it at all costs. He preferred to entertain with his music, in a society that had few positions for professional musicians. Patton was good enough to be one and to earn a comparatively decent income. The money stream he depended on flowed through bootleggers and roadhouses, which "in turn were dependent upon the (sometimes) wealthy plantation owners" (28). The lives of Blacks were those of "medieval serfs." Property was white-owned, just as the law was also white. "*On the other hand,*" Fahey writes, "blacks who worked on Delta plantations were always provided with housing . . . and frequently with food. When the depression came and there was no work, the black workers were fed by the plantation owners, protected by the benevolent southern land-owner tradition" (28; emphasis added), a line of argument Fahey extended in the liner notes to his album of the following year, *The Voice of the Turtle*. The irony does not occur to Fahey that it is one and the same society that oppressed Blacks like "serfs" in the first place and fed them during lean times. Fahey continues, and I quote at length here so we can see how "the text is the thing" and the "function" and "performance" of folksong knit together in Fahey's analysis:

> If we search Patton's lyrics for words expressive of profound senti-ments directly caused by this particular cotton-economy, or for words expressing a desire to transcend this way of life . . . or aspirations to "improve the lot of a people," we search in vain. Such a search would not be fruitful with any blues-singers.
>
> Patton was an entertainer, not a social prophet in any sense. . . . He was not a "noble savage." Least of all did he try to express the "aspirations of a folk." . . . Patton had very good relations with white people. . . . They liked not only his folksongs but also his blues. . . . Patton . . . was received into white homes, slept in them, and ate in them. The racial segregation of Patton's day was not as rigorous as it is now, and it was not as insidious. (29)

Patton's experience was too limited and his view too narrow to have any social message, Fahey argues, imputing that Patton simply "accepted [his] oppressed condition" (Cone 118–19). He had no access to an intellectual environment that would promote an awareness of his people and their situ-ation. Curiously, Fahey does not raise the question of the repercussions that could follow, should Patton raise the ire of his (white) audience, whether in person or on his records (cf. Evans, *Big Road Blues*). This stands in contrast to what Fahey actually knew. He noted that Patton's family and many other Black families had to move away from their homes in the town of Drew because a Black man had shot a white man (23). Fahey also acknowledged doing fieldwork in the Delta, collecting records and interviewing African American songsters such as Ishmon Bracey in the same period as the Freedom Rides, when Blacks and out-of-state whites were being abused, harassed, and worse (see Blazek; also Pollard). During the time Fahey was doing research for his thesis, Black workers on Delta plantations were stag-ing walkouts in protest of low pay and bad working conditions, the first such labor actions since those in the 1930s had been violently put down (Janson, "Negro Walkouts," "Striking Negroes"). The question of Fahey's silence is un-avoidable. Even the logic of his passages calls for saying something—why could he not himself entertain the possibility that white people's pleasure in Charley Patton was a reflection of Patton's fear of causing displeasure (or that white pleasure might have been based on that very fear). That plantation hospitality might vindicate the South's "semi-feudal" economy, and that present-day segregation is putatively more insidious than that which came before, hints that Fahey might want a bit of redemption, insofar as he retains a fondness for "Dixie." He still likes something, in other words, that his radicalized peers do not, even while he may have been prepared to agree with the justice of racial equality.

And yet Fahey's writing works hard to attribute agency to Patton and other "blues-singers." In particular, his book seeks to attribute agency in a way that is not prescripted by Movement politics, which Fahey was still trying to sort out.[3] It is clumsy work to be sure, for he trips over a longstanding stumbling block encountered by white America, namely that it historically has struggled to value African American *history* and *humanity* to the same extent as African American *culture*, as Reiland Rabaka argues. It seems to me also, although this comes out in other Fahey texts, that he is preparing the ground for a one-to-one identification with Patton and Patton's emotional intensity, trying to define what might count as a "piece of justice," as Clecak puts it, for them both.[4]

Alternate Endings

There were other analyses from which Fahey might have chosen or with which he might have differed more explicitly (Ryan; cf. Askew). Paul Oliver, the editor of the series that published Fahey's book, had written one of his own six years before Fahey completed his thesis. *The Meaning of the Blues*, which came with a foreword by Richard Wright, ventures everything Fahey does not, even while making the same observation that the vast majority of the blues is devoid of anything construable as *explicit* protest songs. (I am not saying Oliver is even right about this. It's what he does with his materials that is interesting.)

While in its own way *The Meaning of the Blues* is almost unrelievedly patronizing, it still marks out a contrasting critical territory to Fahey's. Oliver approaches the texts of blues songs as social documents representing various aspects of African American life after the Civil War and into the Jim Crow period. Blues songs tell of such experiences as work, migration, loneliness, sex, violence, natural disaster, jealousy, and incarceration. Oliver emphasizes throughout that these experiences are often shaped by racial segregation and discrimination, relationships between Black men and women, but also sometimes by general bad fortune—"victim of the foibles and frailties of human nature irrespective of class or color" (321). Unlike Fahey, Oliver does not seem to expect that a single song will cohere into a single narrative—the evidence he brings from songs is sometimes just two or three stanzas. He breaks songs down in order to make his case that the blues as a whole make up the social document of the (largely male) African American experience. That is one interesting difference from Fahey's treatment, which, to put the point another way, might have considered that one song consists of many "songs."

Another, more important difference can be seen in Oliver's assessment of the lack of protest in the blues:

> When an exhaustive examination is made of recorded blues it becomes apparent that the number of items that are directly concerned with protest themes is exceedingly small. It is scarcely conceivable that the singers, commenting broadly on the multitudinous facets of Negro life, would *deliberately* ignore or reject those that are the result of racial prejudice and intolerance. The segregated waiting-rooms, the Jim Crow Cars, the forbidden beaches, bathing pools, theatres . . . the short measure, the cropper's "share," the stale goods . . . the Race Riot, the hooded Klansmen, the lynch mob, the hit-and-run killer— the countless manifestations of ignorance, brutality, race hatred and violence, of discriminatory practices and segregation by color must have been the raw material for innumerable blues created by a legion of singers. (321; emphasis added)

But all that raw material, all those great many injuries and injustices, was for the most part not directly worked up into recorded song. (Possibly, Fahey was never in the company of, or trusted sufficiently by, any African American blues singer who did use songs to protest more overtly against white racism. The white musicologist and ethnographer William Ferris, in his book about the Delta Blues, reports gaining enough trust to have such songs played for him by musicians with whom he became friendly.) When the "scars" and "wounds" were "most rife and when they would have been uppermost in the minds of the singers that recorded would also have been the times when reference to them on disc would have been most inadvisable" (Oliver 321). Fahey warns against the imposition of an "external standard" that would presuppose the existence of meaning in Patton's songs. From Paul Oliver's perspective, yes, there was in fact an external, constitutive force that determined at least those meanings that were prohibited from direct expression.

Fahey might alternatively have taken a different set of cues from Patton's individuation as a phenomenon that is in itself political. This is African American guitarist and singer Julius Lester's point, made in 1965, when he was active in the East Coast folk scene, before he became a prolific author and a professor at the University of Massachusetts:

> It was not until the twentieth century, possibly as late as World War I, that the group structure of the Negro community began disintegrating. At least, it isn't until the twentieth century that we begin to notice a new kind of music developing—the blues. In this new form, the individual was distinctly separated from the group. His guitar undertook the role of the chorus and he made it answer what he said. In the blues, the group is entertained by the individual and the emphasis shifts from the creations of the group to the creations of the individual.
>
> At the time the blues developed, more and more men were refusing to accept the life imposed upon them by the plantation system. They did not, however, rebel against it by trying to destroy it. Instead, many simply refused to be a part of it. They wandered from town to town, and state to state, working in the coal mines of Virginia, steel mills of Illinois, railroads of Tennessee. . . . They gambled, they stole and they never stayed in one place too long. Within this segment of the community, a few were blues singers, who found they could make their way by playing at the plantation balls and living off women. Robert Johnson and Charlie Patton, two of the greatest bluesman, lived in this way. It kept them out of the cotton fields and that was their main objective. (Lester, liner notes, *Julius Lester*)

Lester's points fit well with a compelling interpretation of Patton's song "Mississippi Bo Weavil Blues," in which the "bo weavil" insect that devastated cotton crops around the South can be read as an African trickster figure. In Patton's lyrics the "bo weavil" travels boastfully to Texas, Louisiana, and Arkansas, warning farmers "ain't going to treat you fair," turning them off their land, and setting up his own family there. "As a trickster figure," Ayana Smith argues, "the boll weevil intentionally cheats the famer of his crops and therefore becomes a role model for the narrator. The narrator identifies with the power of the insect that destroys the financial well-being of the landowner, and in this way expresses subliminally his own frustration and lack of power" (182). Smith's analysis draws heavily on the now classic insights of Henry Louis Gates Jr.'s *The Signifying Monkey*, a book published many years after Fahey's. But Fahey, had he been of a different frame of mind, might have spotted the "bo weavil" as a kind of allegory or metaphor with a great deal of political relevance. Beyond that one song, Patton's or any Black blues singer's mastery of the associative style can be reinterpreted through the double meaning, "signifying" methods of the trickster tradition, Smith shows. Implicitly agreeing while disagreeing with Fahey, Smith writes that "narrative elements can be arranged in such a way as to be inscrutable, enigmatic or even nonsensical. The poet-singer's genius, therefore, lies in weaving together lines and ideas from a much larger oral tome to evoke a particular sentiment in the thread of a new narrative," whose function, among other things, is to "document the newly found freedom of self determination" (183).

A quite different analysis of the blues, Patton's included, belongs to the scholar of Black geographies Clyde Woods, who, contra Lester, documents a long history of Black struggle to dismantle the plantation system, before, during, *and* after the Civil War. Woods argues that the blues comprised a distinctive political consciousness, what he calls the "blues epistemology," widespread in the South and the North. In his view, such an epistemology is captured less by a focus on the individuated bluesman than by blues singers collectively:

> Patton, Son House, and their many contemporaries in the Deltas of the Mississippi, Arkansas, Louisiana, Missouri, and Tennessee were engaged in constructing a regional, and later, national, African American community through a particular constellation of lyrical, musical and performance styles. Through a blues realism they were also carving out a role for Delta blues performers as a collective which seriously contemplated the problems and inequities of the world around them. Their focus on humor, love, good times, religion, and nature allowed them to present a complete worldview to an audience whose boundaries were continually being widened through the wandering of the musicians, through mass migration, and through recordings. (111)

What I am saying here is that even if factual matters are debatable, and even if certain facts eluded Fahey, there were outlooks, framings, within his grasp, that certainly do no harm to Charley Patton, that Fahey seemed to have rejected. It seems to me that Fahey was hell-bent on reading Patton as being as inscrutable as he, Fahey, thought himself to be—both are unclaimable by anyone and, in the matter of their deepest humanity, fiercely emotional. Charley Patton must be kept as far away as possible from middle-class white feelings about Black blues singers, therefore, as Fahey thinks he himself is.

The reader of Fahey's Charley Patton book gets a final fleeting glimpse of such tensions in the last pages. In a direct address to his relevant audience (that is, the audience he is interested in persuading to see his view), Fahey remarks that the older generation of record collectors and the younger adherents of the "folk music revival" think of Patton as the best of all blues musicians. Fahey avers that if the criterion is an aesthetic one, well it's a matter of opinion, and perhaps correct if "applied to Patton's performance of bluessongs" (69). But the *real* Patton occupies a different stage altogether, for he is not a blues singer but rather a songster who, by definition, commanded a vast repertoire of styles beyond blues, and beyond the segregated category of "race" music (cf. K. Miller). And that, Fahey thinks, is what blues fans get wrong about Patton. The songs are the thing, to paraphrase D. K. Wilgus; Fahey is finished with underestimations of Patton's talents as a performer. It is hard to avoid concluding that Fahey wants to move Patton away from the romanticizing white gaze toward a different margin, where Fahey's own words seem to want to find their place too. "Songster"—a new term in folksong study—is a political category for Fahey, in other words, a way to keep the meaning of the past more open, from the standpoint of a present whose meaning Fahey thinks could also be made more open (i.e., shed of the white, middle-class romance with Black music). But this is an impossible project the way Fahey is prosecuting it, demanding a discounting of the racial romance for everyone else, even as he reworks it for himself.

CHAPTER FOUR

The Great Liner Note Breakdown

Look at the old 78 rpm records from the 1920s and 1930s that John Fahey collected and you will see right away a difference from the LP records of the 1950s, 1960s, and beyond that reissued some of those same recordings. The LP's came with explanatory and sometimes highly evocative notes on the songs and artists. The original 78s, with some exceptions, did not. By the 1950s and 1960s, listeners of songs that were of interest to Fahey were largely ignorant of the musical traditions, and social and geographic contexts, from which the songs of the folk and blues revival emerged. They were also largely white. Record producers wanted to educate this market, in fact the market for virtually all music genres, and one means for this was to place explanatory notes on the album covers (usually the back), or print them separately and slip them inside the record sleeve, or sometimes place them inside a gatefold cover. All this was under way when Fahey released his records on his Takoma label, and was standard practice for the labels (Vanguard, Riverboat, Warner Brothers) that issued his work later. The album notes and booklets John Fahey wrote for his records are, compared with his work on Charley Patton, a hybrid of erudition and utter inscrutability. Fahey began this aspect of his writing career in 1963 with the release of his second album, *Death Chants, Breakdowns and Military Waltzes*. He wrote and included notes for the first LP he ever released, *Blind Joe Death*, only when the second edition came out in late 1964 or early 1965. *Dance of Death*, from 1965, held a Fahey booklet, as did *The Great San Bernardino Birthday Party* of 1966 (Guerrieri, *John Fahey, vol. 1*). Many more albums, liner notes, and booklets would follow. Fahey's liner note writing was begun before his days at UCLA, continued during the writing of his thesis, and kept on going. What does it mean that these two sorts of writing projects were happening simultaneously, one being the effort of a student to show his mastery of the scholarly craft, and the other the effort of a recording artist, equally eager to show his mastery of the inscrutable?

A Brief History of the Liner Note

The album note as a genre afforded a certain flexibility to its writers. It was in fact a rather lively, changing phenomenon when Fahey joined in and when his immediate progenitors were writing their notes too. Liner notes as such appeared sporadically in the 1930s—Fahey was born in 1939—when record companies got the idea that they could collect several 78s featuring some artist, band, or genre of music into an "album" to sell, each record sandwiched in its own folder or sleeve (see Piazza). The inside or outside cover of the album would contain the explanatory "liner notes." This was not how most 78s were sold, however, and it was only by the late 1950s that 78s were even being phased out and LPs playing at 33 rpm phased in. (A single LP could easily fit all the songs that used to compose an album of multiple 78s.) So, the printing of liner notes on LPs was a relatively new practice for a music recording medium that was itself quite new. However we look at it, then, we are looking at a kind of writing young enough for experimentation to become the norm, and young enough to respond to, as well as create, specific audiences for different kinds of music. The timing was perfect for John Fahey. And let's not miss the mounting coincidences. He came of essay writing age at the moment when a new form of self-expression was stressed at school and now with the fluorescence of the liner note genre, he could whet his appetite for expression there too. Happy for him as well, we'll see, that he could align the associative theory of folklore with the same creative impulse.

I noted earlier that D. K. Wilgus was an early proponent and practitioner of liner notes. Wilgus himself credits the scholar and record producer Kenneth Goldstein for honing the art. Goldstein in turn credits classical music records for inspiring him, because of the notes they often contained on composers and musicians. Like classical music, folk music deserved thoughtful reflection:

> I didn't care whether it was Black or white. Folk music is beautiful music. . . . Not enough people know what folk music is. . . . Why not give them some information? . . . I could talk about the text. I could talk about the relationships of songs to each other, and I thought also that the singer was important . . . his background, his culture.
>
> My idea was that if you put the information on the backliner then you will develop a more intelligent sounding disc jockey who is going to play that stuff. . . . What we developed was a far more intelligent audience about folk music. They weren't simply reacting to music, they were listening to music and absorbing it in an intellectual as well as in a spiritual and physical sense. (Goldstein and Narváez 456–57)

Informative, intelligent, revealing of what is, so to speak, behind the scene of the songs—these are the liner note traits that Goldstein and Wilgus prized.

The point was to develop a balanced picture of the music genre, including its provenance, and the story internal and external to individual songs. (Goldstein also commissioned authors already known for their writing, like Sam Charters and Leroi Jones / Amiri Baraka, to produce liner notes for his Bluesville label.) Goldstein states his purposes explicitly in his notes to the Folkways compilation record, *The Unfortunate Rake*, for an audience he considers not quite inculcated into liner note culture: "The introductory notes, and headnotes to each of the recorded ballads have been designed to give that minimum amount of information necessary to supplement the recordings, avoiding, as much as possible, long-winded theorizing and discussion. A selected bibliography of important articles containing references to numerous texts will be found at the end of this booklet, and may be referred to by those wishing to pursue the subject further than this album."

Liner notes should be scholarly, but not too scholarly. "It is obvious from the great wealth of material available that an extended monograph on this ballad cycle [i.e., ballads pertaining to the figure of the rake] is long overdue; perhaps some graduate student of folklore will soon undertake such a study in partial fulfillment of an advanced degree. We shall all be the richer for it" (Goldstein). "Partial fulfillment"—the officious phrase that every college student must include on the first page of their thesis—is Goldstein's wave to the reader that proportionality is the name of the game. He would not want his notes to overwhelm or overthink the ballad culture he sought to illuminate.

As Dean Biron shows, by the 1960s writers were experimenting ever more with liner note style. To the didactic format perfected by Goldstein (which in the 1950s could also be found on classical music and jazz records) were added others befitting the imagined audiences. Some writers attempted to be more literary or artistic, others "expository" but without the didacticism, and others more political or, in Biron's words, "propagandistic," while others simply wanted to stoke fans' interest, assuring them the music is groovy, hip, and so forth (Biron 10). Writers might be the actual musicians (e.g., Bob Dylan, Julius Lester, John Fahey), music critics (Goldstein, Ralph Gleason, Nat Hentoff), promoters, producers, or agents. Fahey's style is a mash-up and a parody of many modes. At first, before Fahey entered UCLA, his notes lampoon what he finds on the records of the folk and blues revival, including in them little stories and character sketches involving himself and his friends, often giving them invented names. Once he is deep into his graduate program, Fahey lets the influence of the academic environment show. The whole time, though, he lards his notes with so much inscrutable, garrulous content it's quite clear that disc jockey's and record buyers are not meant to get what Fahey means by it all, at least not without substantial effort. This is not to say there is no meaning. Fahey's notes are, on the one hand, very legible: they invoke and parody common narrative structures found in the liner notes of many records. On the other hand, individual paragraphs, sentences, and words abound with obscure references, allusive language, and wordplay, which can convey well, provided readers work at it too, Fahey's idea that a new grammar, perhaps not so much of language but of emotion and affect, is required to reconstruct race relations in America.

Structure, Tricks, and Treats in John Fahey's Liner Notes

Let's start with one example of the kind of notes Fahey would especially come to parody, Samuel Charters's liner notes to the 1963 Folkways album *J. D. Short and Son House*. Charters begins: "Northwest Mississippi is beautiful in the spring and the fall. There is a softness to the air, a distant haze that colors the horizon a faint purple. The grass covers the earth with a deep, rich green; the dried grass of autumn a mottled brown. There are stands of trees left beside the road, and clumps of dogwood and rhodedendron [*sic*] that mingle with the blossoming magnolia in the early weeks of March and April" (1). This is classic Charters, aiming for an evocative, highly romanticized setting of the scene.

Fahey rejoins with a riff on Charters's style in his first-ever notes, for the *Death Chants* record: "In the hot summer months of July and August, dust rises in the quiet streets of Takoma Park. The Sligo River becomes a chain of narrow muddy ponds. The rural Maryland countryside becomes a veritable pot of steam as the temperature passes 110, and the humidity is not far behind. The old southern Negroes who work in the cottonfields there have a volk saying which expresses all this quite well: 'If the temperature passes 110, can the humidity be far behind?'" The parallels are clear. Takoma Park, Maryland, stands in for the Delta; its humidity is the Delta's "haze" (Fahey once traced his often-repeated image of the haze back to Charters); the chain of muddy ponds of an overflowing Sligo River substitutes for a Delta river, maybe the Yazoo in a flood. (The Sligo River is Fahey's inflation of Takoma Park's Sligo Creek.) "Folk" has become "volk," Fahey's eternal barb against the romanticizers, who will take anything the ostensible folk say—high temperature and high humidity—as deep wisdom.

If setting the geographic scene is one structural feature of many folk revival album notes, another is the moment when the story is told of the white fieldworker (usually the author of the notes) going south in search of a "lost" bluesman, or of the white fieldworker (or song hunter or record producer) meeting up again with the "found" bluesman who is now a friend. The fieldworker narrative presumes to distill broader social relations, which are understood to involve vast but bridgeable gulfs between different places, cultures, and societies, into an encounter between two people. Such a narrative attempts to personalize and make manageable these relations. For the reader, too, the narrative lessens the distance, putting us vicariously in the scene. Samuel Charters's notes to the J. D. Short and Son House record offer a twist on this moment, taking the opportunity to talk about the Delta's suspicion toward unwanted white visitors. "A stranger in a town like Avalon or Port Gibson is followed as he goes down a street. If a car is left outside a store a sheriff is leaning against it waiting to ask questions when the driver comes back outside." If you have a camera or are making inquiries, you will be driven out. "In towns where a stranger is able to move more freely it is the Negro who is seen talking with him who suffers. Out in the country, where there is a long established pattern of violence, both the Negro and someone seen with him will suffer together" (1).

If these things happened to Charters he does not say. (Fahey's biographers, Steve Lowenthal and Claudio Guerrieri, report something like it happened to Fahey, though.) When he finally gets to his visit with J. D. Short, Charters writes, "The last time I saw J. D. Short it was a blindingly hot summer day in St. Louis" (2). He uses the same device, the same spectacle of privation, in his 1959 notes to a Folkways record of Furry Lewis's music, writing that the "last time" he saw Lewis was in Memphis "chopping weeds on a highway embankment" (Charters, liner notes, *Furry Lewis* 2). It in fact appears Charters only ever met up with J. D. Short in St. Louis, not in the Delta at all. And Charters's notes on Son House imply that he had not even met Son House personally. The fieldworker narrative as a structural feature of this type of album note now is a mere trope in Charters's notes and this may make it more difficult for some readers to digest his description of Son House's music—its "loneliness," "anger," "desperation," and "torment" (5).

When Charters' welds his hard-hitting critique of the Delta's racial economy to a picturesque, scenic rendering of poverty he draws extended ridicule from Fahey. Charters writes in his final paragraph, "In his 'Country Farm Blues,' with its bottleneck guitar accompaniment, Son House sings his only protest at the harsh farm gang system that has brutalized the lives of himself and the men in the lonely countryside around him. In it is the reality that hung around the poor cabin where he lived, like the drifting smoke from a dying autumn fire" (5).

Now it is Fahey's turn to relate the travels of the white fieldworker:

I stopped in at Whelan's drugstore. "Has anyone seen John Fahey or Blind Joe Death or maybe Gerhaupt Hauffman?" I asked dissolutely. "They were recording stars for Paramount thirty years ago, and I was told that somebody here might know where they are." "No," said the old man with the white beard behind the counter, resolutely, "they've done been here and gone. Maybe if you go down to the first fork in the road and turn left and then when you see the big house painted all over green and turn right and left and go by the railroad tracks and stop at the ethnic-looking water tower where once many years ago Jimmie Rodgers got stranded dissolutely—maybe if you do that, you'll see Heh God, and maybe he can tell you where they are."

It was noontime, and gentle breezes blew across the hot cotton-fields, in the midst of time. There by the water tower, I found Heh God, and I opened my mouth and asked him the same question I'd been asking people for months: "Have you seen John Fahey or Blind Joe Death or Gerhaupt Hauffman?" There by the water tower I found Heh God, and he opened his mouth and said, "No, I haven't seen them lately, but probably if you go down to the next left red light and turn green and ride over the great B&O viaduct and ask at the pool hall, maybe," he said hodologically. (liner notes, *Death Chants*)

In contrast to Charters, Fahey's interest is in exposing a certain inventedness of folklore in folklore studies. Toward that end, it is helpful to know Fahey is writing under the pseudonym of "Chester C. Petranick," a misspelling of an old junior high school teacher of his. This means Fahey's pseudonym is placed in charge of finding the real Fahey, whose name is embedded among yet other pseudonyms, Blind Joe Death and Gerhaupt Hauffman. (Hauffman is likely an adaptation of the 1912 Nobel laureate Gerhard Hauptman, a German writer who was a proponent of German naturalism, who also happened to capitulate to the Nazis.) Together they seem to stand as so many undecidable sides of the one true but unlocatable Fahey. Fahey anticipates the argument that Barbara Kirshenblatt-Gimblett would make twenty-five years later, that folklore doesn't so much discover its object as invent it. Fahey bolsters this idea, intimating that there must also be the invention of a self who is capable of doing the inventing, except that this self has itself become inextricable from the folkloric, defined, in other words, by what it seeks. The confounding of cause and effect is perhaps the "midst of time" Fahey plays on, with Heh, appropriately enough, the ancient Egyptian god of infinity, offering directions that will surely lead nowhere. Or if the sacred thing/person/identity/place is found, it will be misrecognized.

The journey is not just one of crossing the countryside, then, but of crossing back and forth between actual places and persons, on the one hand, and illusions and myths, on the other hand. As the journey narrows and one draws closer to one's aim, well, is this not the very moment that opens onto intricate mental and cultural trickery? When "I" finally come face-to-face with the "resolute" local, what and who am "I" actually seeing? Fahey implicitly claims to spot this trickery, but he also seems to know there is no way out of it, for he is playing to an audience of listeners and readers whose tastes, including Fahey's own, are being formed by that very trickery. He is the product of the very history he would critique. Fahey qua Chester C. Petranick is onto something when he writes:

> This sort of thing was not new to me. I remembered the months and months I had spent the previous winter, traveling across the continent and back again in search of the mysterious and elusive Firk Brothers. . . . As I walked down Maple Avenue, the heat from the blacktop road began to get to me. "Just find them [i.e., John Fahey, etc.]," I said to myself, imperatively, there in the midst of time. "Someday you'll find them. You owe it to all the people in the 13th century who started the whole business; to Jean-Jacques Rousseau and Jean Sibelius. You owe it to Heh God, and to the other downtrodden people of Takoma Park—to locate them hodologically." (liner notes, *Death Chants*)

Fahey (Petranick) strongly gestures here to the meanings that accrete in so-called folk music—the ways of traditional peoples and minstrelsy ("13th century peasants"), the high-culture ideologies regarding so-called primitives ("Rousseau"), the idea of a national folk to be resurrected ("Sibelius"), the notion of a contemporary forgotten and oppressed people (the "downtrodden people of Takoma Park") who have preserved something of the old ways. (Chapter 6 will explain what Fahey means by a "hodological" location.) That these ideas have produced at least as much sentiment as they have genuine insight is clear enough in the stream of adjectives that Fahey then rains down: "[Blind Joe Death] expresses the intensely personal, bittersweet, biting, soul-stirring, volk poetry of the harsh, elemental, but above all human life of the downtrodden Takoma Park volk" (liner notes, *Death Chants*). I don't want to suggest that every utterance Fahey makes can be accounted for, only to point to a narrative structure and tone at work in his liner notes. Half of his tactic is to incorporate recognizable names and places sufficient to establish some familiar territory, while the other half means to confound, to reintroduce some distance between the reader-listener and the scene of the blues and the folk. The author himself is implicated, since he is in the act of discovering obfuscations in which he is hidden from himself or that hide his motivations.

Now, such obfuscations might contain one's own other selves. They might also generate a confrontation with what one has projected onto the ethnographic field, especially the projection that a racial other inhabits a world more fascinating than one's own. I sense that Fahey spots exactly this in writing like Charters's, and later I will show how little Fahey was able to escape it himself (see chapter 6). But neither Fahey's nor Charters's notes adequately recognized how that projection was fed by racial segregation or the debt their labors of discovery owed to Jim Crow. The Delta was a prepared space for the fieldworker looking to find African American musicians. "With the rise of Jim Crow," Karl Hagstrom Miller argues, "scholars turned toward segregated spaces to find isolated racial cultures. It made the job of identifying separate racial repertoires—and by extension racial capacities and temperaments—much easier." Fahey did not subscribe to the idea of fully separate repertoires, but Miller could be writing about Fahey and Charters when he adds that "many white scholars began to suggest that their authority as cultural commentators was based on their ability—some argued courage—to pass into segregated black spaces to record a culture invisible to most white people" (257).

This does not in any way mean that Charters and Fahey were ignorant about racial segregation or, for that matter, racist terms (which I abbreviate in the passages quoted below). Let me take a moment to follow these phenomena in their liner notes. For his *J. D. Short and Son House* record Charters writes, "At the edges of the towns are the run down shacks of the 'n****r towns,' that the white southerner has left to the colored men and women of the town as places to live. Out on the country roads, lining the flat fields are the ramshackle cabins of the 'sharecrop' labor and the hired hands who work long hours for low pay in the cotton fields" (1). The countryside has turned profoundly ugly, but Charters sees this is social more than aesthetic ugliness, since the edges of the towns are a matter of social design: "It is the white southerner's revenge for his defeat at the hands of the North in the Civil War.

The white Mississippian, poorly educated, living in an area of poverty and disease, and crippled with the attitudes of the English servant class from which he has come, tries to overcome his awareness of his own inadequacies by forcing the Negroes of Mississippi into a social pattern uglier than his own. It is a system which has left deep scars on both sides" (1). In the Black neighborhoods on the outskirts is the enforced poverty, "but in the center of the towns is the nervous and frightened white society." White Southerners have become so "warped" that they can convince themselves that their "colored neighbors 'like the life here.'" The white Southerner "has had Negro 'friends,' as he calls the relationship, 'all of his life'; and then uses dogs on the Negro children with the courage to protest against the system and to murder any Negro who raises his voice against him" (1).

Notwithstanding the picturesque scene setting I've already pointed out, for Charters it is essential that anyone interested in historical blues music and in the revived careers of musicians like J. D. Short and Son House understand the harsh reality of the Delta. Clearly, this would be on the minds of many college-age white record buyers anyway—the 1961 Freedom Rides were a very recent memory, and civil rights actions were ongoing. There is nothing like these somber pronouncements in Fahey's *Death Chants* album notes. He opts instead for a wry but also equivocating approach.

Let's look at the headnotes to the Fahey recording "Take a Look at That Baby" on the *Death Chants* record. Fahey correctly states that the song was originally recorded by the Two Poor Boys (Joe Evans and Arthur McClain) in the 1930s, but then jokes that the song was used by "Father Jahn" to incite race riots. Father Jahn—one now wonders who else but Fahey would know this—was an actual historical figure, a mid-nineteenth-century German nationalist and anti-Semite, beloved of the Third Reich, who looked fondly back to the days and ways of some ancient, mythic Teutonic "volk" (see Leerssen). But "in its use by Fahey and Blind Joe," Fahey continues, "the song carried no racist connotations."

> Fortunately, Father Jahn and his disciples have all but disappeared from the world historical scene. This brief but unfortunate page in American history is long gone. Though we read of various racist organizations which are springing up, much to our amazement, such as the Black Muslims, the Ku Klux Klan, the Sons of Pericles, the B'nai B'rith, and the New Lost City Ramblers, it is the editorial policy of this company to oppose all such racist organizations, and merely to present

the volk music of the American people in all its diversity and splendor.
(Fahey, liner notes, *Death Chants*)

Fahey's list of "racist organizations" is rich with intent without being clear about what that intent is. He implies an overarching point that racism has become more insidious, a claim we see him make explicitly in his master's thesis. But the groups he points at here would likely surprise at least some of his readers. The Sons of Pericles, for example, was an offshoot of the American Hellenic Educational Progressive Association, a group of American Greeks formed in response to attacks by the Klan. The New Lost City Ramblers was a folk revival band ("imitators" in folklorist and musician Ellen Stekert's blunt assessment) known for striving to reproduce authentic renditions of American folk songs, while also wearing "authentic," old-fashioned clothes. The idea seems to be that many groups are guilty of concocting essentialist notions. If there is a distinction between those combatting racism and those promulgating it, one would not know from Fahey's presentation. Where he wants to go is not clear. Does he impute that a little racism might be normal and inevitable, or that people don't recognize racism when it's staring them in the face, and that's why it has become more insidious? Does he mean that white, middle-class American musical tastes are unwittingly founded on a racial romance, that notions of the folk are irredeemably racial notions? Or is the point just that racist ugliness and musical beauty can be separated out, that the music is the thing, to paraphrase Wilgus again? The lightness with which Fahey strings out his phrases and references, the way he both states a problem and seems to think it may not much matter, also suggest a general weariness (or rather, a specific white weariness) with talk about race and identity. Fahey will not say for sure what he is up to, but when the needle drops on Fahey's version of the song and you start tapping your feet (his guitar finger-picking on this song is superb), the headnotes dare you *to enjoy the song if you can, but know that the folk revival through which you found your way to it has clouded your judgement about why what you are listening to exists at all.* In short, Fahey's style is to catch his audience off guard without having to say too much about his own views.

Finally, there are two structural features in the album notes that are aspects of what Barry Lee Pearson calls the "bluesman's story"—namely, the moment when the investigator inquires after how the bluesman first learned his craft and the moment when musical lineage and current relationships with other musicians are revealed. (In his own work on how interviews with blues musicians are shaped, Pearson emphasizes that these moments, nearly ubiquitous in interviews, are co-creations of interviewer and musician. The musician crafts the life story with an understanding of what the audience and interviewer expect to hear.) From Charters we learn about the origins of J. D. Short's and Son House's musical talents and how their respective talents were cultivated. We learn about who influenced them and who else plays (or does not play) their particular style, and we find out who else they play and record with, if anyone. It is no different with Fahey, except for more tongue in cheek. Once more, here is a passage from his notes for *Death Chants, Breakdowns, and Military Waltzes*:

> As a little boy, John Fahey had sat at the feet of an old blind Negro known locally as "N****r Joe," listening to the intensely personal blues and religious songs the old man played on his surrogate kithera [*sic*]. . . . In time, Blind Joe's kithera was washed away in the great 1927 flood of the Sligo River, which many of the local volk recall with fear and trembling. . . . When Blind Joe died in 1962 his guitar was passed on by his family to John Fahey, just as Jimmy Rodger's guitar had been passed on to Ernest Tubb, and Charlie Patton's guitar had been passed on to Ely Greene by Bertha Lee.
>
> John Fahey made his first guitar from a baby's coffin, and led the old blind Negro through the back alleys and whorehouses of Takoma Park in return for lessons. . . . In 1952, only a few years before Blind Joe's bodily ascension, Patricia Sullivan . . . recorded the two of them and issued them on the now rare Takoma label. . . . Now, thanks to those who remember, John Fahey has just finished a concert tour, and has won even more friends in his travels through this vast land, especially on the West Coast, singing and playing the intensely personal, urgently expressive music of the downtrodden people of Takoma Park. This record is for those who remember.

Readers of this passage face the typical gauntlet of unfamiliar references and misdirections. The surrogate kithara is the invention of the experimental composer Harry Partch. Bertha Lee was Charley Patton's last "wife." Patricia Sullivan was a close Fahey friend in Takoma Park (and cowriter of the epic song "When the Springtime Comes Again," which Fahey often played during his early concerts), who later moved to Los Angeles, as would Fahey (Lowenthal). The 1927 flood of the Sligo River would be a nod to the epic 1927 flooding of the Mississippi River, about which a number of famous blues songs were written, not least by Charley Patton. Fahey was notably on-again off-again irascible and did not necessarily make friends on tour. And he did not sing. So much for those details. The point of the passage is to poke at the venerable status accorded to musical lineages and time-tested tradition. It shouldn't surprise that where Charters plays it straight, Fahey turns expectations on their head. What Fahey wants to know of his audience is, Could you tell the difference between the real and the fake? Do you get that your expectation regarding the typical blues or folk narrative *occults* real historical content rather than revealing it?

But, as with the Patton book and other sections of the *Death Chants* notes, Fahey is harder to pin down here on his thinking about race. Persistently reminding readers that it is on his mind, only rarely does he say what he really thinks about it. And now is not one of those times. Consider these details. On the one hand, it is easy to spot the racialized social hierarchy announced by the sequence of names in the passage above: "N****r Joe," the blind Negro; Blind Joe, Fahey's minstrelized persona; and John Fahey, revered musician. See how the sequence begins with a racial epithet and proceeds (upward) toward implicit whiteness, moving from the nameless but racialized to the named but racially unmarked. It's harder, on the other hand, to discern what the hierarchy, invoked with just a few drops of Fahey's ink, is actually doing here. Yes, it parodies a line of Black-to-white musical transmission that is a staple of folk and blues revival narratives. But if we are meant to understand that Fahey is parodying the misrecognitions of the cultural scene he relies on, likely parodying himself along the way as someone who at least partly fell for the white racial romance with Black musical performance, this is comedy that doesn't exactly root out the racial epithet and might even want to rely on it. There is a world of difference between Fahey making light of his travels through the "vast land" and the "blind Negro" who just exists as a foil. Fahey gives us a way to posit a difference between his own possibly real self and the Fahey who is a persona or character, but he does not give us a way to think about the difference between the person "locally known as," and that person as they really might be. In Fahey rejecting the racist term himself, preferring "old blind Negro" instead, the man remains *only* a racial character. But if the racial epithet is in fact meant to be stamped out in this parody, because the scare quotes remind us that the N-word shouldn't be used, who would the joke be on when Fahey quotes it? "Local" people who still proudly use racist terms? People who don't but still harbor racist feelings, the point being that Fahey wants them to admit what they actually believe? Fahey himself who admits he is part of America's broken world?

The Exploding Footnote

Some of the narrative conventions I've just discussed are also at work in Fahey's notes to his 1964 reissue of *Blind Joe Death*, but once he was enrolled in graduate school at UCLA, his writing becomes even more elaborate and he adopts some of the more archaic conventions of academic writing. Album notes for *The Dance of Death and Other Plantation Favorites*, a 1965 release, contain an "Appendix 1," whose moldy title — "The Musical History of John Fahey: Gathering Together All That Is Presently Known from Divers Sources" — suggests something one might find in a mildewed tome of the previous century. The notes to his 1966 record, *The Great San Bernardino Birthday Party*, are more than twice as long, though just as farcical, as any of Fahey's notes to preceding albums, and they include footnotes to boot. (The lion's share of the notes is Fahey's grudging mea culpa for his violent outburst at a birthday party that left him estranged from his girlfriend. It is told in the form of an annotated *märchen*, not unlike what he would have encountered during his studies.)

It is in the academic bent of Fahey's album notes where an answer to the question posed at the start of the chapter is suggested. To rephrase that question: If his graduate school experience supplied new material to adapt to his album note style, what does it mean that the scholarly and the farcical take place simultaneously, and to what effect? Let's work this out through an example par excellence, "footnote 2" from *The Great San Bernardino Birthday Party*:

2. This song was recorded by Patton in 1929. Its title was "Minglewood Blues," and was issued on Pm. 12854. Its key verse was
   When you go to Memphis, stop by Minglewood, baby,
   You Memphis women, don't mean no man no good.
   The genesis of the term "Minglewood" has been traced to the linguistic dislocation which occurred at the hands of Mr. Mind during the second World War (see *The Adventures of Captain Marvel*, No. 36, June 1941.) Mr. Mind with his babble machine first used this monstrous device on the City of Memphis. The verbal confusion which resulted from it is well known in the annals of the South. Ever since then Negroes and Whites have had a hard time understanding each other's speech (as well as each other). Mind was finally foiled by Captain Marvel in circa May 1945 at the close of the second World War and was electrocuted in a miniature electric chair. A section of the

city, known previously as Glingles, was now confused in the minds of the local volk (due to Mind's machine) with a portion of the first stanza of the ancient folksong, "Wormwood Flower":

I will grind with my Mingles, swood
graving glack bare.
The rasins so rot, and the brilligs
so hair.
With the myrtil, swerd glight, and the dismembered hue,
Fale! Anle Leader and eyelids of glue.
> The section of the city is still known as Minglewood
> (i.e., from Mingles swood.)

If this is not the most maniacally nerdy and psychedelic of Fahey's parodies, it most surely is a contender, right down to the spray of Jabberwock-like verse at the end. Most remarkable is that in the very center of the delirium that is this footnote, Fahey blithely alludes to one of the central issues of the time: relations between Blacks and whites. Does he mean to be glib or does he mean serious business? In what kind of space can both moods exist?

The writing pivots around a reference to contemporary racial "tension," a failure of Blacks and whites to understand each other's respective speech and therefore, in a more fundamental way, "each other" — ostensibly meaning each other's wants, outlooks, intentions, assumptions, demands, and so forth. But the fact that this tension is announced *inside* a fabulation, a double fabulation actually, casts doubt on just how real Fahey thinks the problem is, or precisely how one should care. For the cause of the communication breakdown is the evil comic book character Mr. Mind (fabulation one), who has created a babble machine. Note the implicit reference to the biblical Tower of Babel (fabulation two). So, is communication breakdown real or just invented as a story people tell? But if mutual communication breakdown, who is to be held accountable? Circumstances beyond people's control (read: Mr. Mind as exogenous force of some kind)? Or, equally unsatisfying, everyone all at once (read: Tower of Babel story)? The footnote is certain about one thing, though, and this is its imputing that there was racial "understanding" at a previous time, before 1945, which would be inclusive of the period when Fahey claims in his thesis that southern whites and Blacks lived together more amicably, an assertion I commented on earlier.

But wait, Fahey supplements these meanings with riffs on the two song references that bookend his footnote. First is a complaining quote about mean women from Charley Patton's version of "Minglewood Blues" (which

Patton actually recorded as "It Won't Be Long")—we sense Fahey chooses it since he feels so aggrieved by his girlfriend. At the other end are some notes on the Carter Family standard "Wildwood Flower" (presented here as "Wormwood Flower," a reference to the reputed psychoactive ingredient in absinthe as well as being a tie back to the Captain Marvel comic book, in which the space alien Mr. Mind takes the form of a worm). "Wildwood Flower" converses with "Minglewood Blues" not only in the Carters' substitution of "mingles" for "ringlets" of hair, but in the story it tells of a broken-hearted young woman left behind by her sweetheart. Fahey's experimentation with the "Wildwood Flower" lyrics—consistent with the history of different musical artists adapting the lyrics to their liking—turns them into nonsensical Lewis Carroll–like mondegreens, even quoting Carroll's "Jabberwocky" with his insertion of "brillig" into the song. And here, it becomes clear that a whole new frame of reference has come to circumscribe the footnote—for the Jabberwock is the name of the well-known folk club in Berkeley, California, where Fahey frequently gave concerts, starting in 1965, while Charley Patton, if he were ever to see anyone in Minglewood, a lumber mill town outside Memphis, could have been playing at the jook joint there (*Dyersburg State Gazette*). In juxtaposing these different venues, Fahey reinscribes communication breakdown: there are largely Black audiences at the jook and largely whites at the Jabberwock. But, hold on. With his "associatively" constructed Jabberwocky word salad, isn't Fahey piling "randomness" of his own on top of Patton's? If so, then Fahey's account of Blacks and whites being unable to communicate spells not so much a failure but a beginning in which two people each take enjoyment in verbal play, a situation in which Fahey in particular—Patton is dead of course—allows his own experimentation to "mingle" with Patton's.

It even seems Fahey may want to take Patton's associative stylings a step further. Observe the way that language in the footnote begins as representational (the words make sense), only to become nonrepresentational (words are broken and rearranged into nonsense verse) and therefore, let's say, musical. "Wildwood" becomes "Wormwood," but words also tense up, break, recombine. They fall apart into syllables and letters, and the syllables and letters change places, becoming nonsensical, yet musical . . . "universal." Language, music, people, at the cellular level it's all the same. We therefore have crossed through the valley where Blacks and whites do not understand each other to the musical landscape where they might.

If this reading holds, then the emphasis of the footnote shifts from "we don't understand each other" to "what makes language play so interesting to people?" And from there, back to communicative abilities after all, since folklore is what is "associatively" transmitted from one individual to another, or one generation to another, or what is adapted without ulterior motives by different cultural actors. It seems obvious that there is a *meta* quality to the footnote; the fact that it is itself a fabulation makes a kind of folklore out of "folklore." If there is one thing, then, that keeps Fahey's critique of the "volk" from utterly demolishing the idea of the folk, it is his interest in the continuing processes—highly localized and promising of mutual pleasure, not unlike the "communist cell" of a previous chapter—that makes for something like the folk, after all.[1]

Requiem for Close Reading

So by now the question has to be asked, Just how much of Fahey's liner notes can anyone tolerate? Assuming the answer is "Only so much," how do we draw the line? What makes reading these notes *at all* worth the struggle? In 1968's *The Voice of the Turtle* Fahey takes things to an entirely new level, so the questions are pertinent. Compared with those of *The Great San Bernardino Birthday Party*, his notes in 1968 are more extensive, exacting, and meticulous. He reproduces photographs of himself, family, and friends, including several African American musicians whom he has sought out in his career to date. Through the now-familiar mash-up of fact and fiction and the allusive land in between, Fahey launches an all-out effort to map the entire network of influences, proclivities, and persons that has made him what he is, some twelve album-size pages of notes bound inside a beautifully produced gatefold cover. The once again arcane subtitle, "Being a Musical Hodograph and Chronologue of the Music of John Fahey," hints that Fahey intends to strike, and skewer, a scholarly pose. In its pages can be found passages like this:

> There is, there will be, there was, there at no time is, was or shall be, and neither shall there not be. A vision, a dream, a memory, a prophecy; an affirmation of all of these, a combination, a disjunction, and a negation of all these. A confusion is perfect clarity; (My) mind sees what (my) eyes think; (My) eyes know, do not know, see and see not. What is now disjunct is, will be, was, was not, neither shall be nor shall not be. Conjunct, all of these. In Riverdale and not in Riverdale, at and not at Magruder Park. I hear and do not hear the voice of the Sligo River turtle. It says and does not say. A turtle and not a turtle. All

of these conjunct. Dogs everywhere but do not bark. Fronds rain in the grass, but no one is wet. The swamp is odorless. I see my mother walking on the swamp. Conjunct, all of these. A rainbow, a recapitulation, a restitution, a reunion, a confrontation, everyone knows everyone. A party, a communion. All of these. If I were not illegitimate I would not see the fog. I would not see that we have lost each other. We have lost our way. We sleep, we wake—it is the same. We prowl like stray dogs. If the sun goes down, we know that the earth is turning from its axis. But all of these, and nothing more. At Margruder Park the sun stands still, and we are together. We have not lost our way. (Fahey, liner notes, *Voice of the Turtle*)

I confess being quite taken by this passage. It is both spell-like and ridiculously silly. It has lithe phrasing and hypnotic little repetitions that invite a reader to see where it all might go. The passage has fun violating Aristotle's law of noncontradiction, that something can't "be" and "not be" at the same time. But do we dare take another stab at clearing the verbal overgrowth to see what comes of it all? (No one has done a finer job of tracking down Fahey's obscure references than Claudio Guerrieri in his two-volume *John Fahey Handbook*.) But in this instance, and perhaps the whole of Fahey's career as a liner note artist, except for when he was commissioned to write authoritative notes for records of other musical artists, it is the overgrown tangle itself that cries out for notice. Perhaps elaboration *is* the point; perhaps *that* is where the real action is. Fahey reports in one of his semiautobiographical essays in *How Bluegrass Music Destroyed My Life* a profound love of words, language, and language games. "Ongepotchket" is a particular favorite, a Yiddish expression for something that is overly embellished and too elaborately put together, a nonharmonious thing. Doesn't Fahey give the game away in that very word? Is this, finally, Blind Joe Death's America, everything, everything all at once?

In the passage from *The Voice of the Turtle* just above—in its rolling rhythm, the beat of its short phrases, the flickering of serial conjugations that move forward and turn back on themselves, offering and rescinding meaning in the same breath—the writing achieves a certain momentum that truly invites reading. And yet the more it goes on, the more it threatens to repel the reader. By the end, it has done the job of being "fascinating and boring" simultaneously, as Sianne Ngai has brilliantly written of this kind of prose. Ngai calls these contradictory affects "stuplimity," that is, a combination of the stupid and the sublime. Stuplimity, Ngai says, is a tense holding together of what dulls and excites. It is a "concatenation of boredom and astonishment" (271). Satisfaction finds no quarter in this bizarre combination, for the effect is to produce a feeling that lies outside our learned repertoire of aesthetic responses. Stuplimity "drags us downward into the realm of words" rather than steadily moving us toward some ineffable, transcendent moment where words are no longer necessary or useful (273). The boredom produced by stuplimity "resides in relentless attention to the finite and small, the bits and scraps floating in the 'common muck' of language. . . . Stuplimity arises in the relationship between these little materials and the operations of repetition and agglutination" (278). Stuplimity can be comical, farcical: "Inducing a series of fatigues or minor exhaustions, rather than a single, major blow to the imagination, stuplimity paradoxically forces the reader to go on in spite of its equal enticement to readers to give up . . . pushing us to reformulate new tactics for reading" (272).

Along the way, if we can hang in there, the "negative affect of stuplimity might be said to produce another affective state in its wake, a secondary feeling that seems strangely neutral, unqualified, 'open.' . . . This final outcome of stuplimity—the echo or afterimage produced by it, as it were—makes possible a kind of resistance" (284). Sometimes resistance is about the way stuplimity results from a lavish and excessive attention to detail, *as if* complying with some authority or some standard. But really such attention indicates false compliance and therefore resistance against some encompassing "system." Following some interpreters of Gertrude Stein and Kierkegaard, Ngai also has in mind the way that stuplimity, through its own sheer buildup, forms its own kind of coherence, a bulwark against an incoherent and demanding world (294, 296).

Writing that is "stuplimitous" lures us in and then exhausts us, a consequence that readers of Fahey's album notes eventually and surely face. His writing, the cumulative effect of it, is shocking and tiring, refusing to try to redeem itself for the sake of a reader looking to be enlightened or even just entertained. For soon enough our smiles freeze up. The jokes are falling flat, the writing seems juvenile and now founders on our better judgment to just look away. And yet Fahey keeps on going, with a persistence that lacks conviction in anything other than persisting with the project of describing the situations and framings in which he finds himself: he knows he is being positioned by his "times" and that he is supposed to take a position. And so he keeps writing about *that*. He cannot get ahead of the game and become the self-centered subject that we all know our culture teaches us we are supposed to be. How else to make a coherent subject out of oneself, under conditions in which one feels oneself to be a symptom, but to keep showing up, as it were, keep echoing the cultural "noise" in sometimes artful, sometimes tiresome ways? Well, that is one kind of solution, and this is the kind of resistance that I think Ngai's idea of stuplimity is capable of showing us about Fahey. He achieves a certain momentum, a mounting attack on "systems" and habits, that the reader might want to follow because he might actually be going somewhere worthwhile.

But ultimately the reader of Fahey experiences something quite different from what Fahey the writer experiences. Ngai is helpful here too, although Fahey's stuplimity might work a little differently than she says of stuplimity generally. For part and parcel of any "open feeling" Fahey's reader might get is that one indeed has to give up reading him at a certain point, has to stop bending to his narrative will, has to stop simply following along, or letting him grab you by the elbow. Moreover, Fahey is no Stein, no Kierkegaard, no Melville, no Joyce. He is not instructive (except sometimes), not clear (except sometimes), not *communicative* (except sometimes). Thoroughly outside any canon that has decided ahead of time that, *Oh, you must read Fahey,* it is, to a point, the combination of mediocrity and persistence that works in his favor. I am saying that *to give up seems to be an essential act of the reading,* and an act that *the writing foretells.* This is far different from the energy and determination it takes to have done the writing in the first place. Fahey's album note writing, which a reader begins to read properly enough because it accompanies an album one has voluntarily bought or borrowed, is a site that prompts a sort of anti-economy in the end. Fahey performs the service of enmeshing you in his system, while you pay him back by going your own way. He does this (maybe) because he wants you to acknowledge there is a system out there, including a system of "common sense" on issues of the day, and it's blinding and subjectivating, and it takes the air out of the room. *So, go your own way but don't just return to the comforts of predigested thought and instructed feelings. Even more, don't return to the comforts of the music thinking these notes mean nothing. Comforts are anathema to the cause. Become intelligent, aware, learned. Like me, but not me.* Fahey once described his liner notes as a joke, an entertainment, a way to sell more records (see Blazek). It can also be true that a statement like that just puts you off the scent. After all, more records, more notes.

PART III | Festivals of Democracy (Variations)

Introduction

With his move to Berkeley in the early 1960s, John Fahey dialed up the volume on his dislike of folk music. In his view—more or less shared by Fahey's contemporaries, such as Charles Keil in his *Urban Blues*, and some of the contributors to De Turk and Poulin's anthology of essays on the folk music revival—the anachronistic attraction to folk music, and especially middle-class white attraction to African American blues artists, was at root symptomatic of repressed emotion. "Friendship does not exist here. Because Berkeley people regard the expression of emotion 'bad form,'" Fahey writes in the essay "Skip James" (Fahey, *How Bluegrass* 214). "You must never show love or hate or even affection. Mellow. You can—in fact you must—always project mellow. . . . Berkeley people are cursed by this imprisonment in mellow. But they do not know it" (214). They are aware of emotions, but "because they cannot locate them within themselves, they assume that they exist elsewhere. And where better than in the bosoms of country blues singers, who they have noted exhibit a wide range of affect, mostly incomprehensible to themselves, the Berkeley-ites. After all, these primitives are the repositories of the Folk-soul, the collective unconscious. . . . Therefore let these strange effusions and emanations of *Geist* emanate from forgotten black entertainers" (215). Repressed emotion, Fahey went on to argue, made "Whitey" susceptible to the "Madison Avenue" commercial hyping of blues and blues singers.[1]

In chapters 5 and 6 I offer an extended sketch of the themes of emotion in Fahey's work, particularly the idea that there are emotions people are not supposed to have: anger, bitterness, resentment, the desire to vanquish others, and so on. But he is also attuned to feelings of love, fellowship, and connectedness that tend to get suppressed or degraded or diminished, or simply viewed as trite. What Fahey fights against is a form of false acceptance—rife in "Movement" culture, he argues—that refuses to accept the whole person, the good and bad.

> "Underground," "folk" this and that, "hippie," and "folknik" were
> marketing terms.
> This sales pitch and thought-control capture the entire populace.
> All of these "expressions" of alternative living or the folk soul or
> whatever—all could be bought. The prices were very high.
> Hippie didn't know all this . . . Worse, Hippie didn't know that he
> didn't know much about anything.
> And nobody told him.
> But Hippie did have one or two things: money and a bunch of
> pretensions.
> All Hippie was pretense.
> It seems as though I was the only person who noticed this perversity.
> . . . They and their Madison Avenue bosses were always telling me that
> I should celebrate.
> "Celebrate what?" I asked.
> But they couldn't answer me.
> They told me to make love not war. They told me that Black is beautiful.
> Madison Avenue.
> The new hookers wore different clothing. Lots of flowers. Called
> themselves and their pimps "flower children."
> Hookers and pimps have to be fashion-conscious. Part of their trade.
> And so hookers and other criminals were glorified. Automatically made
> part of
> THE MOVEMENT.
> "Love-ins." Everybody said they loved me.
> Sure. (Fahey, *How Bluegrass* 224–25)

Fahey goes on in his long, looping "Skip James" essay to describe how he (and his friends Bill Barth and Henry Vestine) found Nehemiah Curtis "Skip" James in a hospital in Tunica, Mississippi, only to discover that his musical abilities were diminished and that he was a "creep": "I had played a trick on myself. I expected to find something interesting and enlightening. . . . But instead what I found was this obnoxious, bitter, hateful old creep" (245). What irony, though, Fahey's essay denying Skip James his emotional reality, just as Fahey claimed Berkeley "mellow" had denied him his. It's a highly performative claim and further evidence of just how caught up Fahey's writing could be in Movement motifs, since his beef with Skip James arguably *furthers* the case for mellowness. A reader can justly assume there is some connective tissue between the Movement's shallowness and the emotional confusion Fahey revels in.

In the same essay, Fahey also wonders what desire for what sort of enlightenment drove him to go looking for Skip James anyway. What did he think he would find there? he asks. The question itself arguably goes back to what Marybeth Hamilton notes was the intent of the "Blues Mafia" in the first place: to define the Delta Blues as a great, emotive art form uncorrupted by commerce or social intent, and to find in its African American performers not an incipient proletariat but a class of great artists. The point, traceable to the efforts of white record collectors in the 1940s—well before the Movement— was to elevate the blues and keep it clean of politics. Fahey's writing is and is not precisely of this mold. For one could say that what it records is the experience of the Blues Mafia as its sense of a pure blues was becoming unsustainable. Think of Fahey's *Requia* notes. His emphasis on feelings and the authenticity of subjective experience, his way of thinking about them from the standpoint of Movement demands and at Movement demands from the standpoint of his subjective demands, can then register with us as the sense of that very unsustainability. Fahey feels the pressure of the Movement culture and works with its discourse to say so. His reassessment of Charley Patton in "Charley Reconsidered" reveals that feeling of unsustainability too: recall how Fahey insists on Patton's great emotive artistry, in the context of conceding a more political Patton.

The point here is not to judge but to reintroduce the question of how Fahey's focus on feeling and emotion sustained itself, in a conceptual way, once its basic grammar had been learned. Moreover, where can Fahey go with that focus in mind? What intellectual resources did Fahey take nourishment from, and how so? What role do they play in repeated performative acts of taking and ceding ground? Chapters 5 and 6 show Fahey to have been an assiduous reader of the, in a sense, authorities, who he seemed to think underwrote the importance of emotion and collectively composed a sort of field guide to them. Many of these works—those by existentialist philosophers in particular—circulated also among his new left and Movement contemporaries (Aronson). Fahey drew from lesser-known sources too, but whichever texts he drew from he did so in a way that instantly vernacularized and personalized them and made them useful for what he understood the times called for.

Chapter 5 is essentially a decoding of a lengthy Fahey essay published in 1974 in the *Georgia Straight*, an alternative news weekly from Vancouver, British Columbia, and, like most small, alternative presses of the time, a one-stop bulletin board for local Movement culture. The essay, "Performance as War," was published shortly after the *Georgia Straight*'s music critic wrote a glowing review of Fahey's Vancouver concert (Swanson). "Performance as War" requires decoding because it is almost entirely made of ingeniously sequenced but *unattributed* passages from several of Fahey's favorite philosophers—Hegel, Walter Kauffman, Kierkegaard—with a few passages from T. S. Eliot and Richard Wagner thrown in for good measure. Minus the latter two sources, the essay might be thought of as the associative folklore-making process turned loose on a college philosophy syllabus. Fahey used these radically pared, repurposed, and associatively linked texts (yes, think "Charley Patton" here) to identify a struggle of serious interest. How can he remain part of the cultural scene that has claimed him and not be dragged down into the mediocrity he accuses it of? How can he retain self-integrity under such circumstances, honestly express feelings he claims to have, and perfect an art form he believes in? (By the way, these are all goals that would be solidly endorsed by the very scene he loathes.) Having identified the individual expression of human feeling and emotion as his most cherished value, he spots—via Hegel—a fundamental problem with it. If a society believes the expression of *individual* feeling is the person's ultimate goal, how can that same society legitimate the compromises among individuals that are necessary for the society to function? Fahey has already expressed deep dissatisfaction with the dominant form that "compromise" takes in capitalist society: false gregariousness, Madison Avenue, the Movement that says it loves him, and so on. Taking his cue from Hegel, Fahey worries that art (music) has become a hideout for fakers and posers to express false feelings, because the true feelings cannot be expressed. Our society is repressive and not equipped with the proper social forms to let this happen, if such forms can even exist. Perhaps this is why Fahey makes this piece of writing so difficult, and in places irresponsibly ugly: For, does the right reader even exist? As he noted elsewhere, though, he needs an audience, and although he desires to leave the scene, he stops himself short with the realization that there is no exit from it. He is in and of the culture, after all. "All will be well," he writes at the end, channeling T. S. Eliot's *Four Quartets*. He has not solved the problem he began with, but, as Albert Camus claimed of Sisyphus, he might try to see and live with it more clearly. And if along the way he can entertain . . . well, there you have it. Just reverse the words of the essay's title.

Even decoded, "Performance as War" is essentially a riff that does not bring us close enough to the deeper framework on which Fahey is building. The essay seems held aloft by some set of supports not yet revealed. A feeling-based society is problematic, Fahey worries. But how did we (he) get there in the first place, so oriented to emotion and feeling? Chapter 1's recounting of expressive writing tells part of the story, and his immersion in Movement spaces tells another, even if he struggles there with his own emotional states. Chapter 6 reconstructs what could be considered Fahey's basic intellectual worldview of emotion—that is, the fact of emotion's irreducible existence, our projection of emotion outward into the world, the world itself as always already a palimpsest of other people's feelings and emotional states made concrete in the landscape. Access to this point of view is granted via two key-words that recur in Fahey's writing: "hodology" and the "edge." Of course, it appears these could be keywords only for someone like Fahey. But what is Fahey like? Ever the collector, he gets the first from his reading of Jean Paul Sartre and the second from the renegade urban planner and theorist Kevin Lynch, whose 1960 book, *The Image of the City*, became canonical for the theory and practice of participatory city planning (Klemek; Reitan and Banerjee).[2] These are my best educated guesses anyway. I have commented before that Fahey's writing can be incredibly allusive and secretive, as if up to something he doesn't want to spell out for you but he might not mind being asked about. It is an approach whereby one gets to have one's cake and eat it too: hodology and the edge might only be verbal flavorings and additives with which to tickle people's brains, or they might be a gateway to a mode of understanding what the human being is like, really like, in its natural habitat, so to speak. Well, the great thing about keywords is that they can be light and heavy at the same time, uttered quickly but conjuring worlds. This is what Fahey's stories of hodology and the edge are all about, fulcrums for heavy lifting.

Hodology and the edge are at one and the same time geographical and psychological concepts. Hodology concerns the emotional bearing human beings bring to their everyday, actual physical comings and goings (*hodos* = path), including the emotional relationship to everyday objects, be these objects noticed in passing or objects to which one has an established attachment. It is the idea that the totality of the human environment (hodological space) is so imbued. The "edge" is one term in Kevin Lynch's vocabulary of urban spaces. His book, replete with studies of hand-drawn "psychological" maps by city residents, was a highly influential attempt to say something about how urban dwellers actually live in their cities. Lynch proposes that all space circumscribed by a given city, about which people form a general image, can be divided up into discrete kinds of sites, each characterized by certain patterns of thought, perception, and behavior. Among these, an "edge" is a space between other spaces where normal patterns do not apply. "Hodology" and its variations (e.g., hodolog) are strewn across Fahey's early records and liner notes; the "edge" is something he picked up later, appearing for the first time in 1979, in his liner notes for his *John Fahey Visits Washington, D.C.* record. A defining link to Kevin Lynch is, I think, a hand-drawn map of Takoma Park by Fahey, which includes a mixture of vocabulary and ideas from Sartre and Lynch. The map only appeared posthumously in the endpapers of the Fahey CD box set, *Your Past Comes Back to Haunt You*. Perhaps the most evocative and significant use of the edge concept is in *How Bluegrass Music Destroyed My Life*, in a subtitled section — "Adventures on the Edge" — of the long, concluding chapter, "The Center of Interest Will Not Hold."

A particularly notable adventure on the edge occurs on Ritchie Avenue, in one of the segregated Black neighborhoods of Takoma Park, Maryland, where Fahey's friend Elmer Williams lived. According to Fahey, the two met one day (likely in the late 1950s) when Fahey was canvassing for records in Takoma Park on Sligo Mill Road in another of Takoma Park's segregated Black neighborhoods (Guerrieri, *John Fahey, vol. 1*, rev.). The Ritchie Avenue neighborhood, in other words, is an edge, bound on all sides by a majority white Takoma Park. Fahey's edge narrative builds to a description of a late-night outdoor party during which, at Williams's invitation, Fahey plays guitar for a while, while everyone dances to his music. I explore a number of meanings that accrue around Fahey's account, one of which is the way it works as a Fahey-approved folk festival that improves on the much-scorned Movement.

Fahey's "adventure on the edge" is part and parcel of his attempt to imagine a relationship between Blacks and whites that is free of pretense and slogans. This is what he seeks in his Charley Patton book and in the liner notes I discuss in chapter 4. In obtuse but unmistakable ways he tells us he thinks he has found it out there on the "edge": a hodological reset where people come together to authentically express what they authentically feel when they let go of the pretense and slogans of the era—from the pretense and slogans of Madison Avenue to the pretense and slogans of Black Power to the pretense and slogans of leftists who, according to Fahey, would rather twist the meaning of African American music than see what it has to say on its own terms.

The "reset" is not fully convincing. (It would have helped, for example, if Fahey had actually acknowledged Black writers on the subject. Works by Leroi Jones / Amiri Baraka and Julius Lester, both of whom were making their careers at the time Fahey was making his, would have been good to consult.) Fahey's account of the party is steeped in atmospheric, dreamlike imagery. It's an imaginative glimpse at a liberated future but fails because it is stuck in retrograde sentiment and depends on there being a Black segregated space to locate the imagining. Just as Fahey noted years ago it was too late to march for civil rights, he now says it's too bad that such communing as happened in the edge didn't happen more often.

If Fahey's texts are an extraordinary testament to the blinding power that emotional attachments have, they are also warning shots about what it means—for a reader, listener, spectator, consumer—to value expressed forms of feeling just because they are deeply felt. This is another trap to fall into in Fahey's writing. In his handling, the concepts of edge and hodology are ultimately levers that recirculate a malaise. The point of these ideas in Sartre's and Lynch's hands is that a person does not only project feeling out there into the real world. The real world is also a place where *other* people have their feelings for whatever reasons they have them. The idea is that this might be a starting point for making practical changes, given the illusions that purely emotional relationships can foster. For Fahey, though, these ideas at their best only model person-to-person relationships that make it possible for a John Fahey to commune with a living Elmer Williams, and for that matter a dead Charley Patton. They open no line of flight, no passage, from these small-scale interpersonal forms of communion to larger projects of social change, which in John Fahey's eyes are always suspected sites of co-optation.

It is one of the trickier aspects of Fahey's legacy that he claims not to have mixed music and politics. This is only partly true. It is belied by his songs for Martin Luther King Jr. I have also been arguing that there are aspects of some of his written texts that simply goad readers into putting the writing and the music together. In particular, his complaints about repressed emotion are lodged in a wider critique of crass commercialization and the warping of youth in capitalist society. So, to have said he aimed to play emotions and to have gone ahead and played them is to act politically in that context and, maybe hoping no one will notice, to enter the Movement through the back door. Fahey's tactics enact a point repeatedly made by Jacques Rancière about what he calls art's "aesthetic regime": the very attempt to create and reinforce divisions between different spheres of social practice—art, politics, economy, and so on—virtually ensures that attempts to define what art is will also create discourses about its relationship to those other practices.

Art in our time runs roughshod over conventions, wants to involve a greater palette of sensibilities and continually revolutionize what they can mean and how they can work. This means art is not autonomous but heteronomous, Rancière says, and will always return to the question of how it is to be sorted out from among other activities, a process that will bind them together in some way in the end. To play emotions, to play them in the society that you think finds them difficult, and to have a critique of why that society behaves as it does is to bump one's art against (or for) one's politics.

Listening Session Three

"Dance of Death" (*Dance of Death*, 1965)
"Dance of Death" (Live, *Andy Kershaw Show*, BBC, October 8, 1987)

"Tell Me, Who's Been Fooling You" (John Fahey, Elmer Williams, and "Kelly," recorded in Takoma Park, MD, 1958), http://digital2.library .ucla.edu/viewItem.do?ark=21198/zz000959dv

"John Henry" (John Fahey and Elmer Williams, recorded in Takoma Park, MD, 1958), http://digital2.library.ucla.edu/viewItem.do?ark =21198/zz000959hd

"John Henry (1)" (John Fahey, solo instrumental, recorded in Takoma Park, MD, October 1958) (*Your Past Comes Back to Haunt You*, 2011)

"When the Catfish Is in Bloom" (*Requia*, 1967)
"When the Catfish Is in Bloom" (Live recording, Swarthmore College Folk and Rock Festival, April 5, 1968, Swarthmore Reel 36 track 7)

"Fare Forward Voyagers" (*Fare Forward Voyagers (Soldier's Choice)*, 1973)

Because Fahey was so vociferous in excoriating the Movement and much too quiet about his dependency on it, the former has always been easier to spot. So it is in a headnote he wrote for "The Dance of Death," a song appearing on his 1965 album of the same name:

The Dance of Death is a European peasant song sung before lighting the bonfires on many a pestilent occasion. Quite naturally no record- ings survive of the original 12th century performances but they live on in the folk traditions of Takoma Park. . . . Joe Death heard the old massa gently strum this piece on an old baby's coffin while watching the mansion burn in 1865. Moved, the youth subtly shifted the rhythm to a more Afro-centric style and using the folk process, which he had learned from his father he changed the dirge into a dance. Many in Takoma Park recall seeing the old d**ky shuffling his feet and humming the only surviving song from the white slave tradition. The white slaves in America after their liberation . . . migrated to New York and Berkeley, and their descendants, yet living in their quaint shanties, are known as White Negroes or "hippies". The failure of American society to integrate these people into national life can only have serious consequences in the future, and this piece is included in hopes of increasing intercultural understanding and friendship of all people. (Fahey, liner notes, *Dance of Death*, abbreviation added)

Listen now to "Dance of Death." Is it the confidence with which Fahey plays this song on his record that upholds the intense and even ugly sarcasm of the headnote? As if his virtuosic playing somehow allows for it, or forgives it? The song is a difficult one to play. Fahey's tune is based on Benny Goodman's version of Louis Prima's 1936 tom-tom-propelled "Sing, Sing, Sing (With a Swing)." In Fahey's descending bass notes a listener can also pick up a bit of Camille Saint-Saëns's "Danse Macabre." Fahey rarely played this song live, although given his tetchy headnote, nothing would have been more fitting to play to an audience with which he was at "war" (chapter 5). The one live version that circulates among Fahey fans — played during BBC radio host Andy Kershaw's radio 1 session, in the fall of 1987 — is missing the difficult segment that Fahey plays on the album. About three minutes and twenty seconds into the album version, this segment includes a series of hammer-ons and pull-offs on the top string (the thinnest) that Fahey would have to be in good form to accomplish live *and* that would require a PA system sophisticated enough to transmit the full effect. On the record the effect is outstanding. Fahey's playing emphasizes a very jumpy rhythm that would go well with any twitching, lurching skeleton. ("Dance of Death" alludes to medieval and later allegory, depicting death as a skeleton leading a dance procession of people from all walks of life, be they peasants, princesses, or popes, illustrating that death is the great equalizer.) Only in this one segment, though, does the song's rhythmic drive devolve into the woozy spin that sends home the point of the danse macabre genre — we're all going down, people. Fahey's approach is exquisite. Nowhere else does he get the orchestral effect (a brassy, reedy big band effect in this case) he often claimed for the guitar.

Ostensibly, the point of the dance macabre allegory is that people are failing to take their lives seriously, or, they take them seriously but for the wrong reasons. This is what brings us to Fahey's note about the song, in which Movement sensibilities inaugurate a crisis around what equality means. What Fahey is doing in his note, obviously, is lampooning "Whitey," who is drawn to African American country blues, by flipping the script. For it is a Black man, Joe Death, who has adopted the song of the "white slave," Fahey's satirical rendering of white suburban hippies who imagine themselves to be victims, and whose rescue Fahey, again reversing the relationships, requires integration. (The use of "White Negroes" is a reference to Norman Mailer's 1957 essay of that name, in which Mailer defends white Americans' fixation on an urban Black underworld.) Note, though, that Joe Death is Fahey's minstrelized alias in the first place. Meaning to implicate himself in a complex, highly performative process of misrecognition, the point Fahey seems to be driving at is that Blacks are not the mere victims most white people make them out to be, and that white people are different victims than the ones they make *themselves* out to be. To wit, there are expressive traditions in Black culture not reducible to social and economic status; and white people who fail to get this are victims of their own ideological idiocy.

There is a sort of false equality at work, Fahey is hinting. But he has not quite worked out his meaning. One can raise questions about what he actually thinks about integration, which he will again raise in his later album *The Voice of the Turtle* (see chapter 3), when his notes worry about cultural homogenization and cultural loss. Again there is a reference—winking? ironic?—to the "d**ky" "shuffling" his feet, shushing himself in the presence of "old massa," and so on. Is this, for Fahey, how the "White Negro" secretly imagines African Americans? Is it Fahey telling us himself that it's perfectly cool to use such expressions because he secretly knows better? And what about "Blind Joe," Fahey's alter ego? "Blind Joe" takes his place in a complex history of modern white performers who developed a range of stylistic affinities to Black music and musical performers, from attempted imitation to denial or distraction (Mack). There is sufficient play in Fahey's meanings to consider that he was performing what Sumanth Gopinath has called "radical minstrelsy," a knowing, self-critical blackface that wants to weaponize it for antiracist purposes but, by the same token, also circulates the blackface trope for popular consumption. This is a dangerous game for Fahey to have played. In an interview given a few years before he died, he explains that "Blind Joe Death was my death instinct" (detectable notes of Patton's "uncanny" right there). "Blind Joe Death was also all the Negroes in the slums who were suffering. He was the incarnation, not only of my death wish, but of all the aggressive instincts in me. Initially he was everything that had to do with life and death that a person in our society is not supposed to feel. You're not meant to feel miserable in American society, you're supposed to keep the smile up. With Blind Joe Death I was secretly throwing hatred and death back in the faces of those people who told me I was bad and sinful because I had these feelings" (qtd. in Pouncey 27). In other words, "Negroes in the slums" and "d**ky" are vehicles for the expression of some feeling *Fahey* has? Note how quickly empathy and righteous anger about harm done to others turn into a self-absorbed interest in his own misery. Thinking back to previous chapters, whatever sympathy Fahey may feel for racially oppressed people, whatever validity there may be to his cultural/political critique of the happy American dream, whatever reasonable critique he may have of white mimics of Black music, these things go down the hole of his own emotional fixations, which are, after all, legitimate fixations when feelings are precisely what one is supposed to express. In the struggle for equality and freedom, in other words, Fahey wants justice too. His expressions fit comfortably within the parameters of the Movement as he internalized them. Recall from *Requia* Fahey's riff on the new social justice preachers: in his mind they dealt primarily with obvious forms of unfreedom, whereas the less noted form is the existential kind experienced by individuals. How easily these two modes have slid into each other, though, for Fahey experiences the social oppression of not being allowed to feel the feelings he has.

Now, there is another dance that interested Fahey, the one in which he participated on Ritchie Avenue in Takoma Park, and around which circulate some of the same concerns about race, equality, and emotion. What I would like to do is try for an imaginative reconstruction of what Fahey might have played that night. A close look at his description of what Elmer Williams was playing at the party, before Williams handed the guitar over for Fahey to play, reveals Williams was doing an Arthur Crudup "imitation." Fahey writes that since he knew how to play like that too, that is how his hour of playing began. As luck would have it, in 1958 Dick Spottswood, the record collector whom Fahey and Williams knew, recorded them playing Crudup's "Do You Know Who's Been Fooling You?" in Takoma Park. (Spottswood was with Fahey when they met Williams during a record-collecting trip to another segregated neighborhood of Takoma Park.) The song is available for public streaming in UCLA's online ethnomusicology archive.[3] Because the recording also includes an unidentified "Kelly," we don't know who is doing what. There is one vocalist, either Williams or Kelly, softly singing about a man

whose girlfriend was lured away by someone who has fooled her into thinking he loves her:

> Tell me, who? Tell me, who's been foolin' you?
> Tell me, pretty mama, tell me, who's been foolin you?
> Yes, you three times seven and you don't know what you want to do?

Two guitars, likely one played by Fahey, do their best to imitate Crudup's boo-
gie style, and someone is tapping their foot to the beat. No one seems especially confident. The whole performance is careful, studied, not wanting to
screw up in front of the tape recorder, which seems fitting, given Fahey admitting to feeling a little nervous during his "adventure on the edge."

Regardless, the song fits how Fahey describes the Ritchie Avenue party.
When Elmer Williams and Fahey first drive up, there is no one around. Elmer begins to play slowly but then speeds up. As we saw above, people come
out of their houses and start dancing. Chapter 6 reviews more of the details
and stresses what Fahey feels is the magic of the scene. But what might come
next after the Crudup imitation? Possibly "John Henry"? Fahey knew this
song too and recorded a few different versions. In 1958 Spottswood recorded
Williams and Fahey playing an instrumental duet of that song (also available
to stream).[4] They more or less follow Mississippi John Hurt's version, "Spike
Driver's Blues." Maybe the most memorable of Hurt's repertoire, the song is
rooted in a G chord but contains a short riff—B, Bb, B, G, E—that while
seeming like it might run off in many directions always hurries back to the
tonic G, shaping the song's sublimely prayerful groove. But in 1958 Fahey had
also worked out for himself a far different version. He announces it with a
couple of rapidly picked high notes to get your attention, like, say, an an-
noying railroad crossing signal might. Fifteen seconds' worth of that and
then the fingerpicked chords arrive, but not that distinguishing tonic G. The
chord is glimpsed but never comes to define the song; we hear only dissonance and variations on dissonance. It's a "rough cut gem," in Malcolm
Kirton's words: "The melody is in the key of G but the piece never settles into
the key center. Using partial chord shapes moved up the neck, Fahey centers the tonality of the third (the B notes), giving the entire piece an unresolved, off-kilter sound" (27). Given the dreamlike quality of the scene as
Fahey narrates it, perhaps he played the *traditional* version of "John Henry"
with the singular version of his own creation running hodologically in
his head.

The account of the Ritchie Avenue party is interesting because Fahey includes it as an example of the "edge." This concept, I have said, is of a piece

with his adjoining interests in the philosophy of emotional, existential human space: hodology. Hodology was meaningful enough for Fahey to have copyrighted the music on a number of his records under an invented "Hodolog Music" trademark: *Dance of Death, Requia,* and *Voice of the Turtle* are examples. With this as a provocation I want to pivot toward one of the organized music festivals at which Fahey played, and one "Hodolog" song he played there, "When the Catfish Is in Bloom." I'll say a bit about the song first.

The title "When the Catfish Is in Bloom" riffs on Jimmie Rodgers's "When the Cactus Is in Bloom." Musically, it is one of Fahey's triumphal, completely transporting guitar compositions. Listen and hear his capacity to create and pull you into a veritable sonic landscape, to envelop himself and his audience in a cascade of lush and, near the end, pounding sound. He is helped enormously by tuning his guitar to C modal: CGCGCC, a tuning that is big, moody, and rich in harmonic surplus. Over its seven-plus minutes Fahey plays for all he and his guitar are worth. The song is a great example of the influence of classical music ideas on Fahey, here a variation on the structure of the sonata form—introduction, exposition, development, and recapitulation of themes. The playing is stately and march-like at first, with a succession of pull-offs that sound like little drum rolls. It transitions into sunny banjo-like phrases, and at intervals is blanketed with deeply satisfying overflows of sound in and around the key center. Over the course of the song he varies his speed and volume, but always against the inevitable, amplifying drone of C notes. Fahey paints this song on an auditorium-size canvas and creates a virtual place for himself and his audience. It holds you there for what seems like the turning of a season.

This song might have been what Jerry Fogel, the Stanford University student and music reviewer we met in the introduction to part 1, was thinking about when he wrote that Fahey seems to be coming from a place of deep emotional experiences. I don't doubt it. "When the Catfish Is in Bloom" appeared originally on 1967's *Requia,* the Hodolog music album in which Fahey reports, in a rather self-serving fashion, his thoughts about the "social action theologians" and what might be missed if the idea of freedom pertained only to social struggle in the streets.[5] After the album came out, the song was for a time a regular feature of Fahey's concert repertoire. He played a rousing version at Swarthmore College's Folk Rock Festival on April 5, 1968. Students gave him a full thirty seconds of applause.

Fahey and at least a few people in his audience might have made the link between *Requia*'s notes and Martin Luther King Jr.'s racially motivated murder the night before the Swarthmore music festival. Song meanings change over time and space, for performers and for audiences, and surely this presented Fahey with an example right on his doorstep. Was April 5 the moment when he thought a song dedicated to King might be a good idea? The moment when marching might have made sense? It is impossible to say, but the thought arises nonetheless that Fahey's "hodological" feeling about the Swarthmore festival might have been tweaked. Fahey's audiences were almost always white, the last exception probably being the party on Ritchie Avenue (provided it actually happened) in Takoma Park. Would Fahey have attributed a little more meaning that evening to the whiteness of his audience at Swarthmore, a predominantly white liberal arts college with a primarily Black custodial staff? (After the weekend festival, the college, aware that King's funeral was to be held on Tuesday morning, canceled classes and gave staff the morning off. In the afternoon, the Swarthmore African American Student Society led a discussion session about race.[6] Black students were a small minority at Swarthmore in 1968, and their numbers were in decline.)[7]

Maybe Fahey had a different sense of what his performing was about this time. He does not say. On the audiotapes of Fahey's set you can hear him voice his concern that the set was short and that he had to leave the stage so that Joni Mitchell, the other headliner of the evening, could go on. He tells the stage manager that he could come back after her set and play some more. Apparently he did. Dave Huntington, the student reporter, writes that Fahey played until 1:15 a.m. "All semblances of a performance disappeared; formal relations between performer and audience disappeared. John Fahey was just playing and we listened. Finally bringing the evening to a close, he abandoned open tunings, tuned to the standard tuning and played a hymn: 'In Christ There Is No East Or West'" (Huntington). It was typical for Fahey to close with a hymn; he does it on a number of his records too. Did it feel different that time? Years and years later, in 2009, someone with the handle "Luke" posted an online remembrance of the April 5, 1968, concert at Swarthmore: "What a great show, i walked there from my home at the time. April 1968, sad time. Going to see John Fahey and Joni Mitchell was wonderful, a moment of truth in my life, came about that night. A moment of Change, became America. God bless John Fahey, a master of the guitar, may he be at peace and rest. Joni another time you saved us from our collective sorrow. America in her shame. A lot of us cried that night together with no one (we thought) to blame."

I think it is probably clear that there are arenas of meaning that simply cannot be pinned down, but it is just as probable that affects and ideas are passing close to one another, maybe even touching without knowing: thoughts and feelings in the mind and body of John Fahey tweaked who knows how on April 5, 1968, projecting toward and picking up on the minds and bodies of his audience that night, projecting their somethings toward him, and the ensemble of all that stored in the memory of "Luke" and other unnamed someones.

CHAPTER FIVE
Performance as War

"Turtles are my favorite animal," John Fahey confessed to a *Rolling Stone* reporter in 1970. "Everybody runs over them on the highway and that's why I want to kill everybody. That's *one* reason why I want to kill everybody" (T. Ferris 8). Well, a few years later, for the *Georgia Straight*, a counterculture newspaper in Vancouver, British Columbia, Fahey would explain in an essay of his own one or two of the other reasons. Is "explain" too generous a word, though? "Performance as War" begins easily enough but then devolves into total encryption. (Its less dense first part was reprinted by *Guitar Player* magazine as "Horizontal and Vertical Playing" a year later.) The essay is a crush of ideas, many of which struggle to survive in sentences that are dense, dense, dense. The tone is so uneven and leaden, it seems not the work of one author but many. The essay is college-boy arrogant, *Jeopardy*-smart, bratty, and utterly irresponsible in its provocations. The whole of it might be brilliant satire on a dim-witted culture or a tough-love manifesto on the zeitgeist fueled by some very earnest bookishness. It is bits of all these things. And whatever else it might be, it is, in methodological terms, a raid on the undergraduate philosophy syllabus (the Existentialists), a stealthy heist of Hegel and Heidegger, Nietzsche and Kierkegaard, Karl Jaspers and Walter Kaufmann. (Richard Wagner's writings on orchestra conducting are thrown in for good measure.) I say stealthy because not one of these figures is mentioned by name and very few of their quoted passages are presented as quotes; and because the ideas of these philosopher kings are like so many strings on Fahey's guitar, plucked, he imagines, so he might crush his loathsome audience. It might be, in fact, the world's first Existentialist murder ballad, and it is most certainly the first Hegelian interpretation of Charley Patton. Once inside "Performance as War"—itself walled in by advertisements for bell-bottoms, "Root" shoes, tips for natural living from *Mother Earth News*, and coverage of the developing rift between Timothy Leary, possible FBI informant, and the trio of Allen Ginsberg, Jerry Rubin, and (son) Jack Leary—you are in a centrifuge pressing you against the limits of your tolerance for high jinks, and all you can do is grimace while your reactions separate out.

Fahey begins as if it were Aggregate Execrable Nemesis himself at the lectern: "I, the writer, for reasons which will ultimately make themselves manifest, draw a distinction, at the outset, regarding the manifold aspects of guitar-playing, and composition, on the one hand, and on the other the ultimate sound and *Gefühl* [feeling] which is produced—by means of two definitions" (14). First, there is something he describes as "horizontal" playing, which is simply the action whereby the fingers of the right hand (or a pick held in the right hand) sweep across the guitar strings in order to sound them as such. Every guitar player must do this, but the greats—for example, Charley Patton when playing "Mississippi Bo Weavil Blues"—excel in "vertical" or "percussive" playing. In a motion perpendicular (vertical) to the plane of the fretboard, the strings are so vigorously pressed down or pulled up that "a snapping sound accompanies the tones" (14).

"Rhythmically," and especially when playing fast, Fahey explains, it is the feeling of that particular song that he is trying "to get." (Readers may want to listen again to "Charley Bradley's Ten-Sixty-Six Blues" and recall the discussion of it in the introduction to part 3.) More generally, though, the idea is that *performance is war*. In this war, the first thing you do is to "lay siege" to a song. Fahey wants—this is a boilerplate account of blues playing— neither to play the same song twice in the same way nor to play it exactly the way someone else does. "Rather," now enter the deathly dialectics of Hegel, "I try to bring life to a song, by means of Aufhebung" (14). "I lay siege to the song. I try to destroy its previous existence-identity with itself; by taking the previously-existing and destroying it with the Dasein of the moment" (14). Sometimes, Fahey muses, he is successful in achieving the new, um, design. But many times he fails. And that's fine, more or less. After all, his playing is sometimes strong and other times weak. What annoys him and brings out that inner killer is that the slavish public for whom he performs cannot tell the difference.

Read enough of Fahey, whether the album notes or the essays in *How Blue-grass Music Destroyed My Life* and *Vampire Vultures*, and it makes sense that he majored in philosophy while an undergraduate in college. References to the likes of Georg Hegel, Martin Heidegger, Karl Jaspers, and Paul Tillich pop up like mushrooms in Fahey's humid pages, first as a joke but then you realize he means it. It is no accident that these are the thinkers Fahey regularly deferred to. For all of them, the question of how, and why, to proceed with living, in full knowledge of one's finitude, is a prominent question. Since Hegel has already surfaced in the passage above, let's see what he in particular is saying that Fahey wants to make use of. Obviously it has something to do with overcoming "fixity," with a refusal to allow the perpetuation of the same. Why that refusal? The answer is partly to be found not in Hegel but in the history of blues playing revered by Fahey, the fact that blues singers performed their songs differently when they performed live. (Virtually the only way to hear a blues song played the same way, and repeatedly, is by playing the record it was recorded on. Blues records, we have already seen, are clearly valuable documents.) What draws Fahey to Hegel, however, such that his interest continues beyond the undergraduate years studying philosophy at American University, is the parallels he can draw between his experience of playing music in front of an audience, including his coming into being as a performer at all, and certain of Hegel's ideas about what it means to be and become in relation to other human beings. I should say that this is not a matter of being faithful to Hegel in general, whatever that might mean. It is more a matter of Fahey having found particular motifs he can use and running with them for a while.

John Fahey and the Philosopher Kings

A central question of Hegel's philosophy, particularly in *The Phenomenology of Mind*, is where self-consciousness comes from and what it needs to subsist. Let me develop this question and Hegel's thinking about it for a few paragraphs before digging further into Fahey's essay. Self-consciousness, Hegel argues, does not subsist on its own nor can it self-originate. Rather, it can only originate through engagement with external others, both nonhuman and human. This partly involves the transformation of external matter for human use ("activity" in Hegel's parlance), but more profoundly, indeed essentially, it involves engagement with another self-consciousness in the making. Self-consciousness, in other words, has its founding principle outside of itself. "Instead of an original self, to which the consciousness of an other, or the consciousness of otherness in general is added, Hegel tries to show that the consciousness of that other is the very condition for the emergence of an individual self—and, therefore, for any form of cognitive activity ever to take place" (Ferro 2). The nature of this engagement is one of negation, however. That is, self-consciousness comes to be by recognizing what it is not, and ruling it out, discarding and negating it. It is the "negative acknowledgement that I am not another" (4). Negation of the other so as to posit oneself is not a onetime act. If that were the case, this would be an admission that self-consciousness can self-subsist and be self-identical after all. Instead, "the self is a result of a process; it is itself a process, whose result is simultaneously a new starting point. Therefore, personal identity does not represent, so to speak, a safe harbor, or individual refuge against the otherness of the outer world. Personal identity is at first nothing more than a desire to be oneself, faced with a reality that is always something else," yet this very desire means that self-consciousness is a "self-moving entity, born out of the dialectical interchange of self-sameness and otherness" (5).

Walter Kaufmann, a favorite modern philosopher of Fahey's who wrote widely on Hegel and Nietzsche, and whose *full-page portrait* Fahey included in his guitar instruction book, *The Best of John Fahey, 1959–1977*, was a prime force in introducing postwar American readers to existential philosophies. (Fahey dedicated the book, I repeat, a book of instruction on how to play his guitar compositions, to Hegel.) Kaufmann emphasizes the meanings of the word "self-conscious" as a way to more intuitively grasp Hegel's meaning, as well as the link to Hegel's famous "master-slave" dialectic:

> It is relevant that the connotations of the term are different in English and German. While being self-conscious often means being unsure of oneself and embarrassed, *selbstbewusst sein* means just the opposite: being self-assured and proud. Of course, the primary meaning in both languages is the same: self-awareness. But while this sense is most important, the other connotations are relevant.
>
> As self-consciousness encounters self-consciousness, pride meets pride, and each resolves to destroy the other in order to grow in self-assurance. Each aims at the other's death and risks his life. . . . What matters to Hegel is the comprehension of one particular relationship between one self-consciousness and another, namely that between master and servant. He construes it, in the first instance, as the result of the fight. The loser prefers servitude to death.
> (Kaufmann, *Hegel* 152–53)

Alexandre Kojève, in his reading of Hegel, stresses that each self-consciousness, in requiring recognition of its value by the other, requires being recognized as the "supreme value." "Accordingly, their meeting can only be a fight to the death" (Kojève 7). (That is, it is not a question of fighting over each other's possessions. They do not each desire the objects desired by the other; they each desire the other's desire as such.) This idea is a restatement of Hegel's essential idea that self-consciousness is not self-originating. If so, it cannot also be self-valuing if it is to be certain of its value. To be certain requires recognition, and that certainty needs to be, as it were, absolutely certain. Only risking one's life will do. But inasmuch as one thereby risks having no life at all, one of these selves chooses to give in and become the servant of the other. Thus, Hegel's famous couplet of master and servant or, variously, master and slave, lord and bondsman. "This slave is the defeated adversary," Kojève notes, "who has not gone all the way in risking his life, who has not adopted the principle of the Masters: to conquer or to die. He has accepted life granted him by another. Hence, he depends on the other. He has preferred slavery to death, and that is why, by remaining alive, lives as a Slave" (16).

But right away things become more interesting. The master, now an ostensible "Being-for-itself," exists as such only "*in* the slavish Consciousness" (Kojève 21).

> The Master is fixed in his Mastery. He cannot go beyond himself, change, progress. He must conquer—and become Master or preserve himself as such—or die. He can be killed; he cannot be transformed, educated. He has risked his life to be Master. Therefore, Mastery is the supreme given value for him, beyond which he cannot go. The Slave, on the other hand, did not want to be a Slave. He became a Slave because he did not want to risk his life to become a Master. In his mortal terror he understood (without noticing it) that a given, fixed, and stable condition, even though it be the Master's, cannot exhaust the possibilities of human existence. . . . He is ready for change; in his very being, he is change, transcendence, transformation, "education." (21)

There is a great deal more to the *Phenomenology*, but these are the essential features concerning self-consciousness and identity that Fahey will riff upon (as he already did, albeit briefly, in his *Requia* notes), including who exactly is master and who is slave in his performance war.

"One must take a song and struggle with it," then. "Make it new," Fahey insists, or "the performance is mediocre" (Fahey, "Performance" 20). So, the first fight to the death is with a sort of external object. This is within Hegel's remit, as I just noted. Hegel extols human beings' transformation of the world in a way that confirms human values and worth. But Fahey admits only varying success. Most of his songs are "mediocre, in public or on record," he says. Consequently, his conscience is turned against itself—"offended," he says (15). With himself as the lesson in what can go wrong, he instructs other song composers to move beyond whatever unique pain has led them to write their songs. "But surely," Fahey imagines them objecting, "another person can't have THIS pain!"(15)—a uniqueness that they believe gives songs their life. Fahey responds, cribbing Hegel's own discussion of the problem with the word "this," "The answer to this is that one does not define a criterion of identity by emphatic stressing of the word 'this'" (15). If there is a something (pain) to return to, the point, Fahey says, is to do so in a way that overcomes it, that posits identity as a process, a movement (and a Movement, I am tempted to add).

If Fahey finds only variable success himself, what is worse is how the public reacts. Don't believe the congratulation of the public, "they don't know anything" (15).[1] Thus begins a long diatribe, a foreshadow of his screed against Berkeley "mellow" in *How Bluegrass Music Destroyed My Life*. Fahey rails against audience members expecting they can get to know him and be his friend, when really what they want is to drop his name at parties. "I have no desire to relate to them . . . on an individual basis. To me they are just the audience, a mass, a despicable object, the collective 'Other'" ("Performance" 15). Contemporary "groupies" have "no depth to plunge into, no commitments, or beliefs held strongly, with which one can toy" (15). "One must think of the audience as an invading army . . . to be slaughtered quickly, during a lyrical passage, or immediately after it, while they are in a state of torpor. Otherwise they get the upper hand" (15). In all of this, Fahey proclaims a veritable Hegelian ache to be recognized, *properly* recognized, by a *proper* foe, an enemy with commitments, beliefs. "Public performance must be seen in its essential constituents as a WAR" (15). There is no overcoming of this. And actually, what's to be overcome (or prevented) is the settlement reached in the master-slave relation. "It is the very overcoming . . . of that which is comprehended by the apparent duality of master-slave, the righteous warrior and the Enemy. At the end of each and every performance the Enemy must lay defeated at the foot of the stage. The performer must approach the podium with being-towards-death[2] for it may be, after all, that very performer who is vanquished at the end," falling victim (betraying oneself) to the audience's satisfaction with mediocrity (15).

What Fahey seems to fear most is that he will fail by coming to believe in the audience's approval. Wouldn't it be better to play for a *discerning* audience? An audience capable of deciding whether he is up to the musical task he has set for himself?

Here is how the musician would slay his audience, then:

The great artist must be pied-piper AND exterminator simultaneously. . . . His finale **must** create obituary. *Hold them firmly, terribly. One did not write them in jest or because he was at a loss how to proceed. He indulges in the fullest, the most sustained tone to express emotions in the adagio. The very lifeblood of the tone is to be extracted to the* *last drop,* **by** the performer **from** the audience. . . . *I arrest the waves of the ocean, but the depth must not be visible, or I stem the clouds, disperse the mist, and slow the pure blue ether and radiant eye of the sun. For this I put fermatas—sudden, long sustained notes—into my allegros. Ponder them here in the first announcement of my theme. Hold the long E flats firmly after the three short tempestuous quarter notes, and learn what the same thing means when it occurs later in the work, and at the ending (all is directed and in the service of that same ending).* . . . Music as revenge, as mass-murder, audience-o-cide. Breathing exercises help but they are not enough. (Fahey, "Performance" 15; italics added, bold in the original)

Fahey says not a word about it, but most of this passage—the part I have italicized—is taken from Richard Wagner's 1887 book *On Conducting* (see Wagner 31). It is the passage in which Wagner imagines how Beethoven might explain to a conductor his intent in composing a certain section of the C minor symphony (i.e., Beethoven's Fifth). But for one important change, Fahey drops Wagner's passage as is into his own text. Fahey's modification is that where Wagner imagines Beethoven wanting to extract the lifeblood of a particular tone "to the last drop," Fahey, armed to the teeth with his reading of Hegel, wants to extract the lifeblood of the audience to the last drop.

But lacking authentic recognition from his audience, which is always ready to settle for less than great music, preferring instead to be merely "mesmerized," Fahey continues to turn the knife:

My guitar is a device of execution, of willful mass murder, like the young man who disposed of so many good citizens and good students from the podium of a tower at a Texas University. Would that I had been born with a stronger physical constitution, such that I could have passed the draft exam, or the police physical. This paltry killing I do. It is not enough for me. So many are left over. Ah, for the days of Nazi Germany when a man could accomplish something of note. This music I play is paltry, stupid. These songs are not very good. Why then does the ignorant public praise me? What do they know? What do they think they know? It is in the execution, overcoming, the destruction of the song—not in the stupid bare fact that a song exists—that the merit exists. The public is worse than I am; they should all be shot. (Fahey, "Performance" 15, 20)

I presume these mordant historical references—to the Nazi program of systematic extermination, to the 1966 shootings by Charles Whitman on the

University of Texas campus — are there to shock Fahey's readers into acknowledging they do believe in something, they do have values and priorities, depth and commitments. Fahey does, anyway: there is for him something at stake in the cultures of music. And the love of "folk" music is a sign that something quite serious has gone wrong.

A moment ago we read Fahey stating that the public is worse than he is. But if he has not yet succumbed to the low expectations he thinks his audience has of him by creating low expectations of himself, what does he think his problem is? Why not proclaim victory and get on with it? Alas, the problem is deeper and infinitely more tricky, striking at the heart of certain postwar conceptions of art and artists, musicians and songwriters. The problem Fahey wants to name is that the arts, even for him, may not be the domain of authentic expression they are made out to be but might instead be domains of repressed feeling that actually occlude what their creators feel. If only Fahey would lay these ideas out straightforwardly, we might get to his thesis straightaway. Alas (again), he does not. But this may be part of his purpose; no doubt it is his purpose to make the reader work for it.

Immediately after the passage above, wherein the public is to be shot, Fahey launches into a strange, strange discourse on the human skull. If, right now, you are thinking, "But of course," you know your Hegel. The rest of us have to read, reread, and re-reread Fahey's essay until we decide that the non sequitur might not be Fahey's creation. It happens that in *Phenomenology of Mind* Hegel included a long section on phrenology, the (pseudo)science of reading skulls. In phrenology, the assumption is that the external features of the skull, its little bumps and depressions, express the inner lives, the passions, emotions, proclivities, and overall character of the person it belongs to. Nowhere does Fahey say that his disquisition on the skull comes from Hegel. He simply pastes Hegel's passage right into the essay:

> The skull-bone is not an organ of activity, nor even a process of utterance. We neither commit theft, murder, etc., with the skull-bone, nor does it in the least distort its face to suit the deed in such cases, so that the skull should express the meaning in the language of gesture. Nor does this existential form possess the value even of a symbol. Look and gesture, tone, even a pillar or a post stuck up on a desert island, proclaim at once that they stand for something else than what they merely are at first sight. . . . Doubtless, even in the case of a skull, there is many an idea that may occur to us, like those of Hamlet over Yorick's skull; but the skull-bone by itself is such an

indifferent object, such an innocent thing, that there is nothing else to be seen in it or to be thought about it directly as it is, except simply the fact of its being a skull. (Hegel 359–60)

Fahey does modify the second sentence to read, "For we neither play the guitar, commit theft, murder, etc., with the skull-bone" (20). But after that it's all Hegel's paragraph. Hegel's discussion of the skull is the central part of his lengthy refutation of phrenology, and an aspect of his critique of self-identity that we saw a moment ago. The mind and brain might be *associated* with the skull, but this does not mean the skull is directly involved in the formation of consciousness. In a neat pun, though, Hegel writes that "the poorer the idea we have of mind, the easier the matter becomes in this respect; for, in part, the fewer become the mental properties, and, in part, the more detached, fixed, and ossified, and consequently more akin to features of the bone and more comparable with them" (360–61). In other words, inadequate ideas and poor reasoning are, metaphorically speaking, ossifications, mere bones, inactive, and incapable of helping human beings become truly active. What is Fahey's interest in this passage? He is drawing on Hegel to remake his case that real guitar playing cannot result from low expectations, failing to "lay siege," and so on. The guitar cannot be played with ossified ideas.

The discourse on the skull in Fahey's essay, on the one hand, just confirms the idea that music should involve an overcoming of received musical ideas and drab audience opinions. On the other hand, it helpfully raises the question of what aspect of the inner life artistic creativity expresses and what values such creativity ought or ought not to be based on. The inner life, like the skull, is hidden. The possibility exists that not only is everyone's inner life hidden from each other, but also from themselves. The skull discussion also marks the point at which Fahey shifts to a more hurried and frenetic mode. He rushes through some core ideas of Karl Jaspers, returns briefly to Hegel, then Wagner again, and finally to Kaufmann ("my teacher"). These ideas are stitched together with awkward and obtuse sentences, but there is still the detectable flow of ideas.

Jaspers next, then. Here are the passages from Karl Jaspers's book *Reason and Existenz* that Fahey will quote, almost verbatim:

We always live and think within a horizon. But the very fact that it is a horizon indicates something further which again surrounds the given horizon. From this situation arises the question about the Encompassing. The Encompassing is not a horizon within which every determinate mode of Being and truth emerges for us, but rather that within which every particular horizon is enclosed as in something absolutely comprehensive which is no longer visible as a horizon at all.

The Encompassing appears and disappears for us in two opposed perspectives: either as Being itself, in and through which we are—or else as the Encompassing which we ourselves are, and in which every mode of Being appears to us. The latter would be as a medium or condition under which all Being appears as Being for us. In neither case is the Encompassing the sum of some provisional kinds of being, a part of whose contents we know, but rather it is the whole as the most extreme, self-supporting ground of Being, whether it is Being in itself, or Being as it is for us. (Jaspers 52)

What interests Jaspers is not unlike what interests Hegel. This is something like the question, Why would human beings not want to remain just as they are, content with their empirical existence as it appears to them and as they understand it in relation to all else in the world as it appears to them? A crucial part of Jaspers's answer is that philosophy makes it possible to think that there is and will always be a something just beyond what we accept as reasoned, settled knowledge; that a domain of unreason lurks just on the other side of reason and is the inextinguishable from which reason seeks to distinguish itself. It is this something, this territory, that makes thought itself possible, even though this condition of possibility cannot itself be known. The Encompassing, as Jaspers calls it, is in fact never empirically indicated; what Jaspers's concept expresses is the notion that there is always a something else to be gotten at. Without implying that Jaspers's ideas can be equated with Hegel's, they nonetheless have companionable aspects, such that one can imagine why Fahey puts these unnamed thinkers together. Later in his book, Jaspers writes, "I am not authentically myself if I am merely what I know myself to be. . . . Whenever I objectify myself, I am myself more than this object, namely, I am that being which can thus objectify itself. . . . But in such an object, I recognize only one side of myself, or myself in one particular aspect, but not myself. . . . I have at the same time, lost myself and substituted what I understand myself to be for what I can be" (73–74). This "Encompassing" notion of self as movement, as surpassing boundaries, detecting limits, and so on, is what attracts Fahey to Jaspers and what makes this passage admissible for Fahey's essay.

Now, let's return to Fahey, jumping in right at the point where he concludes his meditation on the skull:

Posterity will demonstrate [the capacity for violence among all peoples in all eras] as man approaches the Encompassing. The latter appears and disappears for us in two opposed perspectives: either as Being itself, in and through which we are — or else as the Encompassing which we ourselves are, and in which every mode of Being appears to us. In neither case however, is the Encompassing the sum of some provisional types of *extermination* a part of whose contents we know, but rather it is the whole as the most extreme, self-supporting ground of Being, whether it is Being in itself, or Being as it is for us *as we confront and annihilate the "Other."*

We always live and think within a horizon. But the very fact that it is a horizon indicates something further which again surrounds the horizon. (Fahey, "Performance" 20; emphasis added)

Noticeable at first is that Fahey inverts the order of Jaspers's passages. Where Fahey writes "extermination," Jaspers had written "being." And where Jaspers had finished one of his sentences with "Being as it is for us," Fahey adds "as we confront and annihilate the 'Other.'" Finally, where Fahey speaks of "posterity," man's approaching of the Encompassing, and the supposed revelation of permanent warlike attitude, it is extremely unlikely that Jaspers would find common cause.

Maybe what most attracts Fahey to the idea of the Encompassing is the suggestion that one always has to struggle against convention, against "horizons," the enclosures that "Others" keep imposing. "Music," Fahey immediately notes, "thus becomes the search for Lebensraum" (20). Fahey wants a good fight, as he has himself noted. He is interested in the very notion of the ineffable, for it indicates the necessity that one must become unsettled. He can join this idea to Hegel, concluding that a true unsettling involves victory over an opponent, who is also unsettled and, as we saw, makes ready to fight for their own ideas and convictions. In this, there is a certain joy. "At the limits of life's possibilities, as they appear, we must all come not to any heavy seriousness," Fahey states in the next paragraph, "but rather a complete lightness as the expression of our knowledge will come to us — The Dance. We must train ourselves such that our lives really feel like they are only beginning as soon as a difficulty shows up. Then, when life seems like at any moment, it may become Serious, heavy, desperate, we pass through such situations to an authentic soaring, the triumph of which is the Free Dance" (20). Turn to Jaspers's book again and we find this is no flight of fancy owing to Fahey. "At the limits of life's possibilities came not any heavy seriousness," *writes Jaspers*, who is summarizing the thinking of Nietzsche and Kierkegaard and noting that "both used the image of the dance" (43).

> In the last decade of his life Nietzsche, in ever-changing forms, used the dance as a metaphor for his thought, where it is original. And Kierkegaard said, "I have trained myself . . . always to be able to dance in the service of thought. . . . My life begins as soon as a difficulty shows up. Then dancing is easy. The thought of death is a nimble dancer. Everybody is too serious for me." Nietzsche saw his archenemy in the "spirit of seriousness" — morals, science, purposefulness, etc. But to conquer seriousness meant not to reject it for the thoughtlessness of arbitrary caprice, but rather to pass through the most serious to an authentic soaring, the triumph of which is the free dance. (Jaspers 43)

Jaspers's passage is all about what it feels like for thinkers like Kierkegaard and Nietzsche to experience original thought, to have broken through prevailing conventions, and to have grasped some sense of transcendence. This must be what it feels like, then, to "lay siege" to a song, to find that the struggle with the music — here maybe a further meaning to Fahey's "The Dance of Death" — yields to a sense of enlargement or transcendence when the struggle seems to be working.

The Heart Seeks a Fellowship It Cannot Accept

No sooner does Fahey seem to be saying something about the joys of struggle and the body rush of pushing through some boundary than the mood sours. Partly, the prose is to blame. It continues to be dense, arcane: "The law of 'this individual heart' is alone that wherein self-consciousness recognizes itself; but the universal and accepted ordinance has by actualizing that law become for self-consciousness likewise its own essential nature and its own reality. What thus contradicts itself within its consciousness has for it in both cases the character of essence and of being its own reality" (Fahey 20). Again, the rare reader might know their Hegel. Fahey has taken verbatim a passage from a six-page or so section of Hegel's *Phenomenology of Mind* titled "The Law of the Heart, and the Frenzy of Self-Conceit." Fahey follows up with two more paragraphs from "The Law of the Heart," word for word, save two modifications that yoke Hegel to Fahey's specific intent to skewer his audience and satirize "art."

"The Law of the Heart" is Hegel's screed against those who would be guided by feeling rather than reason in arranging their affairs with other human beings. For Hegel, whole epochs of human history, whole social and political formations, suffer such misguidance. The problem lies with persons who invest their thoughts and actions in their own self-certainty and self-validation, convinced they are themselves their own measure, and then believing all people should aspire to the same.

The passage Fahey quotes is not easy, but it is possible to get the drift, given where Fahey has already been. It worries that self-consciousness becomes self-satisfied and stops itself in its movement. What's in "this heart" becomes law, a pretended universal, an "ordinance." "Hegel," Judith Shklar explains, "was, in fact, obsessively irritated by the flourishing sentimentality of his own age. In art, in philosophy, and in religion 'beautiful souls,' worshippers of sincerity, and other types of self-cultivating sensitive spirits abounded. Hegel's response to all this was a sustained defense of sanity against what he regarded as pure lunacy" (107). Here is the problem:

> The man of feeling recognizes that one must follow rules in one's relations to other men, not mere impulse. The law he accepts is, however, of a very peculiar sort. It is the creation of his own feelings and it is defined by its utter hostility of all prevailing conventions and laws. In its overflowing concern for other men the heart calls out to all other people to follow their hearts also, and thus to free themselves from the social oppression which stifles individuality by imposing cruel and alien constraints upon it. These spontaneous expressions of the heart, naturally, give much pleasure. They "pass for a display of excellence" and show a fine concern for bringing about "the welfare of mankind." It would seem that the men of feeling must truly show their own perfection. (107)

But the law of the heart has no substantial content other than the bucking of convention. So, as soon as the heart's feeling becomes universal for everyone, and therefore the new norm, it is no longer the law of *one's heart*, no longer *one's own* possession. Then arises the feeling that one must distinguish oneself among others: the man of feeling "denies that 'his excellent intentions' could possibly be those of these 'detested and detestable' people. . . . Its concern for the liberation of others is a sham" (107–8). And there is a second problem. For Hegel, "there is an insurmountable contradiction between the 'heart' and 'law' of any conceivable sort. The heart stands for the supremacy of uniquely personal feeling, while law expresses general rules. . . . That becomes clear as soon as several hearts stake out their claims for general validity. Each insists on its own validity, but because of their personal character, each one of these laws of the heart is different. . . . The heart seeks a fellowship it cannot accept. It is not capable of the self-surrender that any law demands. Without that, a state of war, psychic and social, is inevitable" (108).

Fahey bends Hegel to his purposes in no uncertain terms in the last of the passages he steals from Hegel's "Law of the Heart" discussion. Here is Hegel, with Fahey's additions in italics: "The heartthrob for the welfare of mankind passes therefore into the rage of frantic self-conceit, into the fury of consciousness to preserve itself from destruction *of the audience, the Other*; and to do so by casting out of its life the perversion which it really is, and by straining to regard and to express that perversion as something else, *preferably in some art-form*" (Fahey, "Performance" 20). The first of Fahey's phrases is by now easy to account for. As he has already made clear, he wants to fend off and claim victory over the destructive force of his *audience, the Other*, who wants to share feelings with him, become his friend. They are indiscriminate, detestable. But he goes a step further, proposing to call "art" that which allows the men of feeling to avoid the truth of the situation they are bringing about—that is, the fallacy that durable social relations can be based on sentiment at all. Sentiment, with "art" as its coin, just pushes the law of the heart ever further toward its contradictions. If we can recall Fahey's comments about his audience early in the essay, he brooks no audience that passes off its confused feeling as authentic, defendable feeling. Fahey wants no part of any of it. Insofar as he is himself an artist, his is an art against the arts of the law of the heart. His art wants to cut through sentiment, through self-satisfaction and self-deception, through repetition and habit. We are back to the thesis, then, that "performance is war." It's a brilliant selection from Hegel on Fahey's part, if anyone can be enticed into battle and put the pieces together.

The World Wants to Be Deceived (Also, All Will Be Well)

Fahey will take no time to tarry with these ideas and spell them out more fully. It is just not part of the performance. He prefers to have thrown down the gauntlet and just let the reader figure it out, while he keeps moving forward. But you can also see the essay is ending as you turn the pages; and you can see Fahey just sweating out the last few paragraphs, which by now are mere sticky notes about dance. Fahey reminds us that dance stands for the joy of undertaking original thought and creativity. But now this joy seems called into question if dance, as we saw, is also an art, where art masks the social contradictions that emerge when all individuals aspire to originality. This is just a glimmer of where Fahey might be going when invoking dance again, for he quickly inserts a few words about dance (*qua* rhythms) as a metaphor for all of life (which *is* rhythms). In a passing derogatory note, whose racism he presumably disavows (note Fahey's single quotation marks around the term which I've abbreviated), and which strongly echoes the sentiments of his high-school-era essay, he arrogantly chides that dance is ubiquitous—it's not just "'doing the n****r' to a rock accompaniment" but even Beethoven considered his music the "apotheosis of the dance." (It was actually Wagner who wrote this of Beethoven's Seventh Symphony.) He throws in a note about dance as both vertical and horizontal motion, linking this in the same breath to the two axes of transcendence (vertical and horizontal) argued for by Jaspers (see Schrag), implicitly cuing the horizontal and vertical modes of guitar playing, with which the essay actually began: ergo guitar playing is also . . . dance. There is, in short, no escape from dance, as the multitude of blink-and-you-miss-'em metaphors and references imply. Dance—cue the potentially proliferating dialectics of "The Dance of Death"—signals not originality but its opposite, ubiquity.

If dance, we can reasonably think, is mentioned as an example of "art" into which the law of the heart is displaced, it quickly metastasizes into all of human activity and all of human desire, enveloping even Fahey. He too is a human, after all; he too experiences and manifests rhythms. It becomes impossible to name what art should be about and not about. It becomes impossible to say that art is a special domain of human activity, more truthful than all others. If this is what Fahey wants us to see, then Hegel's law of the heart does not limn a *choice* of action, with Fahey having chosen smarts and truth over sentiment and cover-ups. The law of the heart really is the dominant state of affairs, "the spirit of the age" as such, in which Fahey himself is caught up. Putting this in theoretical/psychological terms, there is no real escape from self-deception and no real escape from sublimating it. Moreover, it is not a stretch to hear Fahey saying that to choose a life of art at all, even an art against "art," is to continually take on, and possibly take in, the prevailing conceptions of what art is about: sentiment, feeling, and at least some desire to share these and have them matter, and to let them shape affairs. So, Fahey might not think himself to be the exception to the law of the heart that he claimed having been, or at least seemed to have claimed, just moments before. One begins to get the sense that Fahey might be thinking that to have chosen being an artist (musician) is to be pulled into a domain (the impossible law of the heart) in spite of himself. He is as much a product of his times as anyone else is.

In the essay's final moments Fahey slips in a last quote from an unnamed "my teacher," actually Walter Kaufmann: "Mundus Vult decipi" (Fahey 20)—the world wants to be deceived. Truth is way more complex, much too frightening, than most people can deal with. People prefer the "bad faith" of lowering their expectations (see Kaufmann, "I and You" 9). Is Fahey imputing the behavior of others here? Or his own? No time to decide, because another quote quickly follows. This is also from "one of my teachers," Hegel again, and still unnamed: "We must have the conviction that it is of the nature of truth to prevail when its time has come, and that truth appears only when its time has come—and therefore never appears too early, nor ever finds the public is not ready for it" (Fahey 20). (This quote is from the end of Hegel's preface to *Phenomenology of Mind* [29].) But can Hegel be believed? Given time and tide, do the right ideas usually win out? If Kaufmann is right, would believing Hegel's dictum be self-deception? And how about these, Fahey's parting words in "Performance as War." Do they mean to mock, or something else? "Indeed, the negative has been annihilated in the verticality of the Aufhebung in the GREAT RHYTHMS of the ETERNAL DANCE. We must all learn this dance—sooner or later. For the Dance does not cease. The Dance continues, the sun rises in the East. *All will be well. All will be well.* For many of us the GREAT DANCE has only just begun" (20; emphasis added).

No worries! "All will be well. All will be well"—a paraphrased line from T. S. Eliot's "Little Gidding," the fourth of his *Four Quartets*.[3] Fahey implies in this last passage that the yearning for "transcendence" is real, trustworthy; that the war of values *will* fade into the serenity of eternal time, opposites *can* unite. Does he mean it? Or had he quoted Kaufmann to warn us of such distracting sentiments? *There, there. Now, now.* All is not well. All will not be well. So what if the sun continues to rise? Performance is war. So. Believe what you like, but at least tell me so we can have the battle. End of essay.

Some Reactions to Fahey's Associative Style of Philosophy

Earlier I wrote about Fahey as a collector of texts and likened "Performance as War" to a raid on the Existentialist syllabus, an effort to intellectually source and authenticate his presumably authentic feelings. The two purposes come together in the dualistic style of the essay itself, a narrative arc whose associative flow of (intellectually sourced) ideas we can more or less follow and, at the finer textual scale, where (authenticating his feelings) Fahey occasionally substitutes his own words and intentions for those of his sources. The narrative arc, to recapitulate, goes like so: the guitar player, to play well, should understand that songs are not meant to be played the same way over and over again. The point is to develop them and make them something new that they were not when you started. As in guitar playing, so in life: you won't know who you are and what you can become unless you are willing to become different from what you are now. But you cannot do that by copying someone else or believing you have it completely within yourself to become different. Your capacity to become different involves an incessant process of differentiating yourself from others. And of course other people might be doing the same. A huge problem results from this, which is that being in society requires a lot of compromise. This is tantamount to putting the brakes on every individual's continual becoming. And this presents a problem, too, which is that those activities (the arts) devoted to expressions of individual becoming take place in a context where compromise is necessary, which means that creative activity might be a ruse, a site of self-deception and lowered expectations. (There is yet another swipe at the "folkies" and "false gregariousness" in that last thought.) If one wants to be an artist of some kind, or even a becoming self of any kind, there really is nothing to be done about this other than to explode in fits of rage or other emotional outbursts, or to admit that in the end, life is just like that. One can still get by, of course; scale back one's expectations, and enjoy the "dance" of human foibles. Fahey adapts this overall message to his own purposes by taking a sort of middle course. He warns that he is prone to impulsive feelings of rage but is aware that he cannot act on these feelings without bringing harm to himself. He calms himself down with the thought that all will be well, but you won't know which is the truer, more lasting feeling: the rage or the calm. If "Performance as War" is a kind of confession, then, you won't hear from him what he is actually confessing, other than the ambivalence of feeling.

Readers who can put together these pieces, or just figure out there are differently sourced pieces making up the essay, might be aided in understanding what Fahey is up to, to the extent they already have models for this kind of approach in Fahey's eclectically, associatively sourced music compositions. In contrast to Fahey's music, which on its face is nonrepresentational, it is another thing to be faced with "Performance as War," which is representational and which purports to tell his audience what his music is about. Why be so obtuse about it, though? Some years before, in liner notes to his *Yellow Princess* record, Fahey writes that the more truthful he is, the more unpopular he will be.[4] If that is in fact true, then the obtuseness of "Performance as War" follows as a reasonable compromise: he can keep talking, which the admiring audience wants him to do, and they won't necessarily know what he's saying. Fahey can be happy getting closer to the truth, which not being just one thing anyway, involves a great deal of ambivalence and confusion; and the audience can be happy knowing the Fahey mystique lives on. While it is true that he derides his audience quite clearly in the essay, less clear is the intellectual justification and the literateness with which he goes about "Performance as War." It is clarity on *that* score that I am saying ushers in the essay's obtuseness. This doesn't mean he is not having any fun with his text. But this is not a case of "stuplimity," as we saw in the previous chapter.

Do we need reminding, though, that this essay is just another side of John Fahey? That there are only sides? (Another is revealed by his comments during his Swarthmore College performance in 1968: "The only time I like to play," he tells the audience, "is when I'm doing something new or playing for other people" [Huntington 1].) This fact ties back to the value Fahey has learned in letting his "sides" show at all—back to the postwar aims of self-expressive writing through to the Movement era that, among those other values concerning social justice and social change, encourages a continual process of self-exploration and experimentation. Let me raise the question again, then, of where Fahey sees himself in the "age" during which this essay falls. One can make the case that all this value placed on self-expression produces a certain inertia of momentum in the essay. Fahey gets on a roll with his feelings, and before you know it, wham!—we are reading about the effectivity of Nazi kills, campus shooters, and Army soldiers, and Fahey's . . . wait for it . . . envy of them. You can laugh it all off, very nervously, and say, well, here is another instance of Fahey mouthing off. But we must notice one thing, that prime targets of violence in America, African Americans, are missing, along with the weapons: no police dogs, no fire hoses, no national guard, and so on. Here, as if having invented political correctness for himself, Fahey's romp shows some sensitivity, and a little consistency too, not that this makes his other choices less egregious and irresponsible. At the same time, he also shows how difficult it is for him to acknowledge at any length actual violence against Black people, and most especially his own complicity with it as a beneficiary of school and residential segregation, and as a believer in the secret world of African American lifeways, which depend on the actual spatial separation that segregation instantiates in the first place. Fahey invented none of this complicity. It was there before he was born. There in his education. There at home. There in the thrill of record collecting and "folklore" fieldwork. It was there, as Aldon Morris argues in his important essay, in the educational legacies of even the most ardent white progressive intellectuals, like the enormously influential C. Wright Mills (who would have nodded in approval at several of Fahey's writing junkets), who did not take racial oppression seriously as one of the consequences of American modernity, nor take Black thought or Black people seriously as a source of social critique and political action (see Morris). What is curious about Fahey is that his idiosyncrasies make his complicity a more complicated affair. Never does he seem *satisfied* in any thought he has, never at rest with any conviction, any commitment, any privilege. Everything seems like a game and not a game at the same time. If there is a warrant for disappointment in Fahey, that is it. If there is a warrant for finding inspiration in the writerly Fahey, because he was not just one thing and could change, as one finds inspiration in his music, well, that might be it too. In the matter of where Fahey sees himself in the Movement age, it is not that he rejected his times. (I think of one of his comments that the 1960s had no effect on him, which is yet another ruse.) Rather, it seems to me he perpetuates the moment at which many kinds of broad social changes begin—that is, the moment of widespread discontent (e.g., Blumer). Many of his discontents, as I have been attempting to show, were shared by others. But they did not solidify into an ideology or a single, committed course of action. John Fahey represents something like one of the Movement's moments of emergence that the Movement continued carrying along with it, as if he were in it yet out of step with it at once.

CHAPTER SIX

Some Music. Some Dancing.
Some Unusual Intermingling.

In John Fahey's writings, telling you how he feels, how he feels about his feelings, and what other people think about his and their feelings might be the single most repeated, underlying, and organizing idea. Some of these writings—"My Dear Old Alma Mater," for example—assert personal feelings without necessarily looking to justify them. The justification is implicit, already underwritten by a particular conception of self. Fahey came of age during the protracted historical moment when the capacity to represent, care for, and manage feelings is a significant marker of the proper form of self-actualizing individuality demanded by liberalism. It is a mere swerve from there, as Fahey demonstrates in his "Communism" essay, toward one of the injunctions of new left cultural politics and Movement values more broadly, that one must lay hold of feelings the dominant culture wants you to repress, in order to speak authentically and seek out your fellows. "The leitmotifs that dominate The Movement," wrote Paul Jacobs and Saul Landau in 1966, "extend far beyond politics. . . . To be in The Movement is to search for a psychic community, in which one's own identity can be defined, social and personal relationships based on love can be established and can grow, unfettered by the cramping pressures of the careers and life styles so characteristic of America today" (4). Included in the Movement, as I have already pointed out, are not just the organizers and activists but "unaffiliated supporters, who outnumber by the thousands, and perhaps even hundreds of thousands, those committed to specific groups." These are the "basic strengths" of the Movement (6). So, plenty of room for Fahey, supporter in spite of himself.

That emotions about music so often stand at the center of Fahey's writings is due in part to his being a musician and a scholar of music. Music and musical tastes are a special case of the postwar discourse about selves and bonds that form among selves. They are important ideologically in liberal societies such as the United States because they are a vehicle through which individuals can exhibit tolerable forms of rebellion, dissent, and resistance to conformity—together with the expression of concomitant feelings, be these anger, alienation, stolen moments of bliss or what have you (see Medovoi). As many scholars have noted, the popularity of the 1960s' folk and blues revival among white audiences, including the rise of individual stars and cult favorites, emerged in this nexus (see Cantwell *When We Were Good*; Hale *Nation of Outsiders* and "Romance of Rebellion").[1]

John Fahey is part of these legacies, drawing on and being drawn on, not body and soul, but piecemeal as circumstances become available. There is the sense in Fahey's writings, though, that his piecemeal affiliation is itself a matter of emotions — that is, something about emotion is already going to preclude him from full-on identification with, as he put it, Berkeley "mellow." *Theory* of emotion, in other words, is also what the Fahey project is about, not only the amok-ness of the feelings per se. This sense, if we follow not only Fahey's "Performance as War" essay but also his book on Charley Patton and certain aspects of the liner notes I treated in chapter 4, flows from the notion that any social formation that gels around shared emotions cannot be trusted. It is extraordinarily difficult, we hear Fahey complaining, to form social relationships on the basis of private emotional experiences.

In this chapter I want to recount how this sweeping genre of emotion, because it is already sanctioned as a kind of social and political currency, leads Fahey to certain texts, and especially concepts, that give standing to emotion as a founding principle of human being and becoming. Fahey seems to have found to his liking a few different works in this vein. Sartre's *Being and Nothingness* and *The Emotions* introduce the curious vocabulary of "hodological space" (roughly, the imbuing of geographic space with human meaning and intention). The urban planner Kevin Lynch and the environmental psychologist Stanley Milgram developed the idea that individuals could make "psychological maps" of cities. From his studies Lynch concocted a typology of spaces, including the notion of "edges," that I think had a special appeal to Fahey. These concepts of hodology, psychological mapping, and the edge were in a way keywords or, as I call them in the introduction to part 3, fulcrums for the leveraging of a large variety of observations and claims, including Fahey's attempts to reimagine relations between whites and African Americans. I want to underscore that these concepts are not just about emotions. They concern putative qualities of geographic space and seem — seem to Fahey, that is — to provide a way to cut through the public/private, social/personal dichotomies that limit the value of feelings in the social arena. In other words, these keywords hint that one's feelings are not simply one's own but are properties of the shared world itself, as Fahey perceives them. In Fahey's handling, I argue, these key ideas lend support to the notion that our shared reality is always more complex than it seems on the surface. These ideas are thereby easily recruited to fantasize about alternative, veiled worlds, and of course a hidden African American world, available for discovery by uniquely feeling (white) people, whose emotions are "authenticated" by their appreciation for and possible participation in those marked-off recesses.

One way to think about the arc that I will trace in this chapter, which culminates in the above notion of an alternative world—a reconstituted Movement culture, I believe—is that Fahey is reconsidering his own thesis in "Performance as War," in which nothing of substance can come from the "law of the heart." Maybe something can come from it after all. A number of things are at stake in this new possibility, however, not least the fallacy that social relations are so structured by feelings in the first place that the topic of "feelings" is the most important place to start in reforming them. Excessive trust in feelings obscures important problems around race that these feelings only think they might solve. Furthermore, because emotion narratives are socially sanctioned, they have a performative element. They *play* to the value placed on emotion and feeling that is already in circulation. I will not pretend to tease apart actual from performed feeling, but instead will put together some propositions about the work done by Fahey's engagement with the idea of emotion's significance. Most especially this work seems to be about privatizing his public experience, and then expecting that it might establish the grounds for a new public. While we could say that everyone's experience of public spaces and public events is a private one, Fahey goes further. He seems to want to reinvent and re-present the public on his terms. It is easier and less lonely this way to imagine that there are others who *feel as I do*, as if to posit—as John Fahey seems to have, by the end of this chapter—"We feel, therefore 'We' are."

Bluegrass and Suburbs Destroyed John Fahey's Life

It is best to get this discussion going by taking a step back to ask how, in the first place, Fahey came to be interested in the raw feelings that seem to be at the center of certain strains of rural American music. Here are the issues: What exactly does he think authorizes his own attraction to African American country blues, when he is generally critical of the manner through which white people's attraction to this music arose (except of course his own)? And what problems will Fahey encounter in claiming the more authentic kind of reaction for himself? The questions emerge on three accounts: (a) it is not clear what the basis is for authentically felt emotional attraction to the country blues; (b) if the feeling is authentic, how can this be communicated without falling into the very clichéd expressions that raise doubts about genuineness in the first place?, and (c) the country blues is an art form no longer popular in the culture that originated it. It is, Fahey writes, a musical remnant. The art form of country blues and the contemporary feeling for it are possibly both anachronistic, unless the case can be convincingly made that they are not.

The section heading above alludes to one of Fahey's books. In it is the story of his conversion to an appreciation of, as he saw them, raw, primal emotions in rural American music. "One day in 1954 or '55," an adult Fahey recalls of his fifteen- or sixteen-year-old self, "I was listening to radio station WARL, Arlington, Virginia" (Fahey, *How Bluegrass* 247). As Fahey describes it, to some degree it was a typical day, marked by the feeling of broken, middle-class promises but also shaped by the opportunity that music provides for forming friendships. (In the case below, Fahey writes about his first hearing of a bluegrass song. It was just a year later that he hears the country blues for the first time. The reaction was much the same.)

When I first started listening to this station there was an afternoon show called "Town and Country Time." The DJ played country-western records . . . Eddy Arnold, Webb Pierce. People like that. No bluegrass. None. I was still an innocent. I didn't know about bluegrass music. Yet . . . I was still reasonably happy. Even though I was unhappy. I was loved. I had friends. I was one of the crowd. . . . We were terribly lonely. And we were all excessively social. We were aggressively social. We were compulsively social. (247)

. . . Because almost all of us had "family problems." Divorces, mainly divorces. But some of our parents were criminals . . . and we didn't see them for a long time. Didn't have anybody to counsel us. To understand us. . . . When we got together—us kids, we were all in our teens—what we did was we got together and talked about the hillbilly hit parade we heard on WARL. . . . That show was very important to us. It is hard now for me to believe just how important that show really was to us. (248)

. . . So you might say that me and the other kids were "thrown" together (Heidegger). WE needed each other. And a connecting link. WARL was that connection. . . . That's how important it was. I'm perfectly serious. And you could say . . . the reason why we discussed the virtues of this or that record—was to feel something good. Rather than the despair we felt as a result of the stupid and reckless activities of mom and dad. . . . Anyway, one day the format changed. WARL hired a new guy named Don Owens. AND the programming changed. (249)

. . . But I didn't care about the change. I hardly noticed it. Until one day Owens did this crazy thing which I could in no way have anticipated. (252)

Fahey then describes Owens playing an old 78 record: "Blue Yodel Number Seven," by Bill Monroe and the Bluegrass Boys.

Then I heard this horrible, crazy sound. And I felt this insane, mad feeling. Neither of which was I in any manner acquainted. It was the bluesiest and most obnoxious thing I had ever heard. It was an attack of revolutionary terrorism on my nervous system through aesthetics. . . . I went limp. I almost fell off the sofa. My mouth fell open. My eyes widened and expanded. I found myself hyperventilating. . . . It was like I had woken up to a new and thrilling and exciting horror movie. . . . I had to hear that record again. (253)

Prompted by the experience, Fahey meets the local record collector, Dick Spottswood,[2] and enters the rarefied world of record collectors and the pavement-hitting practice of collecting. The experience of repeated listening was transformative. Note how Fahey's account becomes hyperbolic but also musical, rhythmic, as he pounds out phrase after phrase, each more outlandish than the last:

Yes, bluegrass music made me into a monster. Filled my head with unecological and un-PC concepts and thoughts and desires and reaction formations and obsessions and sex mania and deviousness and Oedipus complexes and inferior complexes and incorporealities and alligators and snapping turtles. (254)

Bluegrass music and blues are full of anger and fear and anxiety and trembling and hostility and propaganda and . . . well, mostly aggressively angry sentiments and stuff. . . . [Bluegrass music is] unhappy music. Discontented music. Nihilistic music. Atheistic music. Terroristic music. Godless music. Irresponsible music. Uncanny music. Sensual music. Unbridled music. Troubled music. Distressful music. Harassing music. Agitating music. Panic music. Demoralizing music. Tormenting music. Instrumental music. Shocking music. Browbeating music. Unfriendly music. Outlaw music. Gloomy music. Heartaching music. Lamentable music. Desolation music. Pagan music. Death music. Electric Chair music. Castrating music. Sadistic music. Nazi music. And bluegrass music gives you liberal ideas, perverse cravings, makes you horny, angry, antisocial, neurotic, criminal, reptilian, sociopathic, lonely, unhappy, un-PC, EVIL. Know what I mean? If you're ever somewhere and you hear some maniac playing minor thirds on a mandolin against an E-major chord on guitar—run. It's bad ecology man. . . . Bluegrass music is the music of PAN. (265)

So, here is a litany of virtually satanic emotions that defy the middle-class injunction that we should keep our shit together at all times. Robert Cantwell would say these are the proper emotions belonging to bluegrass, because of the essential antimony between "wish fulfillment and nightmare" structuring it (*Bluegrass Breakdown* 216). Here, though, nightmare wins (not that Fahey did not want it to be so). Fahey wants us to know that his feelings are genuine because they literally threw him sideways, with a force great enough to cut through the "good" group feeling he had developed with his teen friends. This force singles him out; it individualizes him and his body. It is a musical flash flood stripping him of his old identity and leaving the detritus with which to form a new one. The writing imitates the qualities of the experience too; it becomes musical, "autological," a term (virtually homophonous with "hodological") Fahey also used in his writing. An autological signifier contains the meaning it expresses. That is, the passage tells about the feeling of having one's head filled emotionally while also being a passage that fills one's head with emotional descriptors, arrayed no less in a series of short, pummeling musical phrases.

The point is that Fahey wants us to know that his feelings about the song are of the moment, and an utter surprise, in no way depending on some prior knowledge of or affection for them. For all intents and purposes, they have no context other than what seems to him to be radio randomness. A year later, and now earnestly into record collecting, Fahey had another such conversion experience at the hands of a record, this time a record in the country blues tradition. He and Spottswood found a copy of "Praise God I'm Satisfied" by Blind Willie Johnson. In a 1992 interview with Dale Miller, Fahey, aged fifty-three, recalls the experience for a writer. "We played it and I had this visceral reaction. I almost threw up. I said, 'Please put on some Bill Monroe records so I can get back to normal.' But here's the trick: by the end of the Bill Monroe record the Blind Willie Johnson thing was still going through my head, and I had to hear it again. This time when I heard it I started crying. I couldn't stop it. It was the most beautiful thing I'd ever heard. (Long pause) That's really strange isn't it?" (qtd. in D. Miller 45). A few years later Fahey reported to another journalist, Edwin Pouncey, "It was some kind of hysterical conversion experience where in fact I had liked that kind of music all the time, but didn't want to. So, I allowed myself to like it" (Pouncey 25).

Readers of histories of blues music will immediately recognize a trope at work in Fahey's reports. It is more or less the same kind of thing found in the writings of W. C. Handy, John Lomax, and many a folk music aficionado too. This is the trope of the conversion experience. In Handy's autobiography it appears in the passage where he recounts being deeply affected the first time he hears, from a distance, the blues being played on a guitar in an empty train station in Tutwiler, Mississippi, around 1903. Other writers have their own remembrances, just as Fahey now has his. All of them say, *I am the sort of person stopped in their tracks, felled, by music.* And not just any music, nor felled in any old way. Here, after all, is a genre of music, blues, associated by definition with the spontaneous emotional outburst of the musician, who is himself taken over by the music (e.g., Calt), transmitting his affect to Fahey on the opposite side of the record player, now having his own spontaneous outburst. It is all quite standard, including the widely known value judgment—repeated down the long line from W. C. Handy to Son House and now Fahey. This judgment pronounces the blues are a secular music, versus the sacred songs played and sung at church.

What to make of this? On the one hand, Fahey's language demonstrates he knows how a certain game is played; he knows how to signify in self-mythologizing fashion the trope of blues "authenticity" (see Mack). On the other hand, communicating feeling requires a language after all, and language is not just about using words. It is about the multiple modes of verbal communication: words, yes, and also idioms, tropes, and narratives. Fahey's version of the conversion story is replete with feelings that are not "nice"; he admits to feeling things that put one at risk of being an outcast. Now one can say that even this is another trope, the hallmark of the badass blues musician, who not only feels intensely but has particular, ugly feelings that can ambush anyone who gets too close. In Fahey's recounting, therefore, it may not be possible to sort out what is genuinely felt, if by that we mean strictly personal, and what is a contrivance. There might be no other way than contrivance as the way to convey personal emotional states; there may be no reason to doubt that, as Erik Erikson suggests, emotional states are already public, social. Asking about Fahey's authenticity, then, is too constraining a question in the first place. The important question is what stories *about* feelings are doing and how this links up with the *claim* that these feelings are authentic, amid a field of inauthentic ones, and why that matters. The specific answer Fahey seems to be going for is one that makes authenticity retroactive, after the fact. That is, have your feelings given you the power to act upon others, let alone yourself? Have they shown you were susceptible to change, such that prior flows of feeling have been altered? Have your feelings enabled you to attract other people to you, to form bonds of some kind with them? What, ultimately, will make those bonds trustworthy?

A caveat. One's bid to having emotionally stood out from the pack is more effective if it can be demonstrated that you come from an environment where true feelings are either suppressed or channeled into becoming the good "worker," "parent," "teacher," and so on. (Recall part 1.) The suburban environment, in other words, figures into Fahey's account of himself. In letters Fahey wrote, and in interviews he gave, in the decade before his death, he is blunt: he plays emotions and these emotions have (at least) to do with the suburbs. Here, first, is Fahey the player of emotions:

> I do not, and have never thought of myself as a "folk" musician or a New Age musician, guitarist or sympathizer. I despise all "revivalists" of folk music, and I despise all "New Age" music. . . . Also, I have never used my music or stage or anything to push some kind of politics or ideology or religion or whatever. What I have always tried to do is very simple and there is no reason to make it complex. In all my music, I have never tried to do anything except express emotions, sometimes very dark emotions, depression, hatred, etc., in a coherent musical language. (Fahey, "Letter to Bill Belmont")[3]

> When I play, I very quickly put myself into a light hypnotic trance and compose while playing, drawing directly from the emotions. In fact, I would go so far as to say that I am playing emotions and expressing them in a coherent public language called music. (Fahey, "Letter to Ron Cowan")

Below, the player of emotions places them in a geographic space, the suburbs. Describing what he was trying to do in the late 1950s when he started composing, Fahey explains to fellow musician Stefan Grossman in 1982:

> The more I played the guitar the more I began to really love the guitar and to love virtually any kind of music that anybody played well on guitar. . . . I was trying to put together some distant music, I was thinking mainly of Bartok as a model, but played in the finger picking

pattern, which I still use. So I was trying to put those things together into a coherent musical language which people would understand and it worked pretty good. Everybody else was just trying to copy folk musicians, I wasn't trying to do that. I was using them as teachers for technique but I was never trying to be a folk. How can I be a folk? I'm from the suburbs you know. (Fahey, "An Interview" 9)

Fahey is quite direct with another interviewer, Jason Gross, about what this means. Referring to suburban "folk revivalists" and what they might have done, he states: "The suburbanite who's singing someone else's tradition . . . can't figure out how to express himself on his own. It might be interesting if they expressed the anguish of the suburbs but they didn't. It would be authentic if that's what a suburbanite talked about and sang about. The pathos of the suburbs or whatever [laughs]. But they didn't do that. Believe me, there's a lot of pathos there but instead they adopted other cultures' music which they didn't know anything about. They didn't do a very good job. I never understood that" (Fahey, "John Fahey"). From John Fahey's account of his conversion experiences and from his being a player from the suburbs, we learn something about what he thinks distinguishes himself from other musicians and what makes his emotional style, and expression of emotion as such, especially noteworthy. From "Performance as War," which I discussed in the previous chapter, we also get a glimpse of how Fahey's background in philosophy lends intellectual support to his emotional "worldview." But now we are at an impasse: Why are emotions there at all, so that they can assume a protean importance in human affairs and in the lives of individuals?

Hodological Space

The stress Fahey places on the suburbs is a good light in which to cast his adoption of a spatial/emotional vocabulary he found in his academic pursuits. It is this vocabulary—"hodology," the "psychological" or "mental" map, and a kind of place called the "edge"—that Fahey uses to develop a narrative of the suburban experience. One might say he depended on the very obscurity of this vocabulary to signify the authenticity of his feelings, as if to say he is onto something original and true *because* it comes from an environment that tends to be thought of as producing only copies, banalities, and falsehoods. In the next few pages I explore the intellectual sources of these ideas and their adaptation by Fahey. A point to keep in mind is their suggestion to him of an alternative reality that can be revealed, of hidden aspects and deep recesses of the mind and the ordinary world outside it that can be recovered and shared. These ideas, in Fahey's reckoning, suggest a way to render a much enlarged self, a self that is not simply made up on one's own but appears on a larger canvas, coming from sites and situations outside the private sphere of the mind and body.

I will start with the most basic of these notions, Sartre's idea of "hodological space," because of the presumption of universality it contains. A discussion of Kevin Lynch's notion of the "edge" follows. The "edge" is a more specific kind of space, a world between worlds. My sense is that Sartre and Lynch are linked for Fahey, a telling example being the "psychological map" Fahey drew of Takoma Park, Maryland. (Both Sartre and Lynch were interested in how their ideas could be rendered cartographically.) I'll conclude with a story Fahey tells about Takoma Park, "Adventures on the Edge," where we can see very plainly the role Fahey's spatially informed imaginary plays in imagining that right next door lies a "lost black folk world" ready to be rediscovered (Lorenz 250).

The word "hodological" appears in numerous places in Fahey's writing, especially the liner notes, which we will see below. The word is never defined, only used; dropped in as a bit of esoterica from nowhere in particular, but signaling Fahey as a holder of secret, arcane knowledges. It seems highly likely, however, that Fahey picked it up from Sartre's *Being and Nothingness*, with which he was enamored, according to an old friend (see Lee). What, then, does Sartre say about it? "The point of view of pure knowledge is contradictory," Sartre writes in that book. "There is only the point of view of engaged knowledge." My knowledge is only ever in this, my body, which I have never been without. "This amounts to saying that knowledge and action are only two abstract aspects of an original, concrete relation" (Sartre, *Being* 407). "The real space of the world," Sartre continues, "is the space which Lewin calls 'hodological.' . . . A pure knowledge in fact would be a knowledge without a point of view. . . . But this makes no sense. . . . Knowledge can be only an engaged upsurge in a determined point of view which one *is*. For human reality, to be is to-be-there; that is, 'there in that chair,' 'there at that table,' 'there at the top of that mountain.' . . . It is an ontological necessity" (407).[4] Having more than once written that he learned his ontology before his epistemology, it makes sense that Fahey would find Sartre's idea appealing (e.g., Fahey, liner notes, *John Fahey Visits*). The hodological has a more precise meaning, though. "A being is not *situated* in relation to locations by means of degrees of longitude and latitude. He is situated in a human space" (Sartre, *Being and Nothingness* 372)—that is, a space full of "being-looked-at or as a being-looking-at . . . according to whether the Other is an object for me or whether I myself am an object-for-the-Other. Being-for-others is a constant fact of my human reality, and I grasp it with its factual necessity in every thought, however slight, which I form concerning myself. Wherever I go, whatever I do, I only succeed in changing the distances between me and the Other-as-object, only avail myself of paths toward the Other. To withdraw, to approach, to discover this particular Other-as-object is only to effect empirical variations on the fundamental theme of my being-for-others" (373; see also Mirvish).

Hodological space is also, insofar as I am a "being-for-itself," tool rich, with significant implications for the temporality and geography of the body: "Objects are revealed to us at the heart of a complex of instrumentality in which they occupy a determined *place*. This place is not defined by pure spatial coordinates but in relation to axes of practical reference" (Sartre, *Being* 423–24). "Each instrument refers to other instruments, to those which are its *keys* and to those for which it is the *key*. But these references could not be grasped by a purely contemplative consciousness" (424). The space from instrument to instrument "must be cleared" (424). "The space which is originally revealed to me is hodological space; it is furrowed with paths and highways; it is instrumental and it is the location of tools. Thus the world from the moment of the upsurge of my For-itself is revealed as the indication of acts to be performed; these acts refer to other acts, and those to others, and so on" (424). For this reason, hodological space concerns more than that which is presently perceived; it concerns the future of the For-itself. Sartre will also say that, on these bases, "my body is everywhere in the world . . . coextensive with the world, spread across all things, and at the same time it is condensed into this single point [the body] which all things indicate and which I am, without being able to know it" (419–20).

Finally, hodological space is a space filled with objects that hail us in determinate ways, that make the world difficult, that bring forth emotion and impel us to potentially transform the world. Sartre explains this in his short work, *The Emotions: Outline of a Theory*, itself explained in the translator's introduction (available to Fahey) to *Being and Nothingness*. "One can draw up a 'hodological' map of our *umwelt*," suggests Sartre in *The Emotions*, "a map which varies as a function of our acts and needs. Only, in normal and adapted action, the objects 'to-be-realized' appear as having to be realized in certain ways. The means themselves appear as potentialities which demand existence" (57). The world might thereby appear "strict and narrow" (57), with "decoys and traps scattered around here and there" (58). "This world is *dif-*

ficult," and we perceive it as such (58). This understood, "we can conceive of what an emotion is. It is a transformation of the world. When the paths traced out become too difficult, or when we can see no path, we can no longer live in so urgent and difficult a world. All the ways are barred. However, we must act. So we try to change the world, that is, to live as if the connection between things and their potentialities were not ruled by deterministic processes, but by magic" (58–59). Emotive behavior "seeks by itself to confer upon the object, and without modifying it in its actual structure, another quality, a lesser existence, or a lesser presence (or a greater existence, etc.). In short, in emotion it is the body, which, directed by consciousness, changes its relations with the world in order that the world may change its qualities. If emotion is a joke, it is a joke we believe in" (60–61).[5]

It is undecidable whether the music of whole albums in which the liner notes reference Sartre's concept is an intended expression of hodological space; whether certain songs, because of their titles—perhaps "The Thing at the End of New Hampshire Avenue," "View (East from the Top of the Riggs Road / B&O Trestle)," or "Commemorative Transfiguration and Communion at Magruder Park"—are also so intended. Albums whose liner notes are rich in geographic invention (e.g., *John Fahey Visits Washington, D.C.* or *The Yellow Princess*) might also be informed by the hodological idea but do not say so directly. Then there are songs so directly evocative of geographic space that a hodological sensibility would seem to underlie them. Such might be the case with the thunder claps, the passing trains, and the bird whistles of the extraordinary "A Raga Called Pat, Part II" and with the singing bridge of "The Singing Bridge of Memphis, Tennessee." For a time in the 1960s, Fahey even registered his copyright with BMI as "Hodolog Music." Such is the case with the album *The Voice of the Turtle*, subtitled "a musical hodograph."[6] It might be best to think of the notion of hodological space as in a sense underwriting the many geographic referents Fahey was prone to invoke. It would thus signal a broad emo-geographical sensibility.[7]

Consider, too, that a hodological experience materializes in Fahey's very use of the word "hodological." Here is an excerpt from the liner notes Fahey wrote for his album *Days Have Gone By*:

Texarkana, it should be observed, is rather a schizophrenic city in view of the fact that half of it is located in Arkansas and half of it in Texas. . . . Yet, it has a peculiar charm of its own. There are several factors contributing to its uniqueness, among them the often ignored fact that it could not have a peculiar charm which was not its own, since its peculiar charm must . . . find its ground of being in the place (hodologically speaking) in which that charm of which we are speaking is located, and of course . . . that place of which we are speaking . . . is identical with itself, and not identical with anything else. . . . Were it to have a particular charm which was not its own, Texarkana would not in fact be Texarkana because . . . it could then be some other city. (4, 6)

In one sense, what Fahey is doing here is a Charley Patton–like bringing together of "various unrelated portions of the universe"—Texarkana, hodology, some philosophy-speak about the identical—in order to entertain his audience, by using ridiculously pompous language, or by the enticements of playful non sequiturs, verging on the *stuplimity* of going on about seemingly nothing, as we saw in an earlier chapter. But aren't the liner notes themselves rendered a hodological object too? The notes are a thing to be experienced as nonsense for a 1960s' audience that may already be thinking about the world as a duplicitous place to be. The notes, in their flesh, confirm it. In this way, Fahey can draw readers close while at the same time staying a step ahead, because he has not revealed the philosophical basis of their connection.

But it is not long (the next paragraph in fact) before Fahey draws his readers' attention to a familiar situation whose absurdity—purposeful, planned racial segregation—he seems to want to pay closer attention to. He begins with a digression on the various toxic names given to African American neighborhoods, which I again abbreviate, before then very elaborately describing the euphemism of the "other side of the tracks."

At this point I should like to make another digression, in the interest of Volkspracheology. A definition of terms is I feel, that is to say, I think both necessary and infertrogracious. "Quarters" in the state of Mississippi is functionally equivalent to other local substantives such as "N****rtown," "S****ytown," "C**nville," etc. The same is true in Arkansas. But in nearby Texas towns, the designation of the areas in which Negroes are found residing are (to be more precise) to be for the most part found residing (allowing for discographical/hydrological discrepancies) the term used by both Negroes and whites is "the flats." . . . Some of these are not only not flat, but convex, concave, and concupiscible as well as concourse conduplicated, somewhat condyloidally. In the LBJ ranch and radio station region, the term used is of course the "colloured section" for obvious reasons.

Such areas are for an equally obscure reason, almost uniformly located, by first . . . locating a pair of metallic (sometimes four) girders running parallel and at right angles to "the quarters." These girders are generally the demarcation line which separate the "quarters" from the sections of these towns. Unfortunately, the writer must express his ignorance of the nature or purpose of these girders. . . . This unusual form of hodological town planning seems indigenous to the South. But unfortunately the writer is unable to account for it. (6, 8)

Of course, Fahey has exactly given his accounting of it. The reasons for this form of town planning are hodological; they have something to do with racialized emotions. There is some feeling too that things don't need to be the way they are: if there is nothing discernibly practical about segregation, maybe segregated neighborhoods do not need to exist. The absurdity, then, is in Fahey's text just as, and because, it is out there in the world itself.[8] But just when it seems he might go somewhere with this insight, tacitly confirming that he uses racist terms as smelling salts to shake white people up, he tells a bawdy little "blues" joke about out-of-towners coming to town for some "jelly roll"—that is, sex. What should the reader do now? Metaphorically walk on by or pause over the fact that a joke is being told that depends on the Black slang that segregation helps preserve? In effect Fahey disrupts the flow of his own critical thoughts, and in a flash switches his point of view to engage in a bit of "light talk" about race that comes off as immune to criticism. The writing refuses to acknowledge the consequences of what it noticed about racial segregation and racism, and therefore it appears that the situation is of no real concern to its author.[9] That is one reading, with loud echoes of what we saw in the chapters of part 2. We can also relate the text directly to the period during which it appears, which once again is the era of civil rights, the Movement, the folk and blues revival. From this standpoint, Fahey appears concerned but uninvolved (in civil rights) while also being involved (in folk and blues) but unconcerned in the typical middle-class white way. Here then is a way to publicly acknowledge the seriousness of racism while clearing a path toward thinking about it on his terms.

Edges and Psychological Maps

Notice in Sartre's discussion, he mentions the possibility that a map of hodological space could be made. Such a map would show the hodological existence of the human being in geographical space and would reveal the attractions, repulsions, and emotional/magical transformations of our lived geographies. Sartre and Kurt Lewin, the social psychologist from whom Sartre got the idea, were not the only ones to think along these lines. In 1960, Kevin Lynch published what would become a classic book, *The Image of the City*, in which the notion of the cognitive or mental map figures heavily. Philosophy was not his motivation; he was a planner interested in making cities more humane. His research asked participants in his planning studies to respond to questions and create sketch maps of images, valued landmarks, everyday paths, and so forth associated with different cities. Later, in a quite different field, environmental psychology, the related idea of the psychological map appeared, inspired directly by Lynch. The psychological map was notably promulgated by Stanley Milgram and Denise Jodolet, for purposes of developing an urban social psychology. Even Erik Erikson announces the need for a new spatial sensibility in 1968's *Identity: Youth and Crisis*. "The traditional psychoanalytic method," Erikson writes, "cannot quite grasp identity because it has not developed terms to conceptualize the environment." Tradition, dictating the environment as an "'outer world' or 'object world,'" cannot take account of the environment as a pervasive actuality" (24). But the environment does not simply surround us. It is in us. "From the point of view of development," Erikson hypothesizes, "'former' environments are forever in us; and since we live in a continuous process of making the present 'former' we never—not even as a newborn—meet any environment as a person who never had an environment. One methodological precondition, then for grasping identity would be a psychoanalysis sophisticated enough to include the environment; the other would be a social psychology which is psychoanalytically sophisticated; together they would obviously institute a new field which would have to create its own historical sophistication" (24).

Sartre was deeply influential for Fahey, but it seems there was a broader movement toward space anyway that Fahey might have encountered in his reading. He was sufficiently motivated by this to draw maps of Takoma Park (see figures 2 and 3). These maps were only published after Fahey's death. He apparently referred to them as "psychological" maps, an indication that he might have encountered Milgram's work. But there are several places on the maps denoted with Lynch's "edge." Because of what is also on the maps, a variety of existentialist moods, it seems likely that these are hodological maps in the Sartrean mode too.

Kevin Lynch came to the study of urban space as a planner who had once studied with Frank Lloyd Wright and who had become critical of the osten-

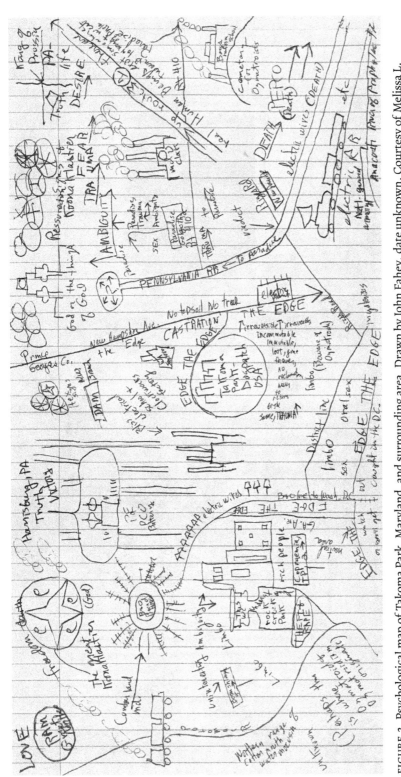

FIGURE 2 Psychological map of Takoma Park, Maryland, and surrounding area. Drawn by John Fahey, date unknown. Courtesy of Melissa L. Stephenson.

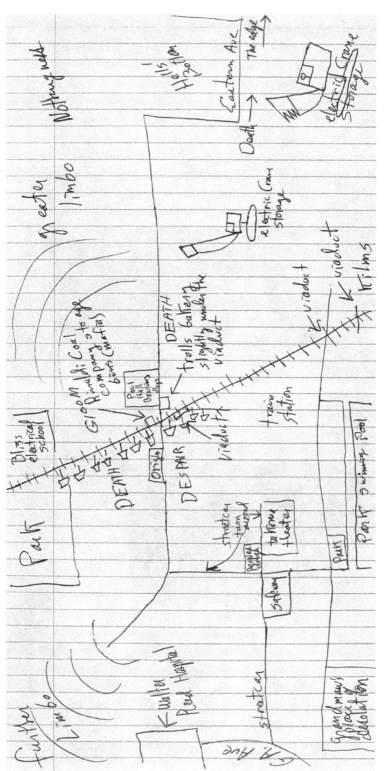

FIGURE 3 Psychological map of Takoma Park, Maryland. Drawn by John Fahey, date unknown. Courtesy of Melissa L. Stephenson.

sibly rational, economistic approaches to planning that came to dominate the field in the early and mid-twentieth century (see Banerjee and Southworth). "We are concerned here with the psychological and sensual effects of the physical form of the city," Lynch wrote in an early statement, irrespective of "functional effects" such as job security, social groupings, and housing quality and of "adequate quantities of the environmental elements" such as houses, stores, and "playfields" (Lynch, "Notes" 135). It isn't that functions and elements of these kinds were unimportant; it's that other functions and other elements required notice. Lynch asks, "What is the effect on us of all that we sense while we loiter or bustle through the city streets and squares? What can we do to make this flow of stimuli more satisfying, more inspiring, more humane?" In *The Image of the City*, he turned these questions into a fully developed analytic scheme.

> Looking at cities can give a special pleasure, however commonplace the sight may be. Like a piece of architecture, the city is a construction in space, but one of vast scale, a thing perceived only in the course of long spans of time. City design is therefore a temporal art, but it can rarely use the controlled and limited sequences of other temporal arts like music. On different occasions and for different people, the sequences are reversed, interrupted, abandoned, cut across. It is seen in all lights and all weathers.
>
> At every instant, there is more than the eye can see, more than the ear can hear, a setting or a view waiting to be explored. Nothing is experienced by itself, but always in relation to its surroundings, the sequences of events leading up to it, the memory of past experiences. . . . Every citizen has had long associations with some part of the city, and his image is soaked in memories and meanings. (1)

That said, Lynch quickly followed these opening paragraphs of his book with the caveat that an American city pleasing to the senses from end to end is nearly unheard of. Most Americans have no idea what such a thing could even mean. They are well acquainted with the dirt, the monotony, and the ugliness and have scarcely a sense of the "potential value of harmonious surroundings" and of what such surroundings would mean for daily life or as a "continuous anchor for their lives" (2).

To a large degree, Lynch argued, humans are hostage to their own adaptability. Unlike animals, which have an instinctual orientation to their environments, humans learn to live in a variety of surroundings. We can therefore do without, so to speak; we can persevere, unaware of what we are missing, unless basic requirements go awry, such as a failure to have any clue as to where one is. In that case, primal responses kick in. "To become completely lost is perhaps a rather rare experience for most people in the modern city. We are supported by the presence of others and by special way-finding devices: maps, street numbers, route signs, bus placards. But let the mishap of disorientation once occur, and the sense of anxiety and even terror that accompanies it reveals to us how closely it is aligned to our sense of balance and well-being. The very word 'lost' . . . carries overtones of utter disaster" (4). It is in this context that the "imageability" of the city becomes so important to Lynch. A clear, distinctive image of one's city, as a whole and in its parts, lends coherence and intelligibility to individuals and to the collective.

At the same time, "there is some value in mystification, labyrinth, or surprise in the environment," so long as the "basic form or orientation" is not lost: a person needs to be able to get out of the labyrinth. "The surprise must occur in an over-all framework; the confusions must be small regions in a visible whole. Furthermore, the labyrinth or mystery must in itself have some form that can be explored and in time be apprehended. Complete chaos without hint of connection is never pleasurable" (4–5). The value of mystification points to the fact that city inhabitants must be participants in creating the image and meaning of the space in which they live. Its meanings should not be final or decided ahead of the experience of space. "What we seek is not a final but an open-ended order, capable of continuous further development. . . . The environment suggests distinctions and relations, and the observer—with great adaptability and in light of his own purposes—selects, organizes, and endows with meaning what he sees" (6).

Lynch's aspirations as a planner steer him away from an overemphasis on individual differences, however.

> Any given form, a fine vase or a lump of clay, will have a high or a
> low probability of evoking a strong image among various observers.
> Presumably this probability can be stated with greater and greater
> precision as the observers are grouped in more and more homoge-
> neous classes of age, sex, culture, occupation, temperament, or
> familiarity. Each individual creates and bears his own image, but there
> seems to be substantial agreement among members of the same
> group. It is these group images, exhibiting consensus among signifi-

cant numbers, that interest city planners who aspire to model an environment that will be used by many people. Therefore this study will tend to pass over individual differences, interesting as they might be to a psychologist. (7)

Note how the open-endedness of meanings now sits awkwardly with Lynch's rigidly devised social groupings. There is no express awareness that individuals belong to more than one "class" simultaneously, nor much interest in how these classes arise and relate to each other, and what hierarchies and relations of power certainly result. Nor how social structuring processes are used to individuate people in the first place (the "hard worker," the "good family man," the "loyal wife," etc.). Ultimately, Lynch's interest is not in individual meanings at all, or much in the supposed class groupings even. Lynch's interest as a planner who is going to help cities develop their imageability is really in the forms and images of forms that, he argues, precede the meanings created around them. The point is for the planner to guide the form of the city, including various forms *within* the city, and to help educate the citizenry's senses so that meanings can accrue around urban forms. "So various are the individual meanings of a city, even while its form may be easily communicable, that it appears possible to separate meaning from form, at least in the early stages of analysis. This study will therefore concentrate on the identity and structure of city images" (9).

Toward this end, Lynch has to find out what images of a particular city residents have formed. But which residents and why? All the participants in the case studies presented in *The Image of the City* were drawn from the "professional and managerial class," although he does not say why. It might be that this is the group to which he has ready access. It might be, as Stanley Milgram hypothesized in 1970, that it is white, middle-class residents in particular who are imagined by Lynch to have the most comprehensive sense of the cities they live in (see "Experience"), and, while Lynch cites the occasional female participant, it is surely white males who compose the majority of the managerial and professional class he studies.[10] In any event, Lynch is clear that he has little doubt that this group's identification of the dominant "landmarks," "edges," "paths," and other features (see below) of the cities studied—Boston, Jersey City, and Los Angeles—would be shared by most city residents. His only disparaging comment is reserved for his brief report of the results of "street interviews" in Boston and Jersey City, the purpose of which was to get a sense of the different regions of these cities and what demarcates them from each other. The respondents' answers, Lynch writes, had "class overtones" and devoted "exaggerated" attention to the "upper-class" areas of their respective city (68). Yet, he offers no comment when respondents identify areas that are socially undesirable, dirty, and so forth. It is not out of the question that Lynch is strongly hinting that a middle-class, white norm is structuring his sense of the reliable informant and consequently the good city.

For Lynch, city imageability implies that the contemporary city ideally can be grasped as a whole. But it is a new kind of whole too. "Primitive man was forced to improve his environmental image by adapting his perception to the given landscape. He could effect minor changes in his environment with cairns, beacons, or tree blazes, but substantial modifications for visual clarity or visual interconnection were confined to house sites or religious enclosures. Only powerful civilizations can begin to act on their total environment at a significant scale. The conscious remolding of the large-scale physical environment has been possible only recently, and so the problem of environmental imageability is a new one" (12–13).

At stake is how planners and urban dwellers alike are going to reckon with this relatively recent capacity of "civilizations" to rework their environments on a large metropolitan scale. Like any other kind of form of which we can have an image (a vase or a lump of clay), the "metropolitan region"—information overload and anonymity, per Milgram, aside—has become a "functional unit" in which daily life is lived (13). Lynch's view of this daily life is extraordinarily romanticized and aestheticized. That is to say, his interest in the aesthetics of urban form is read back into what he thinks the city is actually like: "By the intensity of its life and close packing of its disparate people, the great city is a romantic place, rich in symbolic detail. It is for us both splendid and terrifying. . . . Were it legible, truly visible, then fear and confusion might be replaced with delight in the richness and power of the scene" (119–20). There is no link here back to the social "classes" and the individuals within and across those classes, where daily life of quite other kinds—oppression, marginalization, resistance, and dreams of revolution—is lived. The "image of the city" is an epistemology steeped in whiteness.

What kind of city images, then, are we talking about? Lynch, together with colleagues, developed questionnaires, interview protocols, and a sketch mapping technique for his professional and managerial class participants. Based on some combination of these responses, the suggestive content of the research protocol itself, and the researchers' own field trips, Lynch and colleagues discerned five elements of the city image, including the "edge," which Fahey apparently picked up on:

> *Paths* are to a large degree self-evident. They are the customary "channels" along which people move, frequently or just occasionally. They could be "streets, walkways, transit lines, canals, railroads." (47)
>
> *Edges* demarcate boundaries and breaks but also signify where different areas join. "Such edges may be barriers, more or less penetrable, which close one region off from another; or they may be seams, lines along which two regions are related and joined together." They are important for people in "holding together generalized areas, as in the outline of a city by water or wall." (47)
>
> *Districts* are subsections of city whose interiors have a "common, identifying character." (47)
>
> *Nodes* are "points, the strategic spots in a city into which an observer can enter, and which are the intensive foci to and from which he is traveling." They might be "junctions . . . a crossing or convergence of paths, moments of shift from one structure to another," or sometimes simply a street corner or square where people tend to hang out. (47)
>
> *Landmarks* are "usually a simply defined physical object: building, sign, store, or mountain." They are singled out from among the multitudes of objects in order to confer some kind of identity to an area or to suggest to residents or travelers a general spatial ordering and structure to the city. (48)

Lynch cautions that in a particular study these elements must be understood in a relative, not absolute, way—one person's path might be another's edge, and so on. Elements also interact and overlap with each other. "Districts are structured with nodes, defined by edges, penetrated by paths, and sprinkled with landmarks. If this analysis begins with the differentiation of data into categories, it must end with their reintegration into the whole image" (48–49). The analysis, however, is an amalgamation and an abstraction; there is no one person for whom the objective "whole" actually exists. Lynch's vocabulary is presented as practical, experiential, but also neutral. That a whole other lexicon of urban space might arise from other groups of people based on their histories and experiences—for example, of confinement and fear, of dispossession and forced movement, of arrested motion, of underground, surreptitious, and overt resistance, and, no less, of prevented actions and sites that were not to be—has no place in Lynch's reductive aspirations (see McKittrick; Shabazz).

John Fahey's Psychological Maps of Takoma Park, Maryland

Take some time to pore over the maps of Takoma Park and its surrounding area, drawn by John Fahey. These maps appear for the first time in the post-humous John Fahey CD box set, *Your Past Comes Back to Haunt You*. Much in conformity to Sartre's idea that emotions transform the world, Takoma Park and its surroundings is a world transformed in these maps. The signature existentialist feelings take up residence throughout. "Gloom," "despair," "death," "limbo," "greater limbo," "desolation," "fear," "trauma," and "ambiguity" are in abundance, with small smatterings of "truth," "desire," "freedom," "love," "paradise," and "God." Lynch's "edges" encircle Takoma Park and stretch along the boundaries between Takoma Park and Washington, D.C., and between Prince George County and Montgomery County. Lynch's emphasis on paths, nodes, and districts seems repeated here also. The map is crisscrossed and punctuated by major avenues and railroad lines, important intersections, and local points of interest, several of these being emblems of, as Lynch emphasizes, the power of modern civilization to reshape the environment: the PEPCO power plant (topped by two small objects that look something like the runic symbol drawn by young Nemesis; see chapter 1), Riggs Road, New Hampshire Avenue, Eastern Avenue, the Potomac River, the B & O Railroad and roundhouse, Bliss Electrical School, and the electric crane storage facility. Milgram's (and to some degree Lynch's) prompt to map the spaces of class seems present in Fahey's labeling of Takoma Park as Dogpatch, USA, presumably a reference to the Li'l Abner comic strip about a fictional poor, white southern town. On the second map, there is Hell's Bottom, a "mixed race" neighborhood (see the next section). West of Takoma Park is the place where "rich people live." This is designated by what looks to be some apartment buildings next to a polluted Rock Creek Park, depicted as a large toilet. Underneath is a sign indicating "coproemia" (a toxic condition produced by constipation), pointing back to Takoma Park, perhaps indicating the stuck-up aspirations of the "Ethan Allen" suburbs Fahey wrote about in his "Communism" essay. At a few spots there are created beings — not unlike medieval- and Renaissance-era maps with sea monsters and other fantastical creatures on their borders — that Fahey writes humorously about elsewhere: "ozmatroids," "The Great Koonaklaster" (Fahey's own personal addition of his interest in folklore and myths). But there is also a play on this iconography too: "real human beings somewhere." Lurking in the interstices are possible artifacts of psychoanalysis and/or memories of events and/or desires: "oral sex," "castration," "theft and rape."

Fahey's maps seem to contain a little each of Sartre, Lynch, and possibly Milgram. These sources, while coming from the diverse disciplines of philosophy, planning, and psychology, have in common the premium they place on human emotion and human space as a space of projected affect, but also the physical environment as active in the lives of individuals and societies. They also have in common a fascination with the urban scale[11] and with the modern metropolitan area as questionable with respect to being an inviting home for human feeling. They all share an interest in negative emotions too, as well as the idea that these are aspects of individual agency. This new area of study must have been immensely appealing to Fahey. It is worth noting the specifically urban scale that is the focus. That is, there is no point on the maps labeled "my house," "my friend's house," "my yard," or "the place where I went to school." This is another indication of the consistency with Lynch's and Milgram's prompts to draw attention to the urban, to the city, to public space, as the central concern, albeit perceived through personal experiences, senses, and habits. At the same time, the maps demonstrate the desire to show the city as an "other" world, containing even stranger worlds within it, consonant with the alter-worlds of Fahey's song titles: a "thing" at the end of New Hampshire Avenue, a "view" east from one of the important railroad crossings, a "transfiguration" at Magruder Park, and so forth.

The Edge, in Black and White

The worlds revealed in Fahey's maps live on in his essay "Adventures on the Edge." These adventures tell a story about Takoma Park (based at least partly on factual events) in which race relations, music, the problem of contemporaneity, and emotions and their spatiality all come together. A word about the title "Adventures on the Edge." As Fahey's first map (figure 2) suggests, Takoma Park shares a border with Washington, D.C. (Takoma Park began as a real estate venture in the 1800s. Connected by railroad to D.C., it was billed as a suburban retreat with plentiful fresh air, wooded groves, clean spring water, etc. [see Historic Takoma, Inc.].) Fahey writes that the Edge is the name he and his friends gave to the D.C.-Takoma Park border area, as well as to the boundary between Prince George and Montgomery Counties. Given that there are additional "edges" on his map; that he follows Lynch in noting that edges might not simply be lines but grounds where different kinds of uses meet and interact—"seams, lines along which two regions are related and joined together" (Lynch, *Image* 47); and that Fahey has drawn a psychological map at all, it seems more likely to me that Fahey has adapted, and very much run with, the idea from Lynch and alloyed it to Sartre.

The "adventures" begin with record collecting. After hearing the Blind Willie Johnson record that Fahey had reported momentarily nauseated him, he threw himself into the music of Charley Patton, Mississippi John Hurt, Skip James, Son House, Bukka White, Etta Baker, Elizabeth Cotten, more Blind Willie Johnson, and many other country blues artists. (He kept up his interest too in classical music [Bartok, Sibelius, Holst, Ives], bluegrass, South Asian ragas, and the several others that became so influential in the development of his style.) The early recordings of country blues artists were not easy to come by. Over the next several years Fahey scoured thrift stores and went on door-to-door junkets soliciting at the houses of African Americans throughout much of the American South. The same purpose gave him reason to go door-to-door in the African American and mixed-race neighborhoods of Takoma Park, sometimes with fellow collector Dick Spottswood (see Guerrieri, *John Fahey*, vol. 1, rev.; Lowenthal).

> In the summer of the middle-fifties we [Fahey and Spottswood] had been working local areas in suburban Maryland. . . . I drove us over to Sligo Mill Road [in Takoma Park]. This is an old gravel road right on top of the section called "Hell's Bottom." The racial makeup here was mixed. New Hampshire Avenue, north of the District line, had been built in 1939. It was a short imitation of the Robert Moses-type freeways which were built in New York state. And it served the same purpose. It enabled white urban dwellers to escape the downtown, expanding slums which were mostly black. It paralleled Sligo Mill Road. It was made of concrete and it had four lanes. So all the traffic was on New Hampshire Avenue. Not on dusty little Sligo Mill Road. . . . The old gravel road existed for the sole purpose of the transportation needs of just a few very poor people that lived along it. It was a time warp and we were in it. I was driving . . . slowly down the sandy road when we saw a tall, light-skinned black man walking towards us. I stopped the car and asked him out the window if he had any old Victrola records he would like to sell us. No he didn't, but just as we were about to take off he saw my old Martin "New Yorker" guitar lying in the back seat. "Oh . . . please let me play your guitar. I'll be real careful with it." (Fahey, *How Bluegrass* 266–67)

Fahey identifies the man as Elmer Williams. Williams, I noted earlier, was in fact a local guitar player and song teacher in the area, a member of a large family of musicians. (His younger brother, Warner Williams, stills tours and records [see Spitzer].) Fahey writes that Williams played a slow twelve-bar blues for them, exactly what Fahey and Spottswood expected to hear. But next Williams chose a "coon song," one of the many kinds of songs historically associated with blackface minstrelsy (Lott). "I was surprised," Fahey writes, "but then you see I was born and raised out here. I knew you could never predict what was coming down along the Prince Georges County Line. The Edge. There was always something happening. And it was usually pretty interesting" (Fahey, *How Bluegrass* 268).

Fahey then recounts being taken to a neighborhood party one summer night by Elmer Williams, on Ritchie Avenue, another African American neighborhood in Takoma Park. Also described as an edge location, the Edge is now redefined as anyplace where normal social rules are suspended.

It was a very dark but still warm, late evening. Not a soul could we see.

There was only one streetlight. . . . Elmer told me to park underneath it and turn my engine off.

I did.

Then he took my guitar and went and sat on the right front fender. He started quietly playing that same twelve-bar blues in E which he had played for me the day I met him.

I got out and sat on my trunk, just a little afraid. I didn't know the rules of this game.

Williams was playing slowly and as he did so doors began to open. In the secret houses. Men and women, young and old, began to take tentative gyrations. All danced alone. All danced differently.

Nobody paid any attention to us: dancer, spectator, black, white, musician. This was the original "twist." But it was very slow. Chaos was potentially everywhere, everybody was doing a different "step." But then everybody was in their own "space," as we say nowadays. And nobody "violated" anybody else's space. (272)

You know what I mean.

The music got a little faster. A few more people came out and joined the "dance."

After about fifteen minutes, a few white folks came out of the woods from their settlement below and across Sligo Creek. They lumbered up the hill and found their own territories.

. . . The music got a little faster. [Williams was doing an Arthur Crudup imitation at this point.] The rockers followed along.

Nobody said a word. They just sort of jumped around once in a while. Dancing to the rhythm of my guitar—played by Elmer. Nobody knowing anything, nobody speaking, nobody thinking about what was going on. Everything was simply happening.

It was very quiet out there. Secret and thoroughly mysterious. Like a dream, almost.

Finally, the cat people came out. Just a few. But they leaped and soared over everybody. Over each other and over my car they flew. There in the virtual silence of the forest primeval, the old Negro homes, a barely audible acoustic guitar sound—lost, abandoned, in the midst of time. (273)

Fahey describes the cat people as ordinary human beings, but thin, poor, "poorer than anyone else who lived along the Prince Georges County Line— the Edge, as it was called" (274). Turning seriocomic, presumably referencing Dr. Seuss's *Cat in the Hat*, Fahey writes that they were wrapped in red-and-white-striped cloth. "They wore mittens too" (274). But the narrative quickly shifts the mood again. Elmer Williams "pushes the guitar" into Fahey's hands, and Fahey begins playing, continuing Elmer's Arthur Crudup "imitation" while the people keep dancing.

But after about an hour, some of the people started disappearing into their houses or into the woods. . . . The show was over. . . . Not one word had been spoken or sung the whole time we were in the Ritchie Hollow.

Nobody—black, white, or cat—asked me who I was or said anything to Williams. We could have been locals or we could have been from Mississippi.

. . . All the rules had been suspended. None of the usual stuff had any significance.

For that matter, as far as I could tell, nobody regarded what had happened as particularly important.

Nobody except for me. And how much did I think. . . .

What did I think?

Well, not much I guess. Not very much happened.

Too bad these somethings that weren't very important didn't happen more often.

Just some music. Some dancing. Some unusual intermingling.

Yeah. Too bad. (275–76)

Through his fantastical description of this spontaneous gathering—an alternative folk festival, we might call it—Fahey makes known several things about the nature of his authenticity. He is knowledgeable about music in a way that nobody can be who does not go out into the field; he has established his ethnographic authority. "The field" opens a new hodological path toward a place that has been hiding in plain sight and that has now welcomed him. Fahey has earned the trust of Elmer Williams and, at least for the night, the African American community in Takoma Park. Fahey has been touched by this experience, subtly changed, and he thinks others might have been too, although he is not sure. Anyway, he would like to see more of these "somethings." The cat people . . . well, that's odd. (Fahey really liked cats [Lowenthal].) But don't they serve as a figure for Fahey's wonder, surprise, and piqued awareness of the racial mixing at Ritchie Hollow? And as virtually a third "race," they disrupt and distract from the binary of Black and white, even as the very idea of cat people renders race an innocent construct, as folk notions of race typically do (see Hill).

The Festival of Democracy, Variation

"Too bad" the "somethings" that happened at the party in Ritchie Hollow "didn't happen more often." But what is it that actually happened? For Fahey, his adventure in Ritchie Hollow would seem to settle a number of long-standing scores. For one, there is not a whiff of "false gregariousness." Togetherness is not forced; it has emerged organically. Nothing has been commercialized or advertised; no one has been sold an idea or is trying to sell an idea. There isn't a slogan in sight. There is also complete authenticity of feeling. No one is claiming to feel something they do not actually feel. And the expressions people create about what they feel (their dance) are proportional responses to the gathering taking place: there is no need for authenticity to be *retro*active; it is already active, imminent to the moment. Fahey's worries about the "law of the heart" being inimical to the compromises demanded by properly functioning social relations seem put to rest. Everyone is in their own "space," but they are private together in public: *together* they may witness their privacy. The matter of "Whitey" being the primary audience for the "lost" music of African Americans is put to rest too. The audience at Ritchie Hollow is mostly African American. Nor is the "lost," remnantal music completely lost; it still lives on in places like this. Fahey's own interest in this music is therefore legitimated, the problem of "contemporaneity" is solved. True, this is all happening in a segregated, working-class Black neighborhood, but the oppression that created and maintains such a place appears to be erased: this is a place where a deep-seated culture prevails. Any anger felt by Blind Joe Death can be put to the side, and the tense unity of the double figure of John Fahey / Blind Joe Death splits into the natural persons of Fahey and Williams. Finally, we have a Fahey for whom the pretenses and peculiar verbiage of philosophy can fall away, even while it is these that help show him why this scene, this edge, this hodology that is "nothing much" actually is a lot. When Fahey writes that he wishes the "somethings" at Ritchie Hollow might happen more often, these somethings — this "we feel, therefore 'we' are" — might be what he has in mind.

Now, some other things are happening too, which need to be noticed because they disrupt the settlements just noted. One of these is the artfulness of Fahey's description and the specific sense of its being pre-scripted, as if there were aspects there that Fahey would hope to have seen, and so he does. What seems pre-scripted? Well, the folk festival as a place of a new human becoming, a reinvention of our humanity, as Cantwell puts it (*If Beale Street Could Talk*). One could say that it is this making-new that identifies the scene as a festival. (Further to the narrative's artfulness, only *Fahey* confirms he thinks something new and different is happening. For the other people, it may just be a regular occurrence, truly "nothing much.") Fahey arguably taps a history of festival think that stretches back to Jean-Jacques Rousseau's festivals of democracy. Rousseau, in a now well-worn passage, imagines that individuals who have been freed from old social assignments from before the time of Enlightenment can come together to find out who they could now become (see Berman): "Plant a stake crowned with flowers in the middle of a square, gather the people together there and you'll have a festival. Do better: let the spectators become an entertainment to themselves, make them actors; . . . This way each one sees and loves himself in the others; and all will be better united" (Rousseau 126–27). Given Fahey's educational chops, the possibility exists that Rousseau is an inspiration for how he builds into his story the very criteria he would use to evaluate it. In Fahey's rendering, partygoers are all versions of each other: each indeed "sees and loves himself in the others," and all are "better united" for it.

Tug on another section of the narrative, however, and it is not the future but the past that advances out of the mist: the primeval forest, the old "Negro" homes, the "original twist," the guitar music, all lost in the midst of time (cf. Wells). Forced through the sieve of these minstrelized images, Fahey's narrative is reminiscent of the antebellum plantation frolics engaged in by enslaved Africans for their own purposes and sometimes encouraged by plantation owners (Hazzard-Gordon; cf. Hoelscher). Because Fahey actually knows better, having just told his reader about the segregated space of New Hampshire Avenue (where Fahey used to live) and Sligo Mill Road, he tacitly asks us to allow him the luxury of nostalgically dwelling with the "dreams" and "air" of Dixie, which he wrote about in his 1984 poem "Vignettes, Digressions, and Screens" (see my discussion in the introduction). It can be as if, even for a moment in the mind's eye, the distortions and contortions of *time* never happened in this place apart, as if it is not the result of segregation and white supremacy but rather the surfacing of the "primeval" place of African American belonging. Or, in this imaginary, both can be true, this being one of the signature logics of the "plantation melodies": imagine a world where Blacks are powerless and yet have cultural agency (see Lott). This is an imaginary Fahey knew well.

Recall how quiet the place is too. No one talks or needs to talk. The narrative hopes we agree that silence and awe suit the "primeval" setting. But what would people say if they could speak? What history would erupt? People at Ritchie Hollow might say all sorts of things, about segregated schools, land deeds and restrictive covenants that kept Black neighborhoods Black and white ones white, and informal Jim Crow "customs" that maintained separate eating and entertainment places. They might have talked about the separate suburban communities Blacks built for themselves tucked in and around the other suburban towns of the area, with separate baseball teams, businesses, singing conventions, churches, and beer gardens. They might also have reminded Fahey of a whole other "festival" that had erupted in the Ritchie Avenue neighborhood. It began in 1954 as a protest by Ritchie Avenue residents against the City of Takoma Park. The city's council members wanted to locate a new public works facility in the neighborhood, right there in the egg-shaped cul-de-sac, as Fahey called it, because the existing facility along Maple Avenue was in the path of projected development. Ritchie Avenue's 120 signatories to the petition lost, but they were able to get the city to build a recreational/community center in the neighborhood. It was completed in 1959 and used as a teen club—the Heffner Park Teen Club: "And they would play music and teens from the community in Takoma Park would be there. . . . And we would have a wonderful time, you know, dancing and having a good time" (Rotenstein, "Montgomery County"; also Rotenstein, "An Exhibit" and email).

But Ritchie Hollow people do *not* speak in Fahey's narrative. In this fantasy of what an alternative folk festival might be like, and it is so very mellow, to be sure, the situation is tightly controlled, despite the spontaneity Fahey reports. Nothing gets out of hand. Each Black body dancing alone in its own "space" could be a figure for Fahey's own depths, which we have already seen do not countenance the massing of Black power very well at all. The narrative comes off as an effort to still the world so that Fahey can reconstruct it in his head and assign everyone their places. In view of this, we should be thinking now of an important way that ideology—that imaginary way through which we tend to view our relationship to the real world—tends to work. Ideology, on the one hand, is just *ego* ideology, evident in the imaginary relationship a person has to their social role. On the other hand, ideology also consists of assigning roles to others *within* that ideology (Lott 204). Lott argues that this is a primary way blackface minstrelsy works. White performers in blackface project what Blacks must *actually* be like, while also imagining that as they move in and out of blackface they remain themselves throughout the process. Isn't the Ritchie Hollow party all about this sort of slipperiness? At the time of its occurrence (its likely occurrence in the late 1950s, that is), Fahey was performing his notion of Blackness—recording as Blind Thomas, singing like Charley Patton for Fonotone, and soon to invent, if he had not already done so, Blind Joe Death. As Fahey writes in his essay, Elmer Williams and he could have been "locals" or from "Mississippi." No one cared; they were immediately accepted. Fahey is "primeval" too.

But Fahey tells us that he knows the difference between what is real and what is not. There are leaping cat people, for heaven's sake. And it is not "primeval" times; it is the twentieth century: African American neighborhoods have been hived off by a stretch of "Robert Moses"–type highway construction, "hodologically" relegated to the "other side of the tracks" if we refer to those old Fahey liner notes. The irony, then, is that if the Ritchie Hollow adventure is not merely ideological in the above sense, Fahey provides the necessary pieces to put together a more critical holistic view—but is not going to do it himself. Would we say that makes this "adventure" a confessional moment, in which Fahey admits falling short of his own vision? Or an obstinate moment in which he carries on with a fantasy despite what he knows? Or is he unreflective, not realizing the contradictions of his own perception? Whichever interpretation we choose, and I only mean to be suggestive of possibilities, the moment manifests the power of emotion and feeling as mediators of experience. For Sartre's *The Emotions*, the power of emotion is that it appears to bend reality toward its own will; it pulls us toward what we would probably admit is false once it is pointed out to us. Most important, though, I do not want to miss the cultural-historical, social dimensions of this slippage between the emotional and the rational. The fact is there is no necessity for Fahey to have recognized and resolved the contradiction between the space he professes not to like (i.e., policies that produce segregation) and the space he does like (i.e., "primeval" Ritchie Hollow). There is no necessity, because the contradiction is alive and well in all sorts of ways in the very culture within which Fahey was immersed. As Robert Cantwell argues in *When We Were Good*, the very society responsible for killing off "tradition" invents festivals, concerts, and café performances, where "traditional" personages seem to still exist, because, as it were, there they are *in the flesh*. And as I have also been arguing, Fahey writes during an extended historical moment that encourages emoting, self-expression, and the exploration of inner worlds and wants; a moment that he seems to have interpreted as always already letting him off the hook when he suspects the self he has been encouraged to be has run into the possibility of its ill-suitedness. That a focus on the personal is insufficient in helping make the world more socially just and more livable is something Fahey was aware of at least since the year 1967, when he wrote his notes for the *Requia* album. There he wrote about two kinds of freedom, one social and one individual/existential. There are strong notes of this in the way he sets up his adventure on the "edge," with the same preference for the latter implied. (Even his read of the communal atmosphere in Ritchie Hollow is privatized in its own way, given the fascination with everyone dancing in their solitary space, together entitled to their own reality.) As in 1967, then, so in 2000 when Fahey's essay was published: his reading of politics is, if I can put it like this, emotional and existentialist. But at some point, Fahey did develop the converse, a reading in which the emotional and existential are political. Let's turn now to those reflections.

Coda

The Unintended Story

Looking at the psychological maps where John Fahey spills his hodological guts, reading about his "adventures on the edge," and contemplating once more his claim to have been playing emotions, would we guess that late in his career he came to feel that the music for which he was best known was mere sentiment? *Kitsch*, he called it. To an interviewer he laments, "The things I wrote are kind of beautiful, but they also have these chord patterns and stuff that draw you down. I consider those songs kitsch, because they are a mixture of emotions. They contain no clear statements about anything, and now I find them disgusting" (qtd. in Pouncey 22). He speaks of an unendurable contradiction between the beautiful world that at least some of his music conjured up and the reality of his sadness, anger, fear, and loneliness. The "peaceful element" in the music "was false because I was not at peace. I didn't know what I was doing and felt pretty phony" (qtd. in Pouncey 24). It seems some relief came with psychoanalysis. It brought to the surface the anger he felt and helped him understand why he liked the music of Skip James, Charley Patton, and Son House: they made angry music too (Pouncey 25).

Fahey's choice of word, "kitsch," is idiosyncratic, however, and raises the question of what he means by it when he talks about it as an unresolved "mixture of emotions." It seems that somewhere along the line he encountered the classic essay on kitsch by Marxist art critic Clement Greenberg. Fahey, in his posthumous book of essays, *Vampire Vultures*, quotes one of the well-known passages from Greenberg's essay:

> The peasants who settled in cities long ago as bourgeois learned to read and write for the sake of efficiency (in business) did not also inquire into the cities' views regarding the enjoyment of traditional culture. *They also lost their taste for folk culture and discovered a new capacity* for boredom. They demanded some kind of cultural products for their own tastes. A new commodity was then devised for the new market. Kitsch, destined for those who were insensible to the values of genuine culture. Kitsch uses the debased simulacra of genuine culture. It is a vicarious experience. (qtd. in Fahey, *Vampire Vultures* 69)

On this account (loss . . . discovery . . . new commodity), Fahey would presumably see the folk revival as kitsch—a scene of largely white, middle-class youth cut off from their own past and borrowing a folk culture that did not really exist in the way they thought it did. And now he would toss his own music into the mix. In hindsight, he too had cast about trying to say something, trying to sort out his feelings with unusual tunings and the hodological long march along the fretboard in search of new chord patterns. Kitsch was the living expression of indeterminate and shifting feeling, boredom and loss, of temporary satisfaction with the commodities that happened to be marketed to you, whether country blues, bluegrass, folk, or classical, or even worse, Fahey's simulacrum of all these in the guise of "composed" concert music.

Tempting though it is to write Fahey's self-deprecating valediction off as an advertisement for his new focus on the electric guitar, through which he had been able to revive his languishing career, I want to suggest its significance lies elsewhere. We have seen that for decades Fahey has been critical of the destructive qualities of capitalism. Capitalism derails youthful spirit. It commandeers people's natural propensity to form associations and friendships in order to substitute false gregariousness and "Ethan Allen" suburbs. Fahey celebrates his "bond" with Patton, imaginative and deracinating as it is, in good measure because both have feelings and emotions at odds with waged work and with the ideology of labor discipline. Capitalism ("Madison Avenue") creates slogans about peace, love, and tranquility that confound authentic wants and needs. Twenty years before he died, Fahey told a *Washington Post* journalist that he didn't like capitalism—and didn't like socialism either (see Young). And courtesy of Fahey's nod to Greenberg, capitalism happily sells degraded forms of culture back to the people who leave their traditions behind and yet hunger for whatever need their traditions had met. Turns out Fahey had taken the bait and peddled it to others—"disgusting." It's another performance maybe, but it seems interested in finally trading in the mystery for the history, at least for himself. His geysers of emotion do not originate with him after all; their origin is in the *longue durée* of social history and the historical geography that makes rootless city and suburban people out of rural ones. In expressly Movement terms, or just thinking back to *Requia* and to Fahey's ultimate point in his "Communism" essay, the idea that one's reticence toward "social action" could be offset by prioritizing one's own authentic feelings and experiences is now in crisis. Personal feelings and experiences have been political all along.

What other dots might be connected? In rejecting the label of folk musician, Fahey asks above, how could he be "folk" when he is from the suburbs? In light of his comments on kitsch, we could respond, Well, how is being from the suburbs not a kind of heritage, not a kind of historical space continuous with a certain "genuine culture," to use Greenberg's phrase? The suburb was white and Fahey was a white man within it, reaping a privilege that his writing never puts in the full light of day. Fahey wrote about what he and many other critics thought were the oppressions and alienation of the suburbs and other manifestations of American capitalism, but he did not get so far as, say, W. E. B. DuBois, who also very early developed a critique of American capitalism and who would have been a ready source for Fahey to have thought with. White and Black workers alike were exploited, DuBois concedes, but white worker citizens and property owners helped create and/or enjoy, as they had been doing for many, many years, the conditions that oppressed Blacks (see DuBois, *Black Reconstruction* and "Marxism").

Importantly, Fahey's story is not about a person who is unaware. It seems more accurately a story of how a remarkably intelligent and gifted person's affections can hold them back and slow down their "becoming," in the face of social and political changes they know on some level are asked of them. Contradictions in the society, and not least those in the interdigitated spaces of the counterculture, take root in the individuals caught up in them and create dilemmas that those individuals cannot resolve. Maybe, then, it is a move in the right direction to cut off the very limb you have wandered out on.

Fahey's rumination on kitsch, seen from a distance, is as if one whole arc of cultural and music history, stretching from nineteenth-century minstrelsy to late twentieth-century revivalism, had become conscious of itself and said, "Nothing to see here." But surely there is something to see. For even if the Fahey of *Vampire Vultures* imputes that the emotional content of his long-ago life and music was a mere refraction of the histories and geographies of capitalism, because these had gotten inside him and made him their ground, it was still the emotional world he had, given where he was. The question has to be, What work could these feelings do? And before that question, another: How much does the notion of kitsch *here* jive with the story he tells *elsewhere*? Does it all tally? Fahey's writings identify two errors to avoid at all costs: one, the romanticized sentiments about race that (white) musical artists use to authorize their imitations of other (Black) musical artists, and, two, the imputation of social, political intent where there is none, in songs by the "people," where notions of the "people" are also brined in romanticized sentiment. His response is to try to walk the thinnest line imaginable between the two: reimagining what imitation means and using it to leverage a new source for thinking about the kind of social change he would like to see. I have been arguing that this thin line, Fahey's "festival of democracy," emerges from the logics of Movement culture and his unwitting preparation for it (e.g., his teenage scrapes with learned writing), and that his claim to have avoided being political with his art tells a political story in spite of itself. It might be indicative that too often he anointed himself the only critical voice in the room, understated his own forms of complicity with what he says he abhorred, and downgraded the search for new values on the part of others who also felt disaffected. But I would surmise that what was at stake in John Fahey's project is something like what Jacques Rancière calls art's "singularity"—that is, Fahey's or anyone's hunt for defining the source of art's power *as art*, in the society where it actually circulates, and then discovering what that power can do, and consequently what its political virtues could be (Rancière 23). In Fahey's case, these virtues are muted and have to be excavated, brought to light. They will bring their darkness with them. We are shown the way to them only through a private, whispered sense of them, or better, through a collective, white male legacy individualized, privatized, and problematized in Fahey, not least because capitalist social relations demand individuating work. In this sense, Fahey's writings construct a singular persona that, for all the showiness of "folking" the folk, boogying in hodological space, and deciding not to pull the pin in the "performance as war," wants to shrink the distance and decrease the inequities between Black and white worlds even as it could only deploy aspects of that distance and those inequities in order to do so.

Twenty years on since John Fahey's death, the question of how to settle with him is as alive as ever. One more quick pivot, then, to the music, because it is Fahey's chops as musician, interpreter of songs, and composer of originals that for nearly everyone secures his reputation. During the writing of this book, the issue has arisen within Fahey's listening community of what to make of his art in light of his behavior toward women (e.g., Hopper, "Living with John Fahey"; also Hecht). Listeners can stop listening and maybe wax nostalgic about the pleasures of Fahey's musical art before his boorish behavior was revealed (Hecht). Or listeners can ignore the allegations or challenge or forgive them—there are many ways to try to reconcile difficult differences between revered art and troubling artists. Here is a path worth setting on: listeners can claim the right to enjoy the music because it is indelibly part of their lives. To just give up on it is to forsake part of one's own life and one's struggles. This is the advice of the feminist music critic and scholar Ellen Willis. Forgive the direct address, but, *John, did you know that Ellen Willis, your contemporary who was an unabashed joiner in "the struggle," liked your music? She says in so many words, in her "elegies" for Susan Sontag, that she liked thinking about your records at the startling moment when the sense that life could end, will end, becomes keenly and exquisitely felt.* Willis was strongly attracted to the ways that many varieties of contemporary music, despite patriarchal, commercial, or other origins within sites of privilege that listeners such as herself do not share, nonetheless model the excess that so many people desire—an explosion of libidinal energies, that a listener can appreciate or emulate and take to new heights ("Beginning"). *John, what goes around comes around. Ellen Willis gets you.* To not keep listening is to somehow devalue one's own past and one's involvement in struggles to define what it means to be alive. One source of art's power, Willis strongly implies, has to do with our own power to be affected by it and what it means for that to happen. Ask John Fahey, whose writings tell a story they do and do not mean to tell, and which thereby point to an important aspect of his music's conditions of emergence and its future. *Agreed, John, not all music needs to be protest music, nor all artists social prophets, but all music heard, all things seen, in a time of protest and uprising have their meanings changed. And I know you knew this, at least in secret. I am not religious but shouldn't we call these conditions the state of grace? May you rest in peace but long live your songs.*

Minneapolis, May–June 2020

Notes

Introduction

1. Like John Fahey and many others, I subscribe to the idea that "folk" is an invented category and might always appear in scare quotes. To avoid doing so ad nauseam, however, I will generally do so only for emphasis.

2. Fahey's engagements with so many different fields and genres present certain challenges for any author who wants to connect Fahey's work to its sources in philosophy, psychology, folklore, musicology, and more. My approach is a compromise strategy that surely contains its share of mistakes and sometimes involves informed speculation. Because I aim to balance breadth and depth, readers will find that most chapters repeat the pattern of reading one or two of Fahey's writings along with just one or two "source" texts that he arguably drew from or that his writings can be placed in conversation with. My interpretations are guided by the fact that I do not know for sure how much Fahey knew about the fields he engages. It is certainly fair to say his grasp of the fields of folklore and blues and folk music history was strong, while reflecting certain blind spots in his training. (Beyond this book, see the formidable evidence of Fahey's knowledge in John Jeremiah Sullivan's *Harper's Magazine* essay.) Can the same be said for philosophy and psychology? Was his grasp of each and every field sure-handed? Probably not. My approach, though, is to follow Fahey's lead into the source material and engage with it at what would arguably have been his level of understanding, but with the goal of trying to connect the dots in his sometimes confoundingly allusive style. I suspect his understanding was deeper in many cases, but I choose to remain on safer ground by grappling with the understanding he "must have" had.

3. This is a good place to point out that while Fahey's writings are populated with a wide variety of themes, they reveal a desire to shock the new-left psyche into the realization that, in a sense, all of white America was of a Southern state of mind (see Eastman). The North had its own brand of Jim Crow, Fahey knew, and white people romanticizing African American marginality was itself a racist move. Some of Fahey's writings come from a place that would not be unknown to, and sometimes seem tutored by, W. J. Cash's *The Mind of the South*, a somber book of critical reflection from 1941, pathbreaking in its day. They exhibit guile *and* guilt, with equal doses of resentment and wonder at having been had by the fictional attractions of "Dixie" and the "Old South" of legend—its supposed gentility and manorial grace, its assumed engendering of a real human bond between master and slave. These ideologies seemed difficult for Fahey to let go of even though he understood them to be fictions. On balance—and this is a point worth making as there is relatively little commentary about it—it seems to me Fahey was keenly interested in keeping whiteness in crisis, refusing to accept that the white new left and white liberals, let alone himself, had emancipated

themselves from racism (cf. Yancy, *White Self-Criticality*). One could venture that he was ready to play the sacrificial lamb to make his point too.

4. Dale Cockrell, in *Demons of Disorder*, calls for an earlier "origin" of blackface minstrelsy than Lott. But the two generally agree that the meanings of blackface have always been plural and have changed significantly over time. See Karl Hagstrom Miller's *Segregated Sounds* for a view that challenges Lott.

5. I do not mean to imply Jim Crow is actually over (Alexander).

6. I am very grateful to my colleagues Sumanth Gopinath and Max Ritts for reminding me of these points.

Part One

1. I am indebted to Fahey scholar and sleuth extraordinaire Claudio Guerrieri for sharing Fahey's 1956 essay with me.

2. Fahey was eager for the higher production values afforded by Vanguard than by his own label, Takoma Records (G. Jones, liner notes, *Yellow*).

3. To the extent Fahey is imputing that, say, Martin Luther King—a social-action theologian who had written his dissertation on Paul Tillich—had forsaken the struggle to overcome individual alienation for the struggle to overcome segregation, he would have found strong opposition (see Rathbun).

4. For a video of Martin Luther King Jr.'s funeral service at Ebenezer Baptist Church, see https://www.c-span.org/video/?443156-1/martin-luther-king-jr-funeral -coverage-1968. See also King, "The Drum-Major Instinct" for a transcription of the sermon.

5. In his biography of John Fahey, Steve Lowenthal reports that Sam Charters, renowned blues scholar and executive producer of *The Yellow Princess*, loaned Fahey a tape recorder so he could record the sounds of the "singing bridge" on his way back to California, where he was living. The timing appears to be sometime in February or March 1968 (Lowenthal 82).

Chapter One

1. The growing popularity of psychology instruction in schools also tracks the growth of memberships in the American Psychological Association. In his textbook, Ernest Hilgard reports dramatic increases in the number of member psychologists after World War II: fewer than 500 in 1920, about 1,200 in 1930, 2,700 in 1940, and 7,200 in 1950. The rate of growth during these decades was faster than that of the U.S. population as a whole (Hilgard 578).

2. The 1953 edition of *The Compass* leads with an introduction of the principal and the verses of the alma mater, then lists "student activities," the first two of which are "Expressing our Thoughts" and "Writing for pleasure." In 1954 and 1955, the first years in which academic departments follow the introduction of the school administration, the English department is listed first in both. In 1956 (Fahey's senior year) the English department is again listed first (see Northwestern High School, 1953; 1954; 1955; 1956).

Chapter Two

1. I follow Medovoi's notion of the psycho-political as the conjoining of the political and psychological in the formation of individual subjectivities, consciousness, and identity, rather than the narrower meaning (see Lichter), which is interested in the psychology of overt, conventionally understood political acts, such as participation in political parties, movements, and demonstrations.

2. Compare Fahey's sense of the contradiction between love and hate with the psychologist Ernest Hilgard's comment on class in the United States: "It is usually considered something of an offense to call attention to the class structure of American society. We pride ourselves on equal opportunity in America, on America as the great melting pot. The very doctrine of progress through individual initiative has made us competitive, but it is partly because we are so highly competitive that a class structure has grown up" (530).

Part Two

1. Later came New Age, of which Fahey is sometimes named a progenitor. Splitting the difference, the music critic John Rockwell, in an article on New Age music for the *New York Times*, finds the movement to have been spawned by "folkie-hippies" like Fahey and fellow guitarist Robbie Basho (Rockwell). Numerous sources and individuals claim or imply that, on the contrary, Fahey was comfortable with the label "American Primitive" (e.g., Lowenthal). Primitive referred to "self-taught" and was perhaps a borrowing from the "primitive painters," such as Henri Rousseau. In interviews and letters of later decades, he claimed a preference for the label "alternative" (see Lowenthal). For a brief on "folk" as a sliding and slippery signifier in relation to Fahey's music, see Encarnacao's *Punk Aesthetics*.

2. Folksinger Sam Hinton wrote about many of the same concerns, although without Fahey's acidity (Hinton). For a variety of attitudes and assessments of the folk and blues revival of the 1960s, see De Turk and Poulin's anthology *The American Folk Scene*.

3. If there ever was such an in-group, its symbolic and perhaps real implosion occurred early in Fahey's career. See Denisoff's excellent "Epilogue" in *Great Day Coming*. On the "myth of acousticity" and the presumption of a democratic ethos that seems to belong to the acoustic guitar as a social object, see Narváez's "Unplugged."

4. At a 1976 concert, a drunk Fahey actually did make this suggestion, during some between-song banter (http://delta-slider.blogspot.com/2016/02/john-fahey -live-bootleg-barn-university.html). However genuine an expression it was of Fahey's cynicism, it is entirely possible that it was also a joke directed to the cognoscenti present who might get the allusion to the notorious "Kill yourself!" shouted by the great banjo player Uncle Dave Macon near the end of "Way Down the Old Plank Road," a song included in Harry Smith's 1952 *Anthology of American Folk Music* that Fahey knew so well.

5. I am very grateful to Malcolm Kirton for allowing me access to the "1977 Session" so I could hear for myself where Fahey's "Charley Bradley's Ten-Sixty-Six Blues" actually came from. See also The Fahey Files for Blackwood's comments on *Red Cross*.

Chapter Three

1. In Dan Ben-Amos's view, Wilgus's presidential address was a direct attack on the performative approach (Ben-Amos).

2. Fahey's was the first book on Patton, but not the first study of Patton. Fahey reproduced, and cited, certain details from a booklet of liner notes by Bernard Klatzko, written for some reissued Patton music. He also learned about Patton from blues historians Gayle Dean Wardlow and David Evans. When Fahey was in the graduate program, there were already different interpretations of Patton's personality, including different views on the existence or not of Patton's political consciousness (see Evans, "Charley Patton," *Charley Patton*; Klatzko).

3. In Fahey's view, expressed during folk festival workshops (Guerrieri, *John Fahey, vol. 1*, rev.; Lowenthal) and in his book *How Bluegrass Music Destroyed My Life*, white leftist activists assumed that Blacks of the rural South had no viable culture or traditions through which to express themselves. On the same basis, he was critical of Black civil rights organizers and of the Black Power movement. This is ironic given that Eldridge Cleaver, a brilliant architect of Black Power thought, had written incisively that most leftist thought, Marxism included, could not reckon with the salience of race in addition to class. Cleaver was an advocate of Black experience, precisely what Fahey claimed to be interested in, as the wellspring for a new theory of radical political economy (Cleaver). Regarding Fahey's criticism that only whites were interested in the country blues produced by southern Blacks, Fahey may not have known that Willie Peacock and Sam Block, field operatives for the Student Nonviolent Coordinating Committee, had organized a series of Mississippi folk festivals in the mid-1960s expressly geared to the Delta's Black audience, with civil rights workers (Black and white) also in attendance. So as to celebrate local culture, these festivals featured indigenous blues and gospel music (having discouraged civil rights "freedom songs" for the occasion) and historical African American foodways (see Wesley Hogan on this history; also *Ebony* magazine's "Mississippi Folk Festival" article from 1966).

4. In the notes to *The Voice of the Turtle*, Fahey again attempts to revalue southern culture and heritage by pointing fingers at the North: "Reconstruction and further events such as the invention of television, the automobile, etc., forced upon the South a grotesque conformation to the rest of the nation. Soon (I write in 1968) all regional traditions (value judgements aside, they are interesting) will probably have disappeared. There will be no South. Or North. Only one 'great society' homogenous and perhaps pasteurized also" (n.p.). He also points to northern hypocrisy in enticing African Americans north, only to exploit their labor.

Chapter Four

1. Not all the tensions are resolved, though. The idea that human relationships boil down to interpersonal, (non)communicative relations that can be healed jostles with the footnote's idea of legitimate distinctions between isolated "cultures." There is a dialogue between supposed historical white southern "hospitality" and contemporary

racial "strife" in the South, in which (if we extend this idea out), northerners are not as good as they make themselves out to be and southerners are not as bad as they are made out to be. There is traffic between the idea that the "battle of the sexes" transcends racial difference and the idea that that battle is genetically baked in. Fahey's laser focus on music, which for him represents more or less a sphere of equality, stands in tense relation to an undeveloped allusion to racial injustice, the actual content and consequences of which he leaves blank, except to implicitly incriminate, and then redeem, himself. Fahey seems intent on letting confession and innocence coincide and collide, as if the elaborately confessed racial prejudice is itself a form of innocence, and assertions of innocence are nullified by too much talking.

Part Three

1. Here, with his charges of commercialization, Fahey taps a deep vein of criticism shared by numerous others. See the essays collected in section "iv. folk, rock, cash, and the future" in De Turk and Poulin's anthology (289–331).

2. Fahey's friend and fellow musician Max Ochs suggests that the idea of the "edge" might come from the phenomenologist Edmund Husserl, whom Fahey might have encountered during his study of philosophy in college (Ochs). This is an intriguing possibility, but I think the evidence points elsewhere. Fahey himself identifies the edge as the boundary between Montgomery and Prince George counties, and between Takoma Park and Washington, DC, but, as chapter 6 will show, his actual use of the word points to him as a Kevin Lynch reader.

3. See "Tell Me, Who's Been Fooling You."

4. See "John Henry (Instrumental guitar duet)."

5. In 1973 John Fahey prepared an extended version of "When the Catfish Is in Bloom," some twenty-three minutes, retitled "Fare Forward Voyagers," for his album of that name. The new title borrows from the poet T. S. Eliot's "Four Quartets."

6. See Roberts.

7. See civil rights journalist Paul Good's essay on Swarthmore College after the 1969 Black student sit-in, in *Life* magazine; also Swarthmore Afro-American Student Society, "Early History of the Black Presence."

Chapter Five

1. Howard Becker, in his study of social "outsiders," includes a discussion of jazz musicians' feelings of superiority toward their audience that in some respects parallels Fahey's (Becker).

2. "Being-towards-death" is an expression associated most with Heidegger (e.g., *Being and Time*). While it has its own particular meanings, I will assume Fahey sees a kinship with Hegel's notion of fearless attitude toward death as a desirable orientation in the development of self-consciousness.

3. Fahey's 1973 album, *Fare Forward Voyagers*, had also quoted, in its very title, from Eliot's *Four Quartets*. The passage ("all will be well," etc.) appears first in the writings of the fourteenth-century English mystic Julian of Norwich. It is the voice of

God, as she imagines God speaking to her, during her near-death experience (see Norwich).

4. "I am tired (tonight anyway) of writing humorous record notes," Fahey confesses in a rare mood of candor in the liner notes to 1968's *The Yellow Princess*:

> I am . . . driven to assume that my music has a source, which wants to say something. Many people have asked me what it says (or what it does, if anything, depending on your aesthetic point of view). There are many questions, which seem to admit of no answer. But a rather special sort of "No Answer." Or perhaps the questions, rather than expressing a lack of meaning, express something nonsensical, or contain hidden nonsensical assumptions. How many hours are there in a mile? Is red round or square? Or perhaps the question is properly put. My music does mean or do something. But the answer would be quite unpopular, and, as I said previously, I am a coward. Besides, as an entertainer and/or musician I'm not supposed to be unpopular.

Chapter Six

1. For performers like Ellen Stekert, the gradual shift in the revival toward the individualized art of the singer-songwriter (Bob Dylan is her mark) removed folk music from its shared folk roots, the problem being that the singer-songwriter potentially confirmed the self-centered individualism of America's consumer society (Stekert).

2. Spottswood later became an influential music history scholar, record producer, and radio host. See "Dick Spottswood: Mini Symposium."

3. In fact, some of Fahey's music does have a social-political element, as I have already noted. Recall the discussion about his songs dedicated to Martin Luther King Jr., and his explanation of the Blind Joe Death persona.

4. Sartre is referring to the psychologist Kurt Lewin. See Bollnow for Sartre's existentialist modifications of Lewin's original idea of hodological space.

5. Quentin Smith emphasizes that for Sartre emotion consists of matter (physiological phenomena) and form (consciousness). See Mark Poster for an overview of how Sartre would in later years, through encounters with Henri Lefebvre and other French Marxists, modify his existentialism and along with it his arguably ahistorical notions of the human being and human condition.

6. A hodograph is a technical illustration of the path taken by moving objects, used in engineering.

7. Music scholars will probably recognize some similarity between this discussion and the controversy over the idea of musical "topoi" or topics—that is, the question of whether and how music directly represents in its very sound and rhythm aspects of reality beyond itself. I have no doubt that topoi are present in Fahey's music, but precisely how and to what degree is not something I can settle here. I am grateful to Sumanth Gopinath for alerting me to the theory of musical topoi. For one excellent discussion, see Agawu. Apart from the question of musical topoi, let alone Fahey's "hodology," there seems to be a growing interest in the relationship among music, landscape, and place (e.g., Von Glahn; Watkins).

8. It is possible that Fahey also intends to parody again the didactic liner note styles of Charters (liner notes) and Klatzko, each of whom recounts his Southern journey.

9. Jane Hill identifies "light talk" about race as the way that whites, "while claiming to be anti-racist, are somehow able to acquire and to share with one another negative stereotypes that they use" (31). "Light" talk in particular is, on the one hand, "opaque to criticism," while being a way of producing intimacy among its participants. Hill's argument is worth reproducing at some length. "Light talk among intimates provides an opportunity for White Americans to indulge in explicit 'race talk' . . . including epithets and stereotypes. To the degree that a particular stretch of talk is keyed as 'light,' it is relatively opaque to criticism and censure as racist. This opacity derives from cultural models that associate style, person, and space in simplistic default configuration. Light talk and joking are prototypically private, associated with the spaces of intimacy, where interpersonal solidarity is more important than strict adherence to truth. Indeed, the assumption of a key of 'lightness' actually constitutes intimacy, so to reject the content of such talk is to reject intimacy itself, and thus to threaten important social ties. . . . Light talk and joking are prototypically vernacular, so they are associated with private persons. While . . . evidence of 'bias' is ground for dismissing the views of a public speaker, bias and interest in private space are unproblematic. . . . This kind of intimate talk can, in fact, be used in 'public.' But such a usage constitutes a metaphorical code switch . . . that layers a frame of privacy and intimacy into the interstices of a larger public context. This frame insulates the speaker from many kinds of challenges that might be made of public, serious talk" (108–9).

10. Stanley Milgram, one of the first experimental psychologists to formalize an interest in contemporary urban life, including the use of psychological maps, took cues from themes explored by Georg Simmel and Louis Wirth, two stalwarts of early twentieth-century urban social theory. Milgram suggested that the alleged anonymity, superficiality, lack of trust, and other adaptations to the overstimulation of city living could be put to the test. "The ultimate adaptation to an overloaded social environment," he wrote in a 1970 review article, "is to totally disregard the needs, interests, and demands of those whom one does not define as relevant to the satisfaction of personal needs, and to develop highly efficient perceptual means of determining whether an individual falls into the category of friend or stranger" ("Experience" 1462). Milgram, reviewing recent work by a number of researchers, suggested that a new family of norms may be in the making (none really reflecting the "ultimate" adaptation of "total disregard" just referred to), regarding individual behavior amid the broader canvas of urban social relations. Among Milgram's interests was something he and others called "urban atmospheres." A somewhat amorphous concept, the idea was that city residents and travelers to different cities might be approached, directly through questionnaires or indirectly through journalistic or literary accounts, regarding their overall sense of the "tone, pacing, and texture of social encounters" in a given city (1465). Researchers might also come to understand the legibility of cities to their inhabitants: How well were cities known to those living in them? Which parts were most known and which parts were least known? What aspects of known areas were

emphasized and why? It is through these questions in particular that the psychological map enters. "The psychologist is less interested in the geographic layout of a city or in its political boundaries than in the cognitive representation of the city," Milgram writes (1467). The most salient fact about that representation is that "urban areas can no longer, because of their vast extent, be experienced as fully articulated sets of streets, squares, and space" (1467–68). Impressed by Kevin Lynch's work in *The Image of the City*, Milgram is intrigued by the finding that "while certain landmarks"—of Boston in this case—"as well as paths linking them are known to almost all Bostonians, vast areas of the city are simply unknown to its inhabitants" (1468). But might these generalizations be broken down by "cultural subgroups"? In research conducted for the purpose of generating psychological maps of Paris, Milgram and his colleague Denise Jodolet posed all sorts of questions to over two hundred Parisian residents to get the sense of such differences, especially by class and occupation. Which arrondissements were considered most desirable and by whom? What landmarks are most and least recognizable? What do respondents place on their maps first and why? The point of the study was to understand not just individual differences in how Paris is imagined but how these differences are themselves "social facts" reflecting group sensibilities.

11. The urban scale is a central feature of Sartre's novel *Nausea*. The novel also contains what seem to be numerous applications of hodological space. See, for example, the vignettes concerning the "thing" (54–55) and the chestnut tree (126–33).

References

Adorno, Theodor. *The Jargon of Authenticity*. Translated by Knut Tarnowski and Frederic Will, Northwestern University Press, 1973.

Agawu, Kofi. "Topic Theory: Achievement, Critique, Prospects." *Passagen/IMS Congress Zürich 2007: Fünf Hauptvorträge*, edited by Laurenz Lütteken and Hans-Joachim Hinrichsen, Bärenreiter, 2008, pp. 38–69.

Aggregate Execrable Nemesis (John Fahey). "My Dear Old Alma Mater." *IOTA*, edited by Anthony Lee, 1956, pp. 11–16.

Alexander, Michelle. *The New Jim Crow: Mass Incarceration in the Age of Colorblindness*. New Press, 2010.

Appleton, Sheldon. "Martin Luther King in Life . . . and Memory." *Public Perspective*, vol. 6, no. 2, February/March 1995, pp. 11–13, 47–48.

Aronson, Ronald. "A New Left Philosophical Itinerary: Marcuse, Sartre, and Then Camus." *A New Insurgency: The Port Huron Statement and Its Times*, edited by Howard Brick and Gregory Parker, Maize Books, 2015, pp. 188–201.

Askew, C. Eugene. "Up From Paternalism." *Negro Digest*, vol. 15, June 1966, pp. 12–16.

Banerjee, Tridib, and Michael Southworth. "Kevin Lynch: His Life and Work." *City Sense and City Design: Writings and Projects of Kevin Lynch*, edited by Tridib Banerjee and Michael Southworth, MIT Press, 1995, pp. 1–32.

Becker, Howard. *Outsiders: Studies in the Sociology of Deviance*. Free Press, 1963.

Ben-Amos, Dan. "A Definition of Folklore: A Personal Narrative." *Estudios de Literatura Oral Popular*, vol. 3, 2014, pp. 9–28.

Bendix, Regina. *In Search of Authenticity: The Formation of Folklore Studies*. University of Wisconsin Press, 1997.

Bennett, Andy, and Kevin Dawe. *Guitar Cultures*. Berg, 2001.

Berkeley in the Sixties. "Berkeley Folk Festival — 1966." August 11, 2011. http://berkeleyfolk.blogspot.com/2011/08/berkeley-folk-festival-1966.html.

Berman, Marshall. *The Politics of Authenticity*. Verso, 2009.

Biron, Dean. "Writing and Music: Album Liner Notes." *PORTAL: Journal of Multidisciplinary International Studies*, vol. 8, no. 1, January 2011, pp. 1–14. http://doi.org/10.5130/portal.v8i1.1682

Blazek, Douglas. "Interview with John Fahey." *Your Past Comes Back to Haunt You*, by John Fahey, Dust to Digital, 2011.

Blumer, Herbert. "Collective Behavior." *Principles of Sociology*. 3rd ed., edited by A. M. Lee, Barnes and Noble Books, 1969, 67–121.

Bollnow, O. F. *Human Space*. Translated by Christine Shuttleworth, Hyphen Press, 2011.

Brackett, David. *Categorizing Sound: Genre and Twentieth-Century Popular Music*. University of California Press, 2016.

Brand, Alice Glarden. "Creative Writing in English Education: An Historical Perspective." *Journal of Education*, vol. 162, no. 4, 1980, pp. 63–82.

Braunstein, Peter, and Michael William Doyle, editors. *Imagine Nation: The American Counterculture of the 1960s and '70s.* Routledge, 2002.

Brick, Howard, and Gregory Parker, editors. *A New Insurgency: The Port Huron Statement and Its Times.* Maize Books, 2015.

Bronner, Simon. "Toward a Definition of Folklore in Practice." *Cultural Analysis,* vol. 15, no. 1, 2016, pp. 6–27.

Brooks, Daphne A. "'See My Face from the Other Side.'" *Oxford American: A Magazine of the South,* vol. 95 (Winter), 2016. https://www.oxfordamerican.org /magazine/item/1093-see-my-face-from-the-other-side.

———. "'Sister, Can You Line It Out?': Zora Neale Hurston and the Sound of Angular Black Womanhood." *Amerikastudien / American Studies,* vol. 55, no. 4, 2010, pp. 617–27.

Burke, Patrick. "'Tear Down the Walls': Jefferson Airplane, Race, and Revolutionary Rhetoric in 1960s Rock." *Popular Music,* vol. 29, no. 1, 2010, pp. 61–79.

Calt, Stephen. *I'd Rather Be the Devil: Skip James and the Blues.* Chicago Review Press, 1994.

Camus, Albert. *The Myth of Sisyphus and Other Essays.* Translated by Justin O'Brien, Alfred Knopf, 1955.

Cantwell, Robert. *Bluegrass Breakdown: The Making of the Old Southern Sound.* Da Capo, 1992.

———. *If Beale Street Could Talk: Music, Community, Culture.* University of Illinois Press, 2008.

———. *When We Were Good: The Folk Revival.* Harvard University Press, 1996.

Cash, W. J. *The Mind of the South.* Alfred A. Knopf, 1941.

Charters, Samuel. *Country Blues.* Da Capo Press, 1959.

———. Liner notes. *Furry Lewis.* Folkways (FA 3823), 1959.

———. Liner notes. *J. D. Short and Son House.* Folkways (FA 2467), 1963.

Cleaver, Eldridge. *On the Ideology of the Black Panther Party.* Black Panther Party, 1967.

Clecak, Peter. *America's Quest for the Ideal Self: Dissent and Fulfillment in the 60s and 70s.* Oxford University Press, 1983.

Cockrell, Dale. *Demons of Disorder: Early Blackface Minstrels and Their World.* Cambridge University Press, 1997.

Cohen, Ronald. *Rainbow Quest: The Folk Music Revival and American Society, 1940–1970.* University of Massachusetts Press, 2002.

Coley, Byron. "The Persecutions and Resurrections of Blind Joe Death (revised)." *Perfect Sound Forever.* 2001. http://www.furious.com/perfect/fahey/fahey-byron2 .html.

Cone, James H. *The Spirituals and the Blues.* Orbis, 1991.

Dawe, Kevin. *The New Guitarscape in Critical Theory, Cultural Practice and Musical Performance.* Ashgate, 2010.

Denisoff, R. Serge. *Great Day Coming: Folk Music and the American Left.* Penguin Books, 1971.

Denson, ED. "Finding Fahey." John Fahey: Record Labels and other Trivia for Collectors, 2008, http://johnfahey.blogspot.com/2008_01_12_archive.html.

De Turk, David, and A. Poulin Jr., editors. *The American Folk Scene: Dimensions of the Folksong Revival*. Dell Publishing Company, 1967.

"Dick Spottswood: Mini Symposium." Benjamin Botkin Lecture Series, May 14, 2019. *Library of Congress*, February 29, 2020. https://www.loc.gov/item/webcast -8763/.

Dorson, Richard. "Folklore and Fake Lore." *American Mercury*, March 1950, pp. 335–42.

Dubois, W. E. B. *Black Reconstruction in America, 1860–1880*. Russell and Russell, 1935.

———. "Marxism and the Negro Problem." *The Crisis*, vol. 40, May 1933, pp. 103–4, 118.

Dunlap, David, Jr. "The Cosmos Club," *Washington City Paper*, July 7, 2006. https://www.washingtoncitypaper.com/news/article/13033391/the-cosmos-club.

Dyersburg State Gazette. "Dyer County Historical Society to Host Minglewood Field Trip Sunday." *Dyersburg State Gazette*, April 10, 2015. http://www.stategazette .com/story/2183991.html.

Eastman, Jason T. *The Southern Rock Revival: The Old South in a New World*. Lexington Books, 2017.

Edwards, Brent Hayes. *Epistrophies: Jazz and the Literary Imagination*. Harvard University Press, 2017.

Eliot, T. S. *Four Quartets*. Houghton Mifflin, 1943.

Encarnacao, John. *Punk Aesthetics and New Folk: Way Down the Old Plank Road*. Ashgate, 2013.

Engle, David, et al. "The Contribution of D. K. Wilgus to Ballad and Folksong Scholarship." *The Flowering Thorn*, edited by Thomas McKean, University Press of Colorado and Utah State University Press, 2013, pp. 363–75.

Erikson, Erik. *Childhood and Society*. Norton, 1950.

———. *Identity: Youth and Crisis*. Norton, 1968.

Evans, David. *Big Road Blues: Tradition and Creativity in the Folk Blues*. Da Capo Press, 1982.

———. "Charley Patton: Conscience of the Delta." *Charley Patton: Voice of the Mississippi Delta*, edited by Robert Sacré, University Press of Mississippi, 2018, pp. 23–138.

———. "Charley Patton: Conscience of the Delta." *Screamin' and Hollerin' the Blues: The Worlds of Charley Patton*. Revenant Records, 2001.

———. "The Guitar in the Blues Music of the Deep South." *Guitar Cultures*, edited by Andy Bennett and Kevin Dawe, Berg, 2001, pp. 11–26.

Fahey, John. *The Best of John Fahey, 1959–1977*. Music Sales Corporation, 1978.

———. "Bola Sete, the Nature of Infinity, and John Fahey." *Guitar Player*, vol. 10, no. 2, February 1976, pp. 10, 36, 40, 42, 44.

———. *Charley Patton*. Studio Vista, 1970.

———. "Charley Reconsidered, Thirty-Five Years On." *Screamin' and Hollerin' the Blues: The Worlds of Charley Patton*. Revenant (Revenant Album No. 212), 2001, pp. 46–53.

———. *Fare Forward, Voyagers (Soldiers Choice)*. Takoma Records, 1973.

———. "The Historical Subjectivity of the Guitar." *Grinning Idiot*, 1982, pp. 29–32.

———. "Horizontal and Vertical Playing." *Guitar Player*, vol. 9, no. 2, 1975, p. 48.

———. *How Bluegrass Music Destroyed My Life*. Drag City, 2000.

———. "An Interview with John Fahey." 1982. Interview by Stefan Grossman. *Fingerstyle and Slide Guitar in Open Tunings*, by John Fahey. Mel Bay, 2002, pp. 8–10. Stefan Grossman's Guitar Workshop Audio Series.

———. "John Fahey." Interviewed by Jason Gross. *Perfect Sound Forever*. 1997. http://www.furious.com/perfect/johnfahey.html.

———. "Letter to Bill Belmont of Fantasy Records." *Best of John Fahey, Vol. 2, 1964–1983*, Takoma, 1995.

———. "Letter to Ron Cowan." November 25, 1998. http://www.johnfahey.com /roncowanletter.htm.

———. Liner notes. *Dance of Death and Other Plantation Favorites*. Takoma Records (C-1004), 1965.

———. Liner notes. *Days Have Gone By*. Takoma Records (TAK-1014), 1967.

———. Liner notes. *Death Chants, Breakdowns, and Military Waltzes*. Takoma Records, 1963.

———. Liner notes. *The Great San Bernardino Birthday Party and Other Excursions*. Takoma Records (C-1008), 1966.

———. Liner notes. *Harry Smith's Anthology of American Folk Music, Vol. 4*. Smithsonian Folkways, 2000.

———. Liner notes. *John Fahey Visits Washington, D.C.* Takoma Records (TAK 7069), 1979.

———. Liner notes. *The New Possibility: John Fahey's Guitar Soli Christmas Album*. Takoma Records (C-1020), 1968.

———. Liner notes. *Requia*. Vanguard, 1967.

———. Liner notes. *The Voice of the Turtle*. Takoma Records, 1968.

———. Liner notes. *The Yellow Princess*. Vanguard Records, 1968.

———. "Performance as War." *Georgia Straight*, October 3–10, 1974, pp. 14–15, 20.

———. *Vampire Vultures*. Drag City, 2003.

———. "Vignettes, Digressions, and Screens." *Grinning Idiot*, 1984, pp. 7–14.

———. *Your Past Comes Back to Haunt You*. Dust to Digital, 2011.

Feenberg, Andrew. "Paths to Failure: The Dialectics of Organization and Ideology in the New Left." *Humanities in Society*, Fall, 1983, pp. 393–419.

Ferris, Tim. "Why Fahey Wants to Kill Everybody." *Rolling Stone*, December 24, 1970, p. 8.

Ferris, William. *Blues from the Delta*. Da Capo Press, 1978.

Ferro, Bernardo. "The Return from Otherness: Hegel's Paradox of Self-consciousness in the Phenomenology of Spirit." *Otherness: Essays and Studies*, vol. 4, no. 1, 2013, pp. 1–21.

Filene, Ben. *Romancing the Folk: Public Memory and American Roots Music*. University of North Carolina Press, 2000.

Fogel, Jerry. "Baez: Artist or Activist?" *Stanford Daily Magazine*, November 3, 1967, p. 10.

———. "John Fahey: A Guitarist Like No Other." *Stanford Daily Magazine*, October 27, 1967, p. 6.

———. "John Fahey: The Guitarist of Relevance." *Stanford Daily*, vol. 152, no. 41, November 17, 1967, p. 6.

Frederick, John T. "The Place of Creative Writing in American Schools." *English Journal*, vol. 22, no. 1, 1933, pp. 8–16.

Frith, Simon. *Performing Rites: Evaluating Popular Music*. Oxford University Press, 1996.

Goldstein, Kenneth. Liner notes. *The Unfortunate Rake*. Folkways Records (album no. FA 3805), Folkways Records and Service Corp., 1960.

Goldstein, Kenneth, and Peter Narváez. "Producing Blues Recordings." *Journal of American Folklore*, vol. 109, no. 434, 1996, pp. 451–57.

Good, Paul. "Requiem for Courtney Smith" *Life*, April 9, 1969, pp. 76–89.

Gopinath, Sumanth. "Reich in Blackface: *Oh Dem Watermelons* and Radical Minstrelsy in the 1960s." *Journal of the Society for American Music*, vol. 5, no. 2, 2011, pp. 139–93.

Gordon, Robert. *It Came From Memphis*. Simon and Schuster, 1995.

Grobe, Christopher. *The Art of Confession: The Performance of Self from Robert Lowell to Reality TV*. New York University Press, 2017.

Grogan, Jessica. *Encountering America: Humanistic Psychology, Sixties Culture, and the Shaping of the Modern Self*. Harper Perennial, 2013.

Guerrieri, Claudio. Email to the author, February 13, 2018.

———. *The John Fahey Handbook, Vol. 1*. 2013.

———. *John Fahey Handbook, Vol. 1*. Revised and updated. 2014.

———. *The John Fahey Handbook, Vol. 2*. 2014.

Hale, Grace Elizabeth. *Making Whiteness: The Culture of Segregation in the South, 1890–1940*. Pantheon, 1998.

———. *A Nation of Outsiders: How the White Middle Class Fell in Love with Rebellion in Postwar America*. Oxford University Press, 2011.

———. "The Romance of Rebellion." *The Port Huron Statement: Sources and Legacies of the New Left's Founding Manifesto*, edited by Richard Flacks and Nelson Lichtenstein, University of Pennsylvania Press, 2015, pp. 65–80.

Hamilton, Marybeth. *In Search of the Blues*. Basic Books, 2008.

Hayden, Tom. "Before Port Huron." *A New Insurgency: The Port Huron Statement and Its Times*, edited by Howard Brick and Gregory Parker, Maize Books, 2015, pp. 15–45.

Hazzard-Gordon, Katrina. *Jookin': The Rise of Social Dance Formations in African-American Culture*. Temple University Press, 1990.

Hecht, Daniel. "John Fahey II: A Man on the Edge." July 14, 2014. http://www.daniel hechtblog.com/2014/07/14/john-fahey-ii-a-man-on-the-edge/.

Hees, Peter. *Writing the Self: Diaries, Memoirs, and the History of the Self*. Bloomsbury, 2013.

Hegel, Georg. *The Phenomenology of Mind*. 1807. Translated by J. B. Baille, Harper Torchbooks, 1967.

Heidegger, Martin. *Being and Time*. Harper and Row, 1962.

Hilgard, Ernest. *Introduction to Psychology*. Harcourt Brace, 1953.

Hill, Jane H. *The Everyday Language of White Racism*. Blackwell, 2008.

Himes, Geoffrey. "American Primitive: John Fahey Seeks Out Raw Music Old and New." *City Paper*, September 2, 1998. http://www2.citypaper.com/music/story .asp?id=5679.

Hinton, Sam. "The Singer of Folksongs and His Conscience." *The American Folk Scene: Dimensions of the Folksong Revival*, edited by David De Turk and A. Poulin Jr., Dell Publishing Company, 1967, pp. 67–71.

Historic Takoma, Inc. *Takoma Park: Images of America*. Arcadia Publishing, 2011.

Hoelscher, Steven. "The White-Pillared Past: Landscapes of Memory and Race in the American South." *Race and Landscape in America*, edited by Richard Schein, Routledge, 2006, pp. 39–72.

Hogan, Wesley. *Many Minds, One Heart: SNCC's Dream for a New America*. University of North Carolina Press, 2007.

Hopper, Jessica. "Living with John Fahey aka a Room Full of Flowers." May 23, 2019, *Lost Notes*, produced by Carla Green, podcast, KCRW, Los Angeles. https://www .kcrw.com/culture/shows/lost-notes/living-with-john-fahey-aka-a-room-full-of -flowers.

Huntington, Dave. "Fete Features Unique Folk." *The Phoenix* (Swarthmore College), April 9, 1968, pp. 1, 3.

Jacobs, Paul, and Saul Landau. *The New Radicals: A Report with Documents*. Random House, 1966.

James, Robin. "In but Not of, of but Not in: On Taste, Hipness, and White Embodiment." *Contemporary Aesthetics*, 2009. https://contempaesthetics.org /newvolume/pages/article.php?articleID=549.

Janson, Donald. "Negro Walkouts in Delta Spurred." *New York Times*, June 7, 1965, p. 26.

———. "Striking Negroes Are Evicted from Plantation in Mississippi." *New York Times*, June 4, 1965, p. 17.

Jaspers, Karl. *Reason and Existenz: Five Lectures*. Translated by William Earle, Noonday Press, 1955.

"John Henry (Instrumental guitar duet)." Performance by John Fahey and Elmer Williams. Collected by John Fahey and Richard Spottswood, Takoma Park, Maryland, 1958. University of California, Los Angeles, Ethnomusicology Archive. D. K. Wilgus Collection. Sound recording. http://digital2.library.ucla.edu /viewItem.do?ark=21198/zz000959hd.

Jones, Glenn. Liner notes. *John Fahey, the Legend of Blind Joe Death*. Fantasy Records, 1996.

———. Liner notes. *The Yellow Princess*, by John Fahey. Vanguard Records, 2006.

Jones, Leroi (Amiri Baraka). *Blues People: Negro Music in White America*. Perennial, 1963.

Kaufmann, Walter. *Hegel: Reinterpretation, Texts, and Commentary*. Doubleday, 1965.

———. "I and You: A Prologue." *I and Thou*, by Martin Buber, Scribner's, 1960, pp. 9–48.

Keil, Charles. *Urban Blues*. University of Chicago Press, 1966.

Kierkegaard, Soren. 1985. *Philosophical Fragments / Johannes Climacus*. Princeton University Press, 1985.

King, Martin Luther, Jr. "'The Drum-Major Instinct,' Sermon Delivered at Ebenezer Baptist Church." Recorded, Atlanta, Georgia. February 4, 1968. King Papers, The Martin Luther King, Jr. Research and Education Institute, Stanford University. https://kinginstitute.stanford.edu/king-papers/documents/drum-major-instinct -sermon-delivered-ebenezer-baptist-church.

Kirshenblatt-Gimblett, Barbara. "Mistaken Dichotomies." *Journal of American Folklore*, vol. 101, no. 400, 1988, pp. 140–55.

Kirton, Malcolm. "Notes on the Recordings." *Your Past Comes Back to Haunt You*, by John Fahey, Dust to Digital, 2011, p. 27.

Kitsman, Chuck. "Katzenbach Talks Today, Protest Planned at Dink." *Stanford Daily*, November 17, 1967, p. 1.

Klatch, Rebecca. *A Generation Divided: The New Left, the New Right, and the 1960s*. University of California Press, 1999.

Klatzko, Bernard. Liner notes. *The Immortal Charlie Patton*. Origin Jazz Library, 1964.

Klemek, Christopher. "The Rise and Fall of New Left Urbanism." *Daedalus*, Spring 2009, pp. 73–82.

Kojève, Alexandre. *Introduction to the Reading of Hegel*. Basic Books. 1969.

Kottke, Leo. "Fahey Obit: Interview with Leo Kottke." Noah Adams, *All Things Considered*. February 23, 2001. http://www.npr.org/templates/story/story.php ?storyId=1119026.

Lee, Anthony. "The Wolves Are Gone Now: The Early Musical Life of John Fahey." *Your Past Comes Back to Haunt You*, by John Fahey, Dust to Digital, 2011, pp. 65–68.

Leerssen, Joep. "Jahn, Friedrich Ludwig (1778–1852)." *Wiley Blackwell Encyclopedia of Race, Ethnicity, and Nationalism*. Blackwell, 2016. https://doi.org/10.1002 /9781118663202.wberen399.

Lester, Julius. "The Angry Children of Malcolm X." *Sing Out!* October/November 1966, pp. 21–25.

———. Liner notes. *Julius Lester*. Vanguard Recording Society (VRS-9199), 1965.

Lichter, Robert. "Young Rebels: A Psychopolitical Study of West German Male Radical Students." *Comparative Politics*, vol. 12, no. 1, October 1979, pp. 27–48.

Limón, José. *Americo Paredes: Culture and Critique*. University of Texas Press, 2012.

Lipsitz, George. *The Possessive Investment in Whiteness*. Temple University Press, 1998.

Lorenz, Stephen Fox. *Cosmopolitan Folk: The Cultural Politics of the North American Folk Music Revival in Washington, D.C.* 2014, George Washington University, Washington, DC, dissertation.

Lott, Eric. *Love and Theft: Blackface Minstrelsy and the American Working Class*. Oxford University Press, 1993.

Lowenthal, Steve. *Dance of Death: The Life of John Fahey, American Guitarist*. Chicago Review Press, 2014.

Luke. Comment on "What a Great Show." Joni Mitchell, September, 14, 2009, https:// jonimitchell.com/chronology/detail.cfm?id=1132.

Lund, Jens, and R. Serge Denisoff. "The Folk Music Revival and Counter Culture: Contributions and Contradictions." *Journal of American Folklore*, vol. 84, no. 334, 1971, pp. 394–405.

Lynch, Kevin. *The Image of the City*. MIT Press, 1960.

———. "Notes on City Satisfactions." 1953. *City Sense and City Design: Writings and Projects of Kevin Lynch*, edited by Tridib Banerjee and Michael Southworth, MIT Press, 1995, pp. 135–53.

Mack, Kimberly. "'There's No Home for You Here': Jack White and the Unsolvable Problem of Blues Authenticity." *Popular Music and Society*, vol. 38, no. 2, 2015, pp. 176–93.

McCord, Jeff. "The Collector," *Texas Monthly*, June 2001. https://www.texasmonthly.com/articles/the-collector-3/.

McKittrick, Katherine. *Demonic Grounds: Black Women and the Cartographies of Struggle*. University of Minnesota Press, 2006.

Medovoi, Leerom. *Rebels: Youth and Cold War Origins of Identity*. Duke University Press, 2005.

Milgram, Stanley. "The Experience of Living in Cities." *Science*, New Series, vol. 167, no. 3294, March 13, 1970, pp. 1461–68.

Milgram, Stanley, and Denise Jodolet. "Psychological Maps of Paris." *Environmental Psychology: People and Their Physical Settings*. 2nd ed., edited by H. M. Proshansky, W. H. Ittelson, and L. G. Rivlin, Holt, Rinehart, and Winston, 1976, pp. 104–24.

Miller, Dale. "Reinventing the Steel." *Acoustic Guitar*, January/February 1992, pp. 42–49. http://www.johnfahey.com/pages/ac1.html.

Miller, Karl Hagstrom. *Segregating Sound: Inventing Folk and Pop Music in the Age of Jim Crow*. Duke University Press, 2010.

Mirvish, Adrian. "Sartre, Hodological Space, and the Existence of Others." *Research in Phenomenology*, vol. 14, 1984, pp. 149–73.

"Mississippi Folk Festival." *Ebony Magazine*, vol. 21, no. 5, March 1966, pp. 91–96.

Morris, Aldon. "The Lightning Bolt That Sparked the 'Port Huron Statement.'" *A New Insurgency: The Port Huron Statement and Its Times*, edited by Howard Brick and Gregory Parker, Maize Books, 2015, pp. 167–87.

Narváez, Peter. "Unplugged: Blues Guitarists and the Myth of Acousticity." *Guitar Cultures*, edited by Andy Bennett and Kevin Dawe, New York: Berg, 2001, pp. 27–44.

Ngai, Sianne. *Ugly Feelings*. Harvard University Press, 2005.

Northwestern High School. *The Compass*. H. G. Roebuck and Son, 1953.

———. *The Compass*. H. G. Roebuck and Son, 1954.

———. *The Compass*. H. G. Roebuck and Son, 1955.

———. *The Compass*. H. G. Roebuck and Son, 1956.

Norwich, Julian of. *Revelations of Divine Love*. Dover Books, 2006.

"The Notes on the Songs: *Red Cross*." *The Fahey Files*. https://www.johnfahey.com/pages/rc2.html. Accessed October 18, 2020.

Ochs, Max. Email to the author, September 8, 2018.

Oliver, Paul. *The Meaning of the Blues*. Collier Books, 1963.

Pearson, Barry Lee. *"Sounds So Good to Me": The Bluesman's Story*. University of Pennsylvania Press, 1984.

Piazza, Tom. *Setting the Tempo: Fifty Years of Great Jazz Liner Notes*. Anchor
   Doubleday, 1996.

Pollard, Samuel, director. *Two Trains Runnin'*. Avalon Films, 2016.

Poster, Mark. *Existential Marxism in Postwar France: From Sartre to Althusser*.
   Princeton University Press, 1975.

Pouncey, Edwin. "Blood on the Frets." *The Wire*, vol. 174, August 1998, pp. 22–31.

Rabaka, Reiland. *Civil Rights Music: The Soundtracks of the Civil Rights Movement*.
   Lexington, 2016.

Rancière, Jacques. *The Politics of Aesthetics*. Continuum, 2004.

Rathbun, John W. "Martin Luther King: The Theology of Social Action." *American
   Quarterly*, vol. 20, no. 1, 1968, pp. 38–53.

Ratliff, Ben. "A 60's Original with a New Life on the Fringe." *New York Times*,
   January 19, 1997, p. H38.

Reger, Jo, et al. *Identity Work in Social Movements*. University of Minnesota Press,
   2008.

Reitan, Meredith Drake, and Tridib Banerjee. "Kevin Lynch in Los Angeles:
   Reflections on Planning, Politics, and Participation." *Journal of the American
   Planning Association*, vol. 84, nos. 3–4, 2018, pp. 217–19.

Retman, Sonnet. *Real Folks: Race and Genre in the Great Depression*. Duke University
   Press, 2011.

Richardson, Derk. "A John Fahey Primer: The Triumph and Tragedy of Blind Joe
   Death." *Acoustic Guitar*, vol. 24, no. 11, May 2014, pp. 48–53.

Roberts, Ken. "Morning Classes Cancelled." *The Phoenix* (Swarthmore College),
   April 9, 1968, pp. 1, 3.

Rockwell, John. "New-Age Music Searches for Its Proper Niche." *New York Times*,
   June 22, 1986. http://www.nytimes.com/1986/06/22/arts/new-age-music-searches
   -for-its-proper-niche.html?pagewanted=1.

Rolph, Renton. "A Career of Service." *Stanford Daily*, November 17, 1967, pp. 1, 11.

Rosenberg, Neil V., editor. *Transforming Tradition: Folk Music Revivals Examined*.
   University of Illinois Press, 1993.

Rossinow, Doug. "The New Left in the Counterculture: Hypotheses and Evidence."
   Radical History Review, vol. 67, 1997, pp. 79–120.

———. *The Politics of Authenticity: Liberalism, Christianity, and the New Left in
   America*. Columbia University Press, 1998.

Rotenstein, David. Email to the author, June 7, 2019.

———. "An Exhibit on 1950s Life Reproduces Segregation." *Activist History Review*,
   June 6, 2018. https://activisthistory.com/2018/06/06/an-exhibit-on-1950s-life
   -reproduces-segregation/.

———. "Montgomery County Historical Society BOOM Exhibit Is a Dud." *History
   Sidebar*, June 6, 2018. http://blog.historian4hire.net/2018/06/06/boom-exhibit-is
   -a-dud/.

Rousseau, Jean-Jacques. *Politics and the Arts: Letter to M. D'Alambert on the Theater*.
   Cornell University Press, 1960.

Rowntree, John, and Margaret Rowntree. "Youth as a Class." *International Socialist
   Journal*, vol. 25, February 1968, pp. 25–58.

Roy, William. *Reds, Whites, and Blues: Social Movements, Folk Music, and Race in the United States*. Princeton University Press, 2010.

Ryan, Tim. *Yoknapatawpha Blues: Faulkner's Fiction and Southern Roots Music*. Louisiana State University Press, 2015.

Sartre, Jean-Paul. *Being and Nothingness: A Phenomenological Essay on Ontology*. Translated by Hazel Barnes, Washington Square Press, 1956.

———. *The Emotions: Outline of a Theory*. 1948. Citadel Press, 1989.

———. *Nausea*. Translated by Lloyd Alexander, New Directions, 1964.

Schillace, Nicholas. *John Fahey and American Primitivism: The Process of American Identity in the Twentieth Century*. 2002, Wayne State University, Detroit, Michigan, master's thesis.

Schrag, Calvin O. *The Self after Postmodernity*. Yale University Press, 1999.

Seeger, Mike. *Talking Feet: Solo Southern Dancing*. North Atlantic Books, 1992.

Shabazz, Rashad. *Spatializing Blackness: Architectures of Confinement and Black Masculinity in Chicago*. University of Illinois Press, 2015.

Shklar, Judith. *Freedom and Independence: A Study of the Political Ideas of Hegel's Phenomenology of Mind*. Cambridge University Press, 1976.

Small, Christopher. *Musicking: The Meanings of Performing and Listening*. Wesleyan University Press, 1998.

Smith, Ayana. "Blues, Criticism, and the Signifying Trickster." *Popular Music*, vol. 24, no. 2, 2005, pp. 179–91.

Smith, Harry. *Anthology of American Folk Music. Vols. 1–3*. Smithsonian Folkways, 1952.

———. *Anthology of American Folk Music. Vol. 4*. Smithsonian Folkways, 2000.

Smith, Quentin. "Sartre and the Phenomenon of Emotion." *Southern Journal of Philosophy*, vol. 17, no. 3, 1979, pp. 397–412.

Spitzer, Nick. "Key to the Blues Highway: At Home on Mt. Zion Road." *Blues Highway: Warner Williams Live, with Jay Summerour*. Smithsonian Folkways, 2004.

Stekert, Ellen. "Cents and Nonsense in the Urban Folksong Movement 1930–1966." *Folklore and Society: Essays in Honor of Benj. A. Botkin*, edited by Bruce Jackson, Folklore Associates, 1966, pp. 153–68.

Stryker, Sheldon, et al. *Self, Identity, and Social Movements*. University of Minnesota Press, 2000.

Sullivan, John Jeremiah. "Unknown Bards." *Harper's Magazine*, November 2008, pp. 86–92, 94.

Swanson, Chic. "Jazz Me Blues." *Georgia Straight*, October 3–10, 1974, pp. 17–18.

Swarthmore Afro-American Student Society. "Early History of the Black Presence at Swarthmore." 1987. https://www.sccs.swarthmore.edu/org/sass/history.html.

Taylor, Archer. "The Place of Folklore." *PMLA*, vol. 67, no. 1, 1952, pp. 59–66.

"Tell Me, Who's Been Fooling You." Performance by Elmer Williams, "Kelly," and John Fahey. Collected by John Fahey and Richard Spottswood, Takoma Park, Maryland, 1958. University of California, Los Angeles, Ethnomusicology Archive. D. K. Wilgus Collection. Sound recording. http://digital2.library.ucla.edu /viewItem.do?ark=21198/zz000959dv.

Teodori, Massimo. *The New Left: A Documentary History*. Bobbs-Merrill, 1969.

Thompson, Richard. "Bud Reed Passes." *Bluegrass Today*, February 22, 2011. http://bluegrasstoday.com/bud-reed-passes/.

Virella, Kelly. "'Glee, Satisfaction and Weeping': How America Reacted When Martin Luther King Died." *New York Times*, April 2, 2018. https://www.nytimes.com/2018/04/02/reader-center/martin-luther-king-assassination-memories.html?hp&action=click&pgtype=Homepage&clickSource=story-heading&module=photo-spot-region&region=top-news&WT.nav=top-news.

Von Glahn, Denise. *The Sounds of Place: Music and the American Cultural Landscape*. Northeastern University Press, 2003.

Wade, Stephen. *The Beautiful Music All Around Us: Field Recordings and the American Experience*. University of Illinois Press, 2012.

Wagner, Richard. *On Conducting*. Translated by Edward Dannreuther, William Reeves, 1887.

Watkins, Holly. "Musical Ecologies of Place and Placelessness." *Journal of the American Musicological Society*, vol. 64, no. 2, 2011, pp. 404–8.

Weiten, W., and R. D. Wight. "Portraits of a Discipline: An Examination of Introductory Psychology Textbooks in America." *Teaching of Psychology in America: A History*, edited by C. L. Brewer, A. Puente, and J.R. Mathews, Washington, DC, American Psychological Association, 1992, pp. 453–504.

Wells, Jeremy. *Romances of the White Man's Burden: Race, Empire, and the Plantation in American Literature*. Vanderbilt University Press, 2011.

Wilgus, D. K. *Anglo-American Folksong Scholarship Since 1898*. Greenwood Press, 1959.

———. "The Text Is the Thing." *Journal of American Folklore*, vol. 86, 1973, pp. 241–52.

Willis, Ellen. "Beginning to See the Light." *The Essential Ellen Willis*, edited by Nona Willis Aronowitz, University of Minnesota Press, 2014, pp. 51–58.

———. "Three Elegies for Susan Sontag." *New Politics*, vol. 10, no. 3, 2005. https://newpol.org/issue_post/three-elegies-susan-sontag/.

Wilson, Alan. Liner notes. *Robert Pete Williams, Louisiana Blues*. Takoma Records (B-1011), 1966.

Woods, Clyde. *Development Arrested: Blues and Plantation Power in the Mississippi Delta*. Verso, 1998.

Yancy, George. *Look, a White! Philosophical Essays on Whiteness*. Temple University Press, 2012.

———, editor. *White Self-Criticality beyond Anti-racism: How Does It Feel to Be a White Problem?* Lexington Books, 2015.

Young, Charles M. "Into the Mind and Music of John Fahey." *Washington Post*, May 24, 1981, pp. G1, G8–9.

Index

authenticity, 26–27, 150, 154–58, 168–70, 189–90, 197. *See also* blues persona

Berkeley, California, 127–29
blackface minstrelsy, 13, 15–19, 136, 187, 192, 200n4
Blind Joe Death. *See* Fahey, John — pseudonyms: Blind Joe Death
bluegrass music, 165–67
blues ballad, 88, 94, 100–102
blues music. *See specific blues musicians*
blues persona, 79–84, 145, 164–70, 175. *See also* Woods, Clyde
blues revival, 7, 119, 175. *See also specific blues musicians*

Cantwell, Robert, 14–17, 167, 193
Charters, Samuel, liner notes by, 111–13, 115–16, 118
civil rights, 69, 175, 202n3. *See also* King, Martin Luther, Jr.; new left
counterculture, 5, 9–10, 13, 77, 143. *See also* Fahey, John — Movement; Movement, of 1960s and 1970s; new left

danse macabre, 135–36
Denson, ED, 21, 72
edge, concept of, 131, 138–39, 163, 175–93, 203n2. See also *The Image of the City*; Lynch, Kevin

Eliot, T. S., 130
Erikson, Erik, 52–56, 60, 63–68, 168, 176. *See also* Identity
Evans, David, 73, 75, 80, 84, 98, 102
existentialism, 7, 139, 184

Fahey, John: biography, in Maryland and Washington, D.C., 20–22 (*see also* Berkeley, California; Takoma Park, Maryland; UCLA; Washington, D.C.); capitalism, critique of, 22, 27, 57–63, 68–69, 194–97; cat people, 188; East Coast Blues Mafia, 21–22, 129; folk festival, alternative to, 189–93, 197; "folk" parody, 111–22, 159, 170; kitsch, 194–97; Movement, 22–23, 34–36, 127–29, 132, 137, 161–62, 164, 175, 193, 195, 197; music, interpretations of, 1–5, 23–24, 36–39, 77–84, 134–41; musical taste, diversity of, 6–8, 12–13, 21–22, 164–70, 186, 194; philosophy, 8, 130–32, 145–58, 171–73 (*see also specific philosophers*); record collecting, 95–96, 160, 186; southern U.S. culture and economy, 14, 101–3, 191, 199–200n3, 202n4; spatial representations, 8–9 (*see also* Berkeley, California; edge; hodological space; psychological maps; Sartre, Jean Paul; suburbs; Takoma Park, Maryland); writings, authorial performance in vs. biographical truth of, 24
— music, LP albums: *Blind Joe Death*, 1, 17, 36–37, 108; *Dance of Death*, 108; *Days Have Gone By*, 2–4, 80, 83; *Death Chants, Breakdowns, and Military Waltzes*, 108; *Fare Forward Voyagers*, 203–4n3; *The Great San Bernardino Birthday Party*, 108; *John Fahey Visits Washington, D.C.*, 173; *The New Possibility*, 1–2, 4–5; *Red Cross*, 77–84; *Requia*, 29–35, 69; *The Voice of the Turtle*, 123–24, 173;

CPSIA information can be obtained
at www.ICGtesting.com
Printed in the USA
LVHW091316130521
687347LV00004B/142